Sustaining Social Conflict

Sustaining Social Conflict

Hatred, Money, and Genocide

E. N. Anderson and Barbara A. Anderson

LEXINGTON BOOKS
Lanham • Boulder • New York • London

Published by Lexington Books
An imprint of The Rowman & Littlefield Publishing Group, Inc.
4501 Forbes Boulevard, Suite 200, Lanham, Maryland 20706
www.rowman.com

86-90 Paul Street, London, EC2A 4NE

British Library Cataloguing in Publication Information Available

Library of Congress Cataloging-in-Publication Data

Names: Anderson, E. N., 1941- author. | Anderson, Barbara A. (Barbara Alice), 1944– author.
Title: Sustaining social conflict: hatred, money, and genocide / E.N. Anderson and Barbara A. Anderson.
Description: Lanham: Lexington Books, [2022] | Includes bibliographical references and index. | Summary: "This book examines the roots of hatred, genocide, and mass murder in psychology, history, politics, and economics, including the funding of destructive political campaigns. It provides solutions grounded in moral philosophy as well as possible legal measures"—Provided by publisher.
Identifiers: LCCN 2022035745 (print) | LCCN 2022035746 (ebook)
 | ISBN 9781666918700 (cloth) | ISBN 9781666918724 (paper) | ISBN 9781666918717 (ebook)
Subjects: LCSH: Social conflict. | Violence. | Corporations—Political activity. | Campaign funds—Social aspects.
Classification: LCC HM1121 .A525 2022 (print) | LCC HM1121 (ebook) | DDC 303.6—dc23/eng/20220822
LC record available at https://lccn.loc.gov/2022035745
LC ebook record available at https://lccn.loc.gov/2022035746

Contents

To the people of our nation, our multicultural American family
May we come together
Valuing our rich diversity, innovative thinking, and care for one another

List of Figures

Preface

This book addresses four questions: First, why do people easily fall into hatred and bigotry? Second, who has exacerbated this over time, arousing and mobilizing hate for their own ends? Third, how does the result of this mobilization play out over time? Fourth, and most important, what can be done about it?

Considering these involves extending the inquiry both backward and forward from other books on the world's problems. The book examines the backstory of financial support for social conflict. It then extends forward into application of moral philosophy to solving those issues. The hope is that this will get at least some thinkers beyond the mutual recriminations that seem to have taken over much of political discourse in the twenty-first century.

The human species is a highly social animal. Humans orient to their groups, and depend on them. They need social life, and they treasure it. Innate in humans, and the product of four billion years of evolution, is an ability to defend against threat. Since immediate existential threat must be prioritized over all other matters, people when stressed or threatened are often angry and defensive. Humans have developed a whole range of behaviors, and added such inventions as guns, knives, and bombs. Also basic (and shared with most mammals) is a tendency to compete for control of people and resources, by force if necessary. These responses normally function to keep people safe and alive, but they constantly overshoot: imagined or trivial threats and slights lead to extreme defensive behavior; competition for material goods, control, and power lead to predatory behavior of many types.

Sociability leads most people most of the time to act in a pleasant, friendly, and even loving and caring manner. The basic defensive and acquisitive drives are social too, however. Defense is normally against one's group or a rival group. Acquisitiveness is socially structured, and almost always for social ends, especially power and control. This has led to the classic fable of the two wolves within each person, a good and prosocial one and a savage and wild one, the one that prevails being the one you feed. Even our nearest and dearest may be targets of anger and hate.

The food for the wolves involves working together or working against each other. Other things being equal, making everyone better off is the best way to get more material goods. Power within a social system, especially a hierarchy, is more problematic, because it must often come by getting ahead of others. Maintaining control over people must sometimes be done by incurring costs oneself to ensure greater costs to the controlled individuals or groups, in a negative-sum game.

Individual behavior can be serious enough, but that same sociability guarantees that bad behavior will be enormously magnified by the group. Group violence is common. The extent at various periods is debated, but it rarely escapes any group. This in turn can be improved by formal laws and states, or it can be made still worse, by the development of organized war, genocide, oppression, structural violence, and persecution. This is exacerbated by exclusionary ideologies or totalizing ideologies. Leaders who want to rise in the world, or keep their leadership, quickly learn to take advantage of this, by uniting their people either in good works or in hate. If they choose the latter, they lead their people in attacks on structural opponents of any and every sort. They typically adopt exclusionary ideologies for the purpose.

The translation of ordinary violence to mass murder requires money— a great deal of it. Governments draw on corporations, taxes, or loot. Corporations and individuals donate to political causes, often including extremist groups. Thus, follow the money.

The cure must involve group morality first and last. It also entails democracy with equal rights for minorities strictly enforced, and legal sanctions against hateful violence. This must all be achieved by education in the broad sense, including discourse by leaders and the media.

This book is the fourth in a series on genocide and mass violence (Anderson and Anderson 2013, 2017, 2020). Our agenda began with Barbara Anderson's research on refugees from the Cambodian genocide of the 1970s. She worked in refugee camps in Thailand and among refugees in California. She has also visited and studied Nazi prisons and other sites in Europe. Eventually we went to Cambodia, traveled over the country, saw the memorials to genocide, and developed an interest in understanding this dreadful heritage. Our work has since taken us to Rwanda and other countries where we could further investigate genocide issues on the ground.

We are grateful to Christopher Chase-Dunn, Hollie Nyseth Brehm, Marilyn Grell-Brisk, David Kronenfeld, David Livingstone Smith, Andrea Wilson, and many others for advice and counsel.

E. N. Anderson

Barbara A. Anderson

April 2022

Chapter 1

Definitions

WORLD IN DANGER

The Taliban swept to power in Afghanistan in 1996, was displaced violently by the United States (US) and its allies in 2001, and returned in triumph in September 2021. As the American troops were withdrawing, the whole country fell without significant resistance to Taliban forces, who occupied Kabul before the Americans were gone. Overwhelming popular support may have come more for their anti-foreigner stance than for their extreme program, but many Afghans supported the entire agenda. The Taliban immediately ended democracy, drove women off the streets and into hiding, and restored a reign of terror. Desperate poverty and massive violence ensued.

This was soon followed by Putin's sweep into Ukraine, a violent war to take over a former Russian possession that had become an independent country. Both these episodes are recent and dramatic violence of the extreme right against the forces of democracy, freedom, equality, and human rights. Whether by ballot box, by coup, or by civil war, extremist right-wing regimes have taken over dozens of countries in the past thirty years. Many are outright fascist. Others, like the Taliban, are theocratic. Erica Chenoweth, leading expert on civil resistance, notes "a disturbing global wave of rising authoritarianism, with countries like India, Poland, Hungary, Turkey, Brazil, Thailand, the Philippines, and the United States all backsliding toward autocracy over the past decade. In these and many other countries, aspiring demagogues have rolled back or eliminated civil rights protections for marginalized groups, assaulted judicial independence, threatened political opponents with imprisonment, bullied or persecuted journalists, carried out brazen attacks on elections and the voting process, and turned a blind eye to armed vigilantes attacking their domestic opponents" (Chenoweth 2021: xxii).

This overwhelming swing to the right could not have come at a worse time. Humanity is facing the most dangerous period in its history, a period in which only prompt and resolute action will save the species from extinction through ecological collapse. Global warming is the most obvious threat, but viral epidemics, nuclear wars, and global poisoning by pollutants could all decimate the species.

All these are symptoms of the same condition: ecologically suicidal behavior. The rapid spread of COVID-19 provides insights into what will happen when a more deadly disease, such as the Ebola virus, spreads with equal ease. At the same time, inequality in wealth and power has spiraled out of control, with a few giant firms owning a huge percentage of national and international wealth (Piketty 2017).

A common response to new threats, globally, seems to be regression to right-wing authoritarianism. The leading countries of the world have all had brushes with that form of government in the near past, and many of them are governed by fascist or authoritarian-populist regimes today. Over thirty countries have regimes based on a combination of authoritarianism and discrimination against minorities and the poor. We had hoped, in the twentieth century, for the continuance of progress in the direction of democracy, equity, and care for people and environment. We have faced in the twenty-first century a dramatic worldwide reversal in that progress, and a pervasive regression to the worst of the early twentieth century. The United States is torn between a disunited and soft-spoken Democratic Party and a strident Republican Party increasingly committed to white supremacy, denial of global climate change, denial of the seriousness of COVID-19, and regression to a highly restrictive religious and social climate that increases ethnic and gender inequities.

Worldwide failure to address the challenges of climate change, food production, disease, and war would lead to literally billions of deaths with the next fifty years, as farmland, fresh water, fisheries, forests, and other resources rapidly decline. Totalitarian and fascistic regimes cannot cope with such issues. This failure is due partly to their reactionary style, but also to the fact that they are bankrolled and corrupted by the very interests that produce the problems, including the fossil-fuel industry, the military-industrial bureaucracy, and the big agribusiness interests. Saving the world depends on understanding why the human reaction to challenge has been, so far, to shelter in increasingly repressive, unequal, and antiscientific regimes, and on overthrowing those regimes to bring about rational and decisive behavior.

THE TWO WOLVES

There is an allegedly Native American folktale (widely told, without known origin; Anderson and Anderson 2020) that tells it all clearly:

> "My child, it's time to teach you the most important lesson about life and people. It is that everyone has within him, or her, two wolves: a good wolf that wants to help everyone and do what's best for all, and a bad wolf that wants to do evil and hurt people and the world."
>
> "Father, that's scary. It really worries me. Which wolf wins out in the end?"
>
> "My child, the wolf you feed."

The good wolf is fed by mutual benefit from caring and compassion, and by harmony, help, cooperation, and innocent fun. Good can be simply learning to appreciate richer and fuller personal experiences. It certainly includes helping others enjoy life more. This implies taking responsibility for oneself and others. That in turn requires mutual support and empowerment. Acting out these ethics actually feels good to most of us. Specifically, it triggers an emotion technically known as *eudaimonia*, different from the "hedonic" happiness that we get from partying (Sonja Lyubomirsky 2007, 2014). The task of the present book is to deal with the other wolf, the wolf of harm.

The wolves are equally strong, and equally present. In daily life, the good wolf usually rules, but in bad times the bad wolf tends to take over. The good wolf is gentle and mild, the bad one powerful and tenacious, so the bad wolf usually wins in conflicts.

The savage wolf has a place: it is there to defend from actual attack. The problem is that it is often deployed to hurt friends, family, and neighbors, rather than actual enemies. The bad wolf thus becomes a metaphor for hatred and cruelty. This bad wolf is fed by brooding about minor or imagined slights, ruminating, petulance, offense-taking, frustration—in short, overly negative reactions to the wear and tear of life, and above all to perceived challenges to personhood and social status.

EVIL DEFINED

According to a medieval chronicler, Genghis Khan listened to a debate among sages about the height of human Good—whether it was from helping others, being faithful to God, and so on. Genghis listened politely, then said: "Man's greatest good . . . is to chase and defeat his enemy, seize his total possessions, leave his married women weeping and wailing, ride his gelding, use the bodies of his women as a nightshirt and support, gazing upon and kissing their rosy breasts, sucking their lips which are as sweet as the berries of their breasts." (From Rashid al-Din's "Collected Chronicles"; quoted by Paul Ratchnevsky, *Genghis Khan*, p. 153). Genghis almost certainly said no such thing (Rashid al-Din was known to be creative), but the quote is ideal for demonstrating one idea of good. This book takes the opposite stance. The definition matters less than the explanation. Whether getting rid of your enemy and taking his women and loot is good or bad, it requires some understanding. So does the evaluation one makes of it. If one agrees with Genghis, the present book may still be of interest, to see how such a form of good can prevail.

Evil is defined herein as gratuitous, unnecessary, or disproportionate harm. It usually involves emotional overreaction to negative perceptions: threat, stress, competition, dishonor, attack. Evil can take the forms of theft, betrayal, unprovoked (or trivially provoked) physical aggression, callously causing preventable suffering in others, and insulting others. It also includes prejudice and bigotry, even if hidden. "Evil" includes resentment, hatred, gratuitous cruelty, and desire to harm individuals and groups simply because they are claimed to "deserve no better."

It also includes withdrawing from responsibilities and duties in a manner that harms people. Withdrawing may be appealing, and may look innocent, but it is deadly in many contexts—most famously in genocide, when citizens look on and do nothing, but also in such small things as refusing to be vaccinated during the COVID-19 pandemic.

Above all, evil is seen in genocide, unprovoked war, gang violence, and the many other cases of human groups attacking and devastating other groups. As evolutionary thinker Pascal Boyer puts it, "Observers from outside our species would certainly be struck by two facts about humans. They are extraordinarily good at forming groups, and they are just as good at fighting other groups" (Boyer 2018:33). Culture and natural sociability explain this, in Boyer's thinking. We will have more to say.

"Good" is defined herein as helping. That activity involves caring, cooperating, learning with an open mind, and wanting to make the world a better place. Basic are peace, compassion, and charity. It can include ordinary innocent life: sleeping, breathing, running errands. Obviously ethical philosophers will object to such a rambling definition, so to satisfy them we explain to utilitarians that by "good" we mean what creates the greatest good to the greatest number over the greatest time, with no one counting for more than one and with intention to do this added to actual deliberately doing it, and by "evil" we mean that which causes harm without equivalent benefit. To deontologists (believers in an absolute moral base) we will explain that we consider helping others, or the general welfare, to be deontologically Good, and harming others for no rational reason to be deontologically Bad. This issue will be more seriously considered, and, hopefully, justified, in later sections of this book.

Evil is summed up when a young child hits a smaller one, takes his candy, and laughs when the little kid cries. Good is then restored when the child is talked to, sternly, and made to apologize and return as much or more candy. The world's wars do not necessarily get much more complicated. They usually start from a mix of fear, "honor," greed for land and loot, desire for power and prestige, and simple sadism.

Humans reveal a vicious and cruel streak, even in minor activities like hunting game or breeding and training guard dogs. It is almost never directed at people in general. It is most typically directed at three classes of people: flagrant nonconformists, rivals within one's society, and people the cruel individual wants to control. This latter group often includes family members. More usually, it includes rivals, especially groups seen as structural opponents: groups within one's own society, or near neighbors, that appear to be actual or potential rivals. It sometimes includes superiors, especially if they are acting more oppressive than they usually do and the "inferiors" can unite against them. Again, we will have more to say about these issues.

Moralities generally are about helping one's own, and minimizing hurts to one's own, but often include *maximizing* hurts to one's enemies. All moral codes counsel restraint in dealing with personal enemies; almost all counsel kind and generous treatment of strangers. Most counsel restraint in dealing with group enemies. However, most traditional moral codes express a need to be condign to groups that are traditional rivals. Especially condemned and treated prejudicially are those subgroups of one's own society that do not follow all the majority's social conventions—religion, gender roles, or simply lifestyle—and thus seem enemies, or competitors, within (Baumeister 1997; Beck 1999; Smith 2021). These are the cultural, religious, and political minorities that suffer genocide and discrimination. Finally, at the extreme, many or most traditional moralities powerfully advocate hurting enemies, at least in wartime.

The most obvious and immediate evil involves irrational overreaction to harms, from insults to violent attacks. Aggressiveness and antagonism can be heroic when Horatio stands at the bridge or a revolutionary takes on a tyrant, but more often it is directed as weak or innocent people, thanks to cowardice and scapegoating. Fear and retreat can be desirable too, when threat is real and immediate, but cowardice in the face of manageable threats is a source of harm. Combining both forms of irrational reaction into group hate, bullying, spite, and cruelty, is the commonest form of direct evil.

Those produce deliberate harm for no reason other than to hurt "different" people and make them suffer, through physical harm, mental harm, or taking their possessions. The Viking raiders, Hitler's Nazis, Mao's Red Guards, Mexico's drug cartels, and other such groups may have claimed higher motives, but they exemplify this form of evil.

Physically hurting people need not be evil. Plato and Aristotle pointed out that a surgeon causes much pain, bleeding, and suffering, but (hopefully) for the net benefit of the patient. Other examples are easily called to mind. Philosophers can always find an example of a righteous offensive war, a Robin Hood gang, a raid to free a town. Harm *simply* to hurt, loot, or eliminate other people is the evil.

A less obvious type of harm is striving for short-term, selfish benefits that are taken as more important than long-term, wide-flung ones. The benefits of burning fossil fuels and the costs of global warming are the most conspicuous case today. A classic type of harm by callous bureaucratic cruelty involves displacing large numbers of poor people for a project that benefits a few rich, as is often the case with big dams (Anderson and Anderson 2020; Scudder 2005).

Motivating evil, often, is anger and hatred. Anger has its place in human behavior, as a defense (Tavris 1982); only excessive, irrational anger leads to evil behavior. Much evil, however, comes from simply doing a destructive job without much anger and without questioning orders, as the "good Germans" did under Hitler (Goldhagen 1996; this book caused some debate, but has held up well to challenge). Such evil is notoriously "banal," though Hannah Arendt was aware that the high perpetrators are more deranged than banal (Arendt 1963).

Other things being equal, the more fear and insecurity, the worse people act. All sources that seriously consider human harm agree that fear is a major motive (see, e.g., Baumeister 1997; Beck 1999; Collins 2008). Insecurity even without fear produces aggression.

This book is concerned with violence and cruelty. There are other moral problems. Jonathan Haidt (2012) listed dimensions of moral judgement found in societies around the world: Harm/Care, Fairness/Reciprocity, Ingroup/Loyalty, Authority/Respect, Purity/Sanctity. These break out by factor analysis from a vast range of sources, literary and psychological (Graham et al. 2011; Haidt 2012). Another related list gives us "care/harm, fairness/cheating, loyalty/betrayal, authority/subversion, and sanctity/degradation" (Miller et al. 2019:434). This is not an exhaustive list. Yucatec Maya speakers of Mexico praise hard work, responsibility, and tranquility above all else (E. N. Anderson 2005). East Asians praise social support and solidarity, which is not at all the same as "in-group" and "loyalty" (Cohen and Kitayama 2019; Sasaki and Kim 2011). In short, the present book is not addressing all moral issues; it is concerned with direct, primarily physical, harm.

Another part of the human mix is practical reason. It often wins out simply because people want to survive. As David Hume said, "Reason is, and ought only to be the slave of the passions, and can never pretend to any other office than to serve and obey them" (Hume 1969:437). Daniel Kahneman's book *Thinking, Fast and Slow* (2011) is directly relevant: we react emotionally at a gut level, then may think it over rationally. Evil usually depends on avoiding the latter. We thus cannot count on reason to save us; it should, but it rarely does. It is, in fact, too often perverted to the service of hate. All these various moral and rational issues feed into solving the world problems of violence and hate.

Many people have studied this problem before, but few have presented a comprehensive theory. Roy Baumeister's *Evil* (1997) is basic to the field and to our own work, tracing it to personality and perceptions. Another basic work is Ben Kiernan's *Blood and Soil* (2007), an encyclopedic history of mass murder in all its violent, hateful, cruel forms. Aaron Beck's *Prisoners of Hate* (1999) is psychological, coming from a social framework that integrates cognition and emotion. Similar is *The Nature of Hate*, by Robin and Karin Sternberg (2008). James Waller has written several deep and searching books on genocide and its antecedents, including dehumanization and cultural stereotyping (Waller 2002, 2016). Simon Baron-Cohen's *Zero Degrees of Empathy* (2011) takes a stance that people are basically good, but corrupted by bad examples and cultural and social norms. He provides detail on the neurology and neuropsychology of empathy and the lack of it. Steven Bartlett's *The Pathology of Man* (2005) takes a darker view, mainly listing the doings of the bad side; the book reviews a number of older theories. Randall Collins in *Violence* (2008) discusses the whole scope of violence, from what we call "evil" to violence purely for fun, as in pickup boxing and wrestling.

Ervin Staub (1989, 2003, 2011) has been particularly sharp and incisive in his studies of genocide, evil, and repair. He sees dehumanization, zealot ideology (later to be called "exclusionary ideology"; Harff 2012), and stress as causative of genocide and other evils. He sees a cure in strong, reinforced morality, notably tolerance and empathy, but understands that major national and international legal systems will have to be in place to stop genocide. He has devoted his life to finding resolutions, with considerable success (Staub 2018). Gavin de Becker's *The Gift of Fear* (1997) is a particularly fine investigation of insecurity and its value in a dangerous world. He is a security expert who has found that people usually have a "gut feeling" that something is wrong with dangerous individuals, but convince themselves it is imagination, ignore the feeling, and get hurt. He advises us to go with our intuitions in such cases.

Robert Sapolsky's *Behave* (2017) looks at human evolution and cultural restraint. Kathleen Taylor's *Cruelty* (2009) covers important psychological

terrain. Zeki and Romaya (2008) review the physiology of hate. Albert
Bandura's book *Moral Disengagement* (2016) exhaustively treats that side
of evil: cold-blooded failure of compassion. *Complying with Genocide*
(Anderson and Anderson 2020) expands on the above works; the present
book is a continuation of it, exploring more deeply into the psychology
of violence.

Alan Fiske and Taj Rai's *Virtuous Violence* (2014) argued that most violence is excused by claiming it is necessary and even good. Of course, almost
everyone sees defense of self, family, and nation as sometimes necessitating
"virtuous violence" (to use their term). At the other extreme, the excuses
used by playground bullies are notoriously absurd, often coming to no more
than "those kids were littler, so I beat them up." The excuses for genocide by
Hitler, Stalin, and other sadistic dictators do not bear much scrutiny either.
Fiske and Rai show that people always have an excuse; they do not show
that these excuses are much more than window-dressing. Most violence is
done to people who are considered "unworthy" because of ethnicity, religion,
nationality, skin color, or ideology; excuses for such violence do not hold up
to rational attention.

POVERTY NOT A FACTOR

One thing to get out of the way immediately: all authors agree that the classic
lore about poverty and hardship explaining bad behavior is hopeless. Many
mass murderers, cold bureaucrats, and genocide leaders were raised in afflu-
ence. Conversely, the vast majority of impoverished individuals and sufferers
from hardship do not commit atrocities. They often lead model lives. Poverty
contributes to trouble, if only because the poor have less to lose and may
be desperate, but it does not doom anyone to a life of crime. Poverty often
reduces people to living in unsettled and violent neighborhoods, which is a
risk factor, but even there most survive without committing murder.

The famous correlation of poverty with crime may have as much to do
with the rich getting away with it as with the poor committing it. The rich
often get away with literal murder, but more common is the oft-noted fact that
the murderous behavior of the rich and powerful is not "crime." A poor man
kills a neighbor and goes to prison; a ruler uses lies to start an unprovoked
war (as rulers have done since the beginning of state societies) or commits
genocide (as the military rulers of Myanmar are doing today) and is never
called to account. Even more deadly, and less penalized, are corporate sales
of tobacco and drugs. Pollution deliberately generated by giant corporations
in the full knowledge that it would kill thousands of people is not prosecuted.
The tobacco industry has paid only nugatory sums for their actions over

time. Bureaucrats who eliminate health care for the poor as an "unnecessary expense," or displace thousands for a public-works project and provide no relief, never suffer for it. A poor man who hits his neighbor in a fit of rage, however, may languish in jail for years. If one duly accounts for corporate killings as evil, the rich are well ahead of the poor in murderous behavior. Also, claims for the "peacefulness" of modern times compared to the past (Pinker 2013) are not supported (Fry 2013). Modern governments are murderous, with no "poverty" or "virtue" to excuse them.

WISDOM EXPLAINED: CHINA

Another tradition of explaining evil developed in China. As pointed out by Mencius 2,300 years ago (Mencius 1970; Chinese original fourth century BCE), humans get enjoyment or satisfaction from pleasant social interactions. To Mencius, this is inborn (*xing*) in humanity. Such prosocial acts as expressing gratitude are classic ways of feeding the good wolf and feeling good (eudaimonic) about it. As Mencius pointed out, people could not be prosocial unless they had strong innate tendencies in that direction. We all depend on large, complex social groups for survival. Our joys, sorrows, and angers most often come from interactions within those. Mencius used a tree metaphor: If a tree is cut back and starved, it becomes a miserable shrub, but if it is left to express its inborn nature (*xing*), it grows straight and tall. On the other hand, one cannot make a naturally small weed into a tree.

Mencius's great critic Xunzi (1999; Chinese original third century BCE) had a point too: people have also the capacity for selfish greed and overreactive hate. He put it directly: "Human nature is evil; human good is learned" (ENA translation). For him, human nature "is what is impossible for me to create but which I can nonetheless transform" (Xunzi 1999:199). In almost all societies, the inevitability of hate and selfish greed, combined with the need to maintain one's own society, leads to sending warriors off to loot and kill the neighbors. Redirecting, projecting, displacing, and scapegoating hold societies together by channeling the accumulated anger and petty meanness into raids and war. That forces the victims to organize in their turn and fight back, especially since they often (and reasonably) feel that victimization entitles them to do it (Zitek et al. 2010), and so the world turns to blood. Thus, a society needs an army, but then how do you keep evil leaders from sending it against the wrong people? Only by educating the people to make them prosocial enough to get along.

Both agreed on the necessity of education. Xunzi saw education as the only hope for reforming people: Mencius saw it as necessary to keep people growing straight and true. This introduced wider questions of how to structure

society, with Shen Buhai (Creel 1974) offering a preview of modern management science by strongly arguing for defined positions in hierarchies, with
higher-ups taking charge of general issues, lower-downs having charge of
their specific jobs, and everybody sticking to those roles—no meddling by
superiors, no overweening presumption by people under orders. This led to a
whole question of structure and agency, repeatedly addressed in the Chinese
literature, with Confucians arguing for agency (the moral gentleman or lady
will act right and thus reform society) and Legalists arguing for structure:
not only for strict laws but for the rule of law and for a defined structure of
society: the system must work such that anyone can fill his or her role. Later
the Buddhists and Daoists added religious morality; thinkers combined these
with Confucianism in a comprehensive view of good and evil.

The questions of human goodness and of structure vs. agency are endlessly
with us. Between Mencius and Xunzi, the two wolves of the Native American
story are well covered, but neither is as willing as Indigenous thinker to say
they are both within. Mencius, Xunzi, and the Indigenous storyteller agree
that education is determinative.

Chapter 2

Human Constants

Evolution and Conflict

SURVIVAL AND CONFLICT AMONG ANIMALS

The first rule of life for animals is that immediate threats to life, limb, and genetic investment must take precedence over everything else. Chronic threats must be avoided by constant vigilance. This leads to frequent anxiety in animals with nervous systems sophisticated enough to feel such a mood. The good things of life can generally be postponed; flight from a predator or an enemy cannot be. This affects perception. To use a classic example from Buddhist writings, it is easy to mistake a rope for a snake. Doing so is the safe way to err. Mistaking a poisonous snake for a rope can be deadly. All animals with sharp perceptive skills are primed to make this default: to see danger in anything potentially dangerous (this and what follows depend heavily on Clutton-Brock 2016).

The classic response is the fight-flight-freeze response, which is hard-wired into the brains of all animals that possess a significant nervous system. Animals when attacked will try to evade: they will run away, deflect, lead a chase of a weaker animal, do deferential moves, and otherwise avoid direct physical conflict. They can simply bear trouble by cowering down in their lairs. If intelligent enough to have something like a theory of mind, as higher animals do, they can negotiate. Dogs and coyotes, for instance, do this by trying out threat displays and deference displays to see what works with an opponent. Biologists have identified four stages of conflict in typical mammals: studied indifference, display, sham fighting, and real fighting. In display, the mammal tries to look as big and fierce as possible (Clutton-Brock 2016). A lizard will do these purely by instinct, but a dog or cat will tactically deploy them, testing various behaviors to see how far she can push it without having to risk damage.

Only if forced or cornered will they fight, and even here they try to avoid actual violence. Hair stands up, lips draw back to disclose teeth, claws come out. The animals arch to look tall, and growl or roar. If that fails, an animal may chase the threat—another member of the species, or a predator—or run from it. If there is a conflict, the animals scream and snarl, spit, claw, and may even join for a quick slashing bite, but make little real contact and do not hurt each other. At this point, one usually gives up and runs or makes deferential gestures. In general, mammals fight only in desperate circumstances: fighting over very limited food, territory, or mates. The authors of this book have watched lions and hyenas face off over kills in Africa with absolutely no fighting—the weaker side just waits till the other has fed enough to leave the carcass. We have watched different species of vultures squabble over a carcass, the bigger ones displacing the smaller, but if the carcass affords enough food for a meal for all, nobody squabbles.

Animals assess other animals' strengths with great accuracy, drawing on instinct and experience, and defer to strength. The more desperate the threat, however, the less they defer. Even in quite simple mammals, there is a clear correlation between fear and unreasonable response. An unafraid animal will calmly assess the situation and act strategically. It will challenge by display, and only if that fails will it allow a confrontation. It will instantly drop this and defer or flee, if threatened with superior force, but will fight if necessary or if it sees a good chance of victory. They rarely fight to the death, but, in addition to self-defense in desperate situations, three things will produce serious fighting.

The first, and the only one for which they will regularly sacrifice their lives, is seen in protection of young, as Charles Darwin observed. Attacks on a female's young that she is sheltering will provoke violent defense by a tiny bird against a hungry cat (as we have observed). Animals will also fight in defense of their reproductive advantage by guarding and defending their mates, especially if they are collectors of harems, like red deer and elephant seals. Some few mammals are monogamous enough to allow mates to defend each other; coyotes, for example, will fight to defend mates (personal observation). The most social animals, from wolves to chimpanzees to meerkats, have generalized this defense of reproductive advantage into defense of the entire group, since all members are either related or at least potential mates and helpers (Clutton-Brock 2016). Humans have generalized this beyond all measure. They fight over women, sometimes over men, and always to protect the young but they will also fight to the death in defense of any and all reference groups that become meaningful to them, even huge, vague, ill-defined groups like "Islam" or "the white race" or "the workers." This makes humans truly unique among animals—it is, in fact, the most clear and visible difference between humans and others. No other animal would fight to the death for an undefined abstraction. In fact, to our knowledge, no other animals except trained dogs will fight seriously to protect members of another species. Humans routinely fight to protect their pets, livestock, charismatic megafauna, and even favorite birds.

A long second is defense of a critical food resource—either an actual food item or a critical feeding territory. Humans are not territorial in the sense of mockingbirds—humans do not defend individual territories of a specific size with a specific resource list—but they do defend whatever territory is defined by their immediate sociopolitical group. This can be a band's hunting ground, a chiefdom, or a nation-state. Resources are similarly guarded.

Another common conflict is over dominance. A young, maturing animal will seriously fight an older, declining one, sometimes to the death. This is how dominance hierarchies change in the more combative species. Again, humans have extended this beyond all measure, but also have self-consciously put it in tension with equality and equity (Boehm 1999; Graeber and Wengrow 2021). People will fight to the death for power and glory, but will also fight to the death to equalize power, or even to reduce disparities by small amounts. Social, economic, historic, and other factors lead to huge differences in the cultural construction of dominance, hierarchy, and power (Graeber and Wengrow 2021). Classically, those who favor hierarchy and see it as legitimate and desirable are "conservatives"; those who favor equity are "liberals." This usage has somewhat broken down of late.

Finally, the most intelligent animals remember bad treatment; they can hold grudges and take revenge. Even animals with otherwise short memories may remember sustained bad treatment for a lifetime, though the extent of this is debatable. Vengeance is more long-term and serious among humans.

In most mammals, males are stronger than females, which has its effect on competition. In social species, however, females' roles as mothers and group organizers gives them the real leadership power; this is true of wolves and lions. The lion king with his impressive mane cannot stand up against two united females, a fact which makes lion sisters often stay together. Animal drives for competition over mates, territory, food, and other resources drive their conflicts. They may feel something of cowardice, insecurity, and excessive fear, due to threat, hurt, and stress; we see this in abused animals. The Greek writer Arrian, more than two thousand years ago, wrote a beautiful and moving description of adopting a badly abused greyhound with post-traumatic stress disorder (PTSD) or canine equivalent, and making it an ideal pet by gentle, loving, supportive care (Arrian 1831:81–83). Many since who have worked with animals have had similar experiences. Animals can display psychopathy and aggressive disorder, as many humans do. Some dogs, cats, and other animals, however, are simply and incorrigibly vicious.

Conversely, the higher animals have their simple equivalents of most of the standard human virtues (Bekoff and Pierce 2009; de Waal 1996). Mammals, at least the females, and in some species the males, are usually good and caring parents. They practice reciprocity, a biological prime for responsibility and social life. They are usually peaceful and resolve conflict. Chimpanzees have the glimmerings of the distinction between "feeding" and "eating"; their social feeding is a quite different type of event from solitary feeding (de Waal 1996). Some other intelligent animals may well make this distinction, so critical for human social life.

Dogs, when meeting each other, tend to make friends quickly, using a variety of instinctive and highly stereotyped behaviors. Artificial restraint by humans prevents many of these. Thus, when dogs on leashes meet, they are apt to be much less friendly than when they meet off the leash, and a fenced dog barks and snarls when a free-running one would not. (Human parallels should be obvious.) Dogs have a complex social behavior that includes some of the building blocks of morality. Dogs socialize, play, make friends, reconcile after conflicts, cooperate in hunting, recognize packmates, mutually defend the pack, show deference, and keep their society smoothly functioning (Hare and Woods 2013; Serpell 1995). Most of this is mediated through fixed, instinctive behaviors. For instance, when two dogs are playing and one inadvertently hurts the other, the injured party often lets out a distinctive yip. The dogs immediately stop play, reach out their heads toward each other, and just barely touch noses or do some similar move. They then immediately go back to roughhousing. Clearly, this fixed action pattern is the equivalent of "I'm sorry, I didn't mean to hurt you," and it is clearly an important aspect of dog society—important enough to have evolved through natural selection.

Dogs are superb learners, and seem to reflect to some extent on what they do, but their behavior does not require intelligence of a high order. Dogs certainly love, but they do not think much about it; a literate dog would not write Stendahlesque novels. Yet even dogs must decide when to apologize, when to trick each other, when to play or attack, when to mate or avoid. Instinct cannot answer all questions. Dogs and chimpanzees show shame of a rudimentary sort, grief, caring for family members, and even a certain distributive justice to their young; dogs feed their litters, wolves feed packmates, and chimpanzees sometimes distribute food to their whole troops. Violence is common among these animals, and hatred is certainly known, but the animals are not hatefully biased the way humans are, nor do they commit genocide, though chimpanzee troops sometimes target other troops. Finally, animals vary as individuals. Some are born more aggressive than others of the same species. Some are more timid. We need not go into extremely complex and subtle explanations of human quirks; all higher animals have simpler but similar traits.

SURVIVAL, CONFLICT, AND
EVOLUTION AMONG HUMANS

"The human mind was not designed for impartial beneficence. Morality has evolved, both biologically and culturally, as a device for cooperation *within* groups. Groups of humans who help one another . . . are more likely to survive and outcompete other groups that leave their members to fend for themselves. Cultural evolution has taken our biological capacity for altruism and scaled it up with religion and peace-promoting modern institutions. . . . Our social behavior is overwhelmingly driven by our emotions." (Caviola and Greene 2020).

Human changes in recent millennia have sometimes been rather dramatic—evolution of light skin in the last seven thousand years, evolution of small body size in tropical forest groups—and there have been developments such as lactase persistence, but these are changes involving few genes. The more serious aspects of humanity—the genetic substrate, whatever it is, for emotions, intelligence and cognition, basic needs (Kenrick et al. 2010) and wants—are not known to have changed much in millennia. They are highly species-specific, general throughout the species, and evidently the products of long selection (on evolution, see Henrich 2016; Sapolsky 2017).

Almost all human groups fight (Kissel and Kim 2018). So far as we know, genetics does not encourage but does not prevent the fight-flight-freeze response from going society-wide. Evolution of the group violence so conspicuous in humans may have occurred through group battles (Anderson and Anderson 2020, Choi and Bowles 2007). This theory has been challenged. Mark Dyble (2021) showed mathematically that such a genetic development would require extremely high selection pressure—many fatalities for losers, many benefits to winners, over a long time.

Altruism may have arisen the same way (Bowles 2006, 2009; Choi and Bowles 2007), but that explanation would be subject to the same criticism. Most argue that human altruism and self-sacrifice arose through kin selection, in which benefits to wider kin outweigh self-sacrifice by an individual. Martin Nowak answered Bowles (2006) to this effect, pointing out with appropriate mathematical modeling that "kin selection, direct reciprocity, indirect reciprocity, network reciprocity, and group selection" (Nowak 2006:1560) are enough to account for it, and "group selection," whose existence is debated, is not needed for the model. Bowles has revised his own model accordingly, arguing, with Herber Gintis, for a wider picture including selection acting on reciprocity (Bowles and Gintis 2011). It also appears likely that human "hyper-cooperation" evolved at least in part from coparenting by a group that expanded to include wider and wider kin (Burkart et al. 2014; see also Anderson and Anderson 2020; Henrich and Muthukrishna 2021; it is worth noting that cooperation exists even in amoebae [Santorelli et al. 2008], so may not be so difficult to evolve).

Modern humans (*Homo sapiens sapiens*) appeared about 150,000 years ago, as hunting-gathering populations. Agriculture did not appear until just before 10,000 years ago. During the long period of nonagricultural life, people probably lived in groups of 50–150, which were part of larger groups, often defined by language, of about 500. This, at least, is what was typically found to be true of hunting-gathering societies such as the Australian Aboriginals and north woods Native Canadians. The numbers were independently arrived at by several anthropologists, but classically reviewed and established by Robin Dunbar (2010). Inevitably, they have been challenged (e.g., De Ruiter et al. 2011; Graeber and Wengrow 2021). Human societies are flexible. There is justification for the basic "Dunbar's Number" of 50–150: it is the smallest group that can expect to maintain itself reproductively. Smaller groups are subject to statistical "random walks" to extinction (Dunbar 2010). On the other hand, the challenges have certainly established that there is no need to think modern humans evolved in groups of that size. They probably evolved in groups of various different sizes.

Burton Voorhees and colleagues (2020) explore hyper-cooperation further: "Extensive cooperation among biologically unrelated individuals is uniquely human. . . . We propose that the evolution of human cooperative behavior required (1) a capacity for self-sustained, self-referential thought manifested as an integrated worldview, including a sense of identity and point of view, and (2) the cultural formation of kinship-based social organizational systems within which social identities can be established and transmitted through enculturation." In other words, "a culturally grounded social identity that included the expectation of cooperation among kin." Ideas about kin are extended. Eventually, "deviations from expected social behavior are experienced as a threat to one's social identity, leading to punishment of those seen as violating cultural expectations regarding socially proper behavior" (from the paper abstract). This allows understanding of others and their intentions, and acting accordingly.

In any case, group cooperation and group conflict became universal in known human societies. Very often, the cooperation within the group is deployed in conflict with the rival group (De Dreu et al. 2016). Conflict and cooperation have neurological correlates that give them a biological substrate not dissimilar to that of other primates (Sapolsky 2017, 2018). Later cultural development produced larger and larger wars, as people developed larger social units: lineage-based chiefdoms, early states, empires. Traditional small-scale societies, led by a chief or a council of elders, usually are at tension with neighboring groups, and sometimes fight. War becomes larger-scale and more serious as chiefdoms develop into larger and more productive communities.

Humans are perfectly typical mammals in all these ways, acting like other violent and predatory species, but for us this is only the beginning. First, humans assess threat, stress, strength, and weakness in ways more complex than other animals do. Second, humans are so social that they usually fight as groups, and thus see threat, strength, and weakness at the group level. A few animals, such as chimpanzees and meerkats (Clutton-Brock 2016), fight as groups, but only on a very limited level, rarely much above the extended family.

The human form of animal minimization of fighting is our usual ordering of defensive behavior: 1) Prevent in the first place, by caution and civility. 2) Cope by minimizing reaction to slights, not imagining or exaggerating them. 3) If really hurt, bear it with minimal reaction. The Bible counsels a "soft answer." We may laugh it off, pretend not to notice, or just bear. 4) Talking it out is slightly worth a try, but all too rarely works, and in fact can make things worse. 5) Anger: everything from outrageous comments and passive aggression to cutting off heads. 6) Vengeance, often in the form of generalized nastiness. 7) Displacement, scapegoating, projection, often taking the form of general misanthropy, callousness, and greed.

All this is still within the basic animal response to threat or stress: First, there is a rapid assessment of the situation, triggering a fight-flight-freeze response. Then rational behavior cuts in after that initial reaction, hopefully before major damage is done. The same fight-flight-freeze reaction occurs in the face of long-term threats like famine, flood, epidemics, or war. We face those more rationally and with considered judgement, but we still have strong drives to deal with such crises by attacking someone (often a scapegoat), moving away, or hunkering down, at worst getting depressed. Extreme and continued stress in the absence of support can lead to PTSD, with its varied problems from flashbacks to hyperreactivity. The most obvious difference between humans and other animals is that group hatred is often shown against purely arbitrary groups and is stirred up, led, and organized by particular individuals. These individuals may, indeed, define or even invent the groups to be harassed.

People are usually resilient in the face of disasters (Bonanno 2021). Emmy Werner and Ruth Smith (1982, 2001) found that even being raised under very rough and stressful conditions did not damage children if they had stable families or even just chances to get their lives in order; some were reformed by college or the military or other institutions. On the other hand, chronic abuse,

truly unsettling and ongoing disaster, and lack of support are risk factors for
PTSD; war and rape are particularly common precipitating events. Chronic
abuse also tends to produce more abuse. It is fortunately only rarely true that
"hurt people hurt people"—most victims survive and turn out stronger for the
ordeal—but it is even less true that "what does not kill me makes me stronger," as Nietzsche said (Aphorism 8, from *Twilight of the Idols*, 1990 [1888]).
Those who do pass on the abuse are the cause of an appreciable amount of
the evil in the world.

Despite being evolved for sociability, people remain quite individual,
acutely aware of self-interest as well as family interest and group solidarity.
The tension has been a theme of literature since humanity began. Natural
selection may simply have stopped when it got to "good enough," as it has
with the notoriously imperfect lower back. Or selection may have found an
uncomfortable but still best-possible spot, with people always squabbling and
arguing though they depend on and even love each other.

Humans are excellent at putting themselves in the other person's place—
understanding what others think and feel (Mead 1964). This understanding
is localized in the frontal lobes, and is a uniquely human ability; higher apes
and other social animals have it in very modest amounts, but human abili-
ties in this regard go far beyond any other animal's, allowing us to be highly
empathetic and to know how to help (Tomasello 2016, 2018, 2019). A revealing finding concerns tickling. Only *someone else* can tickle an individual.
Self-tickling seems generally impossible. When tickled, whether laugh or
fight depends on the understanding of the other's motivation. (Chimpanzees
and even rats make this distinction too.) The problem with understanding others' feelings is that it can be put to evil use, as when torturers know exactly
how to do the worst to their victims (Baumeister 1997; Collins 2008). Often,
perhaps more often, evil comes from failure of empathy, a point stressed by
Simon Baron-Cohen (2011).

Culture defines all those variables in complicated and often unpredictable
ways. Male humans are, on average, physically stronger than females, but
culture can make them either far stronger than physique would allow, or far
weaker than it would usually determine. Strange patterns of strength and
weakness develop, according to local contingencies that have shaped culture
over time. Hakka Chinese women, for instance, are the strong and muscular
ones, thanks to a heritage of out-migration for work or soldiering by the men,
leaving the women to do the hard work at home (Oxfeld 2017).

Individual differences in strength, levels of aggression, and other personality traits are amplified by cultural and social differences in solidarity, mutual
support in aggression, social greed and praise of looting, and other such traits.
All human societies have faced the problems of evil and breakdown. All have
figured out how to cope and survive; those that did not are no longer with

us. Therefore, all existing societies have some form of governance and some moral codes. All achievement of human individuals must come because they have been supported, helped, and mentored somewhere along the line. No one grows up without care, and no one is unaffected by the caregivers.

COMMON PRINCIPLES OF MORALITY

Oliver Curry and coworkers looked at ethnographies of seventy societies, finding that there are seven general principles in all of them (and probably all other societies on earth): Help and maintain solidarity with family, similarly maintain the group, practice reciprocity (return favors), be courageous in seeking resources and defending the group, divide resources according to clear rules considered fair, and do not steal or appropriate others' property without permission (Curry et al. 2019). Game theory and economic theory in general predict this. One of the researchers, Harvey Whitehouse, has gone on (with coworkers) to chronicle the universal valuing of shame, empathy, coalition building, sanctions against transgressors, and "prosocial punishment," as well as other well-known building blocks of society. All societies use shaming, ostracism, and if necessary serious punishment to deter free-riders, cheaters, and rule violators (Whitehouse et al. 2019:397). Social markers from language and costume to flags and slogans show group membership. Even the smallest societies today are not much like humans 100,000 years ago, but the worldwide distribution of a common morality must count for something. One can infer that those general moral rules were in force at least that early.

All human societies, though to greatly varying degrees, have some set or subset of in-group killings that they define as murder, and thus repress or prevent. They also discourage theft (taking others' possessions without asking), encourage generosity and sharing, discourage anger and hateful speech, encourage kindness, discourage harm, encourage help. These are recognized everywhere as being necessary for a functioning society, and, also, most people recognize that doing right by others actually feels good (Barasch et al. 2014). It is a self-reinforcing activity in humans.

The differences in morality between the San people of southern Africa and such philosophers of today as Henry Sidgwick and John Rawls are largely in the subtlety and learnedness of the language, not in the morality itself. This is not to reduce Sidgwick and Rawls, but to elevate the San groups to their proper level (see, e.g., Low and |Useb 2022. |Useb is a San scholar; the vertical line in his name represents a click that is phonemic in his language). We have heard many philosophically well-crafted arguments from Maya farmers in the rainforest and Chinese fisherfolk in eastern Asia. No one has a monopoly on moral wisdom.

As with other mammals, the level of fear and stress partially predicts the level of unreason of the response. Culture and society make great differences here (Boyd and Richerson 2005; Henrich 2016; Richerson and Boyd 2005; Sapolsky 2017). A culture of violence and looting, a charismatic leader dominating society, a long-standing legacy of fear of one particular rival group, or a recent challenge by an upwardly mobile competitor lead to increasing fear, and thus to more deference (among the weak) or more fighting (among the strong) than reason would predict. Damping down such situations by forcing reasonable behavior on the actors is the key to preventing violence, but it is difficult to achieve. Humans complicate the matter immensely via cultural models, personal plans, and social scripts, making prediction possible but difficult (Alvarez and Bachman 2016). Humans beings are necessarily social; babies cannot survive alone, and, as noted, human groups smaller than about fifty cannot maintain themselves under simple premodern conditions. They thus must have social rules to minimize conflict and allow cooperation. Thus far the good wolf. The bad wolf appears when people are offended. They tend to be defensive and even suspicious, especially toward potential-rival groups in their own societies. They are usually calm, but will flare up, and will join or support without much hesitation when war or raid are called by their leaders. Those who are usually trustworthy and reliable will lie, cheat, and betray trust when an opponent is thought to deserve no better. This, they will learn, often costs them a great deal later on.

Social fear—fear of being rejected, ostracized, or even simply disliked—is often experienced as existential terror, worse even than the most serious fear of starving or illness. It thus arouses real anger. With recursion, this gets constructed to hate, directed toward any social rival. Hate takes over, through vicious cycles (positive feedback loops), unless deliberately damped down, which requires structural morality plus self-interest.

Self-interest, however, is problematical (Kahneman 2011). No one knows *exactly* what their self-interest is. There are too many variables and contingencies in everyday life for us to calculate well. (What will the inflation rate be in ten years . . . ?) Thus, people often avoid the effort of calculating. Second, people, like other animals, initially react with fight-flight-freeze to everything stressful. (They may not even be conscious of it.) Many people never get beyond that, getting stuck in defensive reactions. This is particularly true if they have weak self-efficacy and a poor sense of ability to control their world (Bandura 1982, 1986). They then may be deluded by politicians into seeing their self-interest solely as gratifying their hate for weaker individuals, or, more commonly, weaker structural-opponent groups. In particular, the commonest human reaction is to be solidary and loyal to more powerful or dynamic people who share their structural opponents. This explains how the plantation owners of the old American South could so easily set the poor whites against Black people, and why that tactic has succeeded so well for evil populists and fascists in the modern world.

Initial reactions are emotional, not rational (Zajonc 1980), and the rational comes slowly and usually imperfectly. If people are too irresponsible, ignorant, stupid, or hyperemotional, or all four, they will go with the irrational first response. This is far worse if evil leaders and media personalities are whipping up evil.

PATTERNS OF VIOLENT BEHAVIOR AMONG HUMANS

Humans need food, shelter, security, and other physical requirements; they also need social life and support, and they need to feel in control of their lives. These needs ultimately lie behind all human action. Social life is obviously necessary at least in infancy, since children, unlike baby turtles or crocodiles, cannot survive alone.

A sense of control of life is a less well recognized need, but is known to be necessary for human survival (Langer 1983; Schulz 1976). Need for control leads to competition for power, which can become obsessive and lead to evil. This book is a preliminary attempt to integrate all conflict into one theory. Rivalry and fear leading to aggression and defensiveness are taken as basic, and somewhat explored. Much more effort is needed on this, but hopefully the present book will be useful. Animal studies, as noted above, have shown that conflict over reproductive advantage, resources, and social place are particularly important. These are essentially control issues: control of—or at least ability to protect—mates and young, of life-support resources, and of social place. These add up in humans into personhood—one's validity as an individual. Fear of loss of control over these causes existential panic in humans, as in animals, unless humans can oppose it with heroic amounts of rational coping. Threats of losing them, especially if the threats are vast, vague, formless things (from "the international conspiracy" to "minorities" to "globalization"), are deadly to such reasoning. As infants, people learn to fear, but they cannot yet learn the reasonable coping methods. Especially if their parents are fearful or bigoted, the infants learn to deal irrationally and emotionally with natural challenges. Then, emotional overreaction is censored by parents and later by wider society, leading to guilt and shame as people grow older; the guilt and shame then cause more fear and anger, and the person can settle into a permanently sour and defensive attitude, initially sparked by failure to engage with better methods of dealing with genuine threat and fear. Existential panic about a spouse leaving can lead to murder. Fear of minorities achieving equality can lead to lynching or genocide.

People are not well described by essentialized terms like "aggressive" or "rational." Human beings are highly adaptable and flexible. They deploy a range of strategies. They do not like to kill, and avoid doing it when possible (Bregman 2020; Collins 2008; Hughbank and Grossman 2013). There is, in fact, a long literature on how rarely soldiers in war, police in action, and criminals in stickups actually fire their guns to kill; Randall Collins (2008) reviews this at enormous length. Yet they are incredibly violent when situations bring that out. Collins argues that the microsociology of events determines this. Normally peaceable people suddenly break out in violence, for instance when drunk and angry, and regret it later (see also Alvarez and Bachman 2016; Baumeister 1997).

Humans react to fear in any of a number of ways; aggression is one. They apply reason or do not apply it, depending more on mood and circumstance than on any innate human nature. They can love their families or avoid them. Modern thinking sometimes sets up two straw men: the idea that people are "basically violent" or the idea that they are kind and gentle until socially taught to be violent. Neither one is even close to the truth. People, like all other mammals, are innately gifted with a range of reactions, from violence to flight to deference. These are deployed according to situation. Humans add a formidable level of intelligence, and a variety of cultural adaptations. These let humans fine-tune the genetically coded responses.

It is impossible to avoid irritation and annoyance. There are always aches and pains, mosquitoes and flies, hot sun and cold wind. No one is totally comfortable for long; irritation is a condition of protoplasm. Families are constantly troubled by minor jockeying for attention, affection, love, support, and special favors. Couple and sibling conflicts are inevitable, and immortalized in millions of poems, songs, and novels. Randall Collins notes the human condition of constant low-level "griping, whining, arguing, quarreling" (Collins 2008:338), and that the setting in which most people are most often violent to each other is the family: at least 80 percent of small children fight siblings; 85–95 percent of parents physically punish, even if morally opposed to it; 50 percent even physically punish teens. "Couple violence occurs in 16 percent of couples per years; more extreme abuse in 6 percent" (Collins 2008:374). This figure is for the United States. The rate is far higher in much of eastern Europe and parts of the Middle East. Moreover, all communities have small-scale (though serious) conflicts, often deadly. In most communities, over time, these conflicts are serious enough to prevent any major progress, or anything forward-looking. Yet they can be controlled, allowing improvement.

Thomas Hobbes (1950 [1657]) was right in seeing people constantly at "warre" with each other, but he was wrong about the level and scale. Our wars are at the level of groups, not individuals. Sheer social hate is the commonest cause of harmful violence and other evils. Crosscutting loyalties help a great deal in modern societies, but people tend to pick the strongest social group as their reference group, and then to stick by it in conflict. People are far too social by nature to allow a state of "warre" of "each against all" to exist. They depend on society, and are happiest in a warm, affirming social world. However, people are resentful, hateful, and mean when their sociability is not validated. Being large, strong animals, they will fight if socially hurt or threatened. This, not the competition of each against all, is the real "warre" that breaks societies down.

Similarly, Sigmund Freud's dismal assumption of the basis of human psychology in the id—a dark welter of violence and sex that occupies the newborn brain and can be tamed only by strict upbringing—turns out to be the exact opposite of the truth; psychology has shown that babies are highly prosocial from birth, and that aggressive violence and unrestrained lust are learned responses (Tomasello 2016, 2018, 2019).

Even so, in human societies, there is conflict all the way up: couples, families, neighborhoods, empires. Conflict over tangible resources is often less important than conflict over respect, social standing, and power. Bigger groups or local leaders intervene and manage reconciliation in most cases, but may intervene to make things worse. Thus, murder and war remain common. (On violence, see Akçam 2012; Alvarez and Bachman 2016, and discussion of this work in Anderson and Anderson 2020.) Mercifully, the farther we get from ordinary minor pains, the less inevitable are the conflicts. Some annoyance in families is inevitable, but can be controlled by negotiation. People easily move from annoyance to conflict, but at every stage the process can be interrupted.

This unity of conflict would be trivially obvious if it were not for one thing: all those levels of trouble have been dealt with by different branches of care. Health professionals take care of individual aches and pains. Family therapists deal with family conflicts. Anger management deals with individual feuds. Sociologists and anthropologists try to understand larger conflicts, and politicians try to deal with them, often by making them worse. The problem with these different views, and the silos that enclose them, is that fear, anger, and conflict translate from level to level easily. Badly raised children can become tyrants and dictators. Neighborhood feuds can turn into wars. Local everyday hatreds can be mobilized for genocide. Individual defensiveness can be integrated into strike-force gangs and war bands.

Alan Beals and Bernard Siegal pointed out long ago (Beals and Siegal 1966) that all societies have conflict, because of rivalry, resource competition, and differences in opinion and viewpoint. Conflict is fluid: new contradictions keep arising, new coalitions are made. Conflict involves constantly shifting factions, loyalties, and identifications. They see conflict as an ongoing process within all societies. Social construction and social pressures determine the actual content and the behavior of people. Conflict leads to the hate and greed that directly produce evil. It also leads to stress, threat, and fear that prevent people from doing good; they are too scared or too involved in the conflicts. Conflict, however, can also lead to negotiation, peace, problem-solving, and ultimately a better-run, more harmonious society (Gelfand and Jackson 2019). Beals and Siegal (1966) suggested that the study of conflict resolution should thus be basic to all human science, and also to education and to improving society.

People usually realize that they need to work with others—to cooperate in working for food, clothing, healing, wealth, and position. Also, vitally important, but behind the other social drives in immediacy, are love, care, and warmth. The prosocial feelings are necessary for humanity (otherwise babies would never survive, and few adults would), but they must take last place, following the more immediate survival urges. The level of self-confidence and security within society then predicts (more than other factors) the level of defensiveness of the individual. Highly defensive individuals who are also aggressive become the evildoers.

Developing self-confidence and self-efficacy appears to be the best way of dealing with evil (Bandura 1982, 1986). These in turn depend on learning rational coping with threats. Other things being equal, the person who is least worried about social threats is the one most prone to provide social help, to appreciate the work of other people, and to value other cultures. Admittedly, other things are never equal—there is always surrounding culture to deal with, and genetic predispositions—but building self-confidence may still be the most basic cure for excessive fear and defensiveness (Bandura 1982; Beck 1999). The trouble is that one must develop it at all social levels to stop genocide. Unfortunately, the bad wolf—the powerful and outside-directed side of defensiveness and antagonism—makes conflict too easy. It often wins against the gentler, more local good wolf. Normally, only a combination of hope, security, social support, and solving immediate survival needs can create a climate where the good wolf can flourish. Things go much better if one can "do well by doing good."

There are several dimensions of good and evil. First is the degree to which people can feel love, caring, and nurturance, with a range from altruistic to psychopathic or sociopathic. Most people are somewhere in the middle: usually caring and reasonably decent, but easily induced to snap, be resentful, be irresponsible, and even fight over nothing in particular.

Second is the degree of confidence. A person raised in a reliable, responsible family, and then trained to deal with progressively more difficult problems while growing up, develops genuine self-confidence, and is extremely unlikely to be evil, with no reason to be defensive or cruel (Bandura 1982,

1986). This is true even if the family is quite stressed and challenged (Werner and Smith 1982). Innate defensiveness is marshaled only when clearly necessary. At the other end is the totally abject, fearful person. The dangerous person is the one in between: the person with brittle self-confidence, who is normally brash and confident-acting but is vulnerable and easily brought down by challenge. Roy Baumeister's theory of evil (Baumeister 1997; Tierney and Baumeister 2019) depends heavily on this perception, and remains the most solid and well-documented theory of the deep psychological background of bad acting.

Third is the degree of conformity. An independent person can resist pressures to act bad, but can also do evil voluntarily, especially when ruthlessly taking something from a victim. A total conformist will do anything, including follow orders to shoot down Jews or Tutsi or African Americans. In this case, it may be the person in the middle that does best, going with social pressures when they reward good or neutral behavior, but resisting pressures to act against others without reasonable cause.

A final problem is the human tendency to discount the future and the distant excessively, in environmental matters and elsewhere (E. N. Anderson 2010). Global climate change will cause untold damage and countless millions of deaths within this century unless countered immediately, but almost nothing is done. Summit after summit has produced a "commitment to make a commitment at some time in the future" (National Public Radio, Nov. 11, 2021). India promises to do something about coal burning by 2070—by which time its major cities will be going underwater. A fight between neighbors on one's own street causes more concern. Again, this makes perfect sense in the light of our animal heritage. If an animal is killed by a snake or predator today, the future is irrelevant, so the prudent animal focuses on immediate threats. The same default applies to wide-flung but not obviously imminent problems. The world's problems are mine and "no man is an island," but attention is often restricted to families and neighbors.

In sum, the ultimate wellsprings of existential fear lie in threats to personhood and control of life and resources. The ultimate wellsprings of evil lie in failure to deal rationally with those threats.

TYPES OF VIOLENCE

Randall Collins (2008) reviews a range of violence, from war to mere fun (boxing, martial arts, and even riotous partying). (See also Alvarez and Bachman 2016, Anderson and Anderson 2013, 2020). A brief summary of these, with standard alleged motives, is necessary at this point.

Common homicide usually involves direct anger breaking out of control. Honor, usually meaning group standing and respect, causes a great deal of it, and will be analyzed at length below. Control within families results in much family violence. Neighborhood fights, drunken brawls, and other homicides are well analyzed by Collins, Alvarez and Bachman, and others; they reduce to similar basic issues, usually control of one's social place and world, and to some extent control of resources or outright robbery. What stands out as common ground in all these cases is control of people and resources; control and management of one's social place; high emotions, mostly fear, anger, and hate; and the extreme importance of social identity and belonging. Following orders, conforming, showing social solidarity, fighting for one's group against group rivals, and hatred of potential rival groups all derive from this. It is a pervasive theme of all studies of evil.

Two important points emerge. First, an enormous number of killings throughout history have been by people simply following orders—soldiers, perpetrators of genocide, police, and others. Second, when motives go beyond that lowly level—as they must for the actual leaders and instigators, and for everyday murderers—they are usually a mix of cold-blooded greed for land, loot, and captives and emotional fear leading to anger and hate. Sorting these out is normally difficult or impossible, in spite of the inevitably doomed theories that talk only of "rational choice" or "uncontrolled passion." People are rational-emotional animals (Beck 1999; Ellis 1962).

From available literature, it is appears that most killing worldwide has been done in war or mass murder. For the United States and other high-resource countries, in recent decades, individual murder is far more common. For countries with recent records of massive civil war and genocide, such as Cambodia, Rwanda, and Syria, war is more common. Dubious records from many nations make comparisons difficult.

War is the main form of large-scale murderous violence in terms of the number of deaths it causes. It is normally multicausal, since rarely is a single cause sufficient to start something so important and deadly. Identified motives include Hitler's classic "blood and soil" (Kiernan 2007), meaning ethnicity and territory; loot; captives, in ancient times often enslaved or sacrificed to the gods; revenge, a highly emotional matter; and sheer desire for power and control. Almost as common is ideology: religion vs. religion, capitalism vs. communism, human rights vs. lack thereof, and many more. Some wars are simply preemptive strikes, meant to disable rivals or potential rivals. Wars of liberation against colonial and other oppressors are also common. Of course, wars have at least two sides, so simple defense is a motive for about half the damage. Given the multicausal nature of war, "rational" greed and irrational hate are maximally mingled here. Russia's invasion of Ukraine, for instance, was a classic "blood and soil" war. Putin and many other Russians saw Ukraine as an integral part of Russian territory. There was also the confounding issue of ideology: Ukraine was rapidly adopting participatory democracy and human rights, which Putin and many others saw as dangerous Westernization.

These motives are surprisingly scale-neutral, animating neighborhood fights and international meltdowns. Gang turf battles and world wars can be analyzed the same way, with allowances for differences in scale and complexity. Civil war (Collier and Sambanis 2005) adds regionalism and local resentment. Civil wars are usually either for independence or for power and control over the whole polity, but ideological problems like religion are well represented.

Genocide has been second only to war as a large-scale killer since 1900 (if not earlier). It is directly caused by sheer hate. In earlier times, it was almost always either religious (minorities being repressed) or settler-invoked against weaker inhabitants of land the settlers were taking over. In all modern cases, the hatred has added ethnic and political issues. Religion and settler colonialism continue. Genocide today is almost always mobilized by strongmen in authoritarian systems.

"Structural violence" (Galtung 1969) is a cover term for abusive, often fatal, treatment by bureaucrats and other faceless entities who deny medical care, evict impoverished people from their homes, and otherwise cause suffering for purely legal and bureaucratic reasons. This is another case of "just following orders," and like war and genocide it directs attention to the back story—the ultimate sociopolitical reasons why the leaders and elites of a social system sacrifice some large and uncertain number of its members on the altar of callousness. Particularly common of late has been coldly murderous behavior by giant firms: tobacco companies who knowingly sell deadly products, drugmakers who flood the market with dangerously addictive opiates, fossil fuel and chemical companies that pollute the air and water and cause global climate change, gunmakers who fight down all attempts to control guns or even study gun violence, farmers and food processors who evade safety standards, and countless lesser malefactors. The worldwide failure to control structural violence puts such firms above the law.

Unlike direct murderous violence, this form cannot be analyzed as basically anger out of control. It is a product of simple greed combined with a belief that some very large percentage of the human race "does not matter," because they are too poor or insignificant to be of concern. In Kantian terms, they are treated as means, not ends.

VARIATIONS IN ANTAGONISTIC BEHAVIOR

People vary enormously in aggressiveness and other problem behaviors, with culture, individual experience, and genetics all involved and all poorly sorted out in the explanatory literature. Some people are saintly, always helping and knowing the best word and action in a difficult situation. They need to hear honesty and moderation and solidarity. The two wolves are equally strong potentially, but the one that is fed does indeed take over. People are not basically "good" or "bad"; they are basically quiet, with the genetically based potential to react cooperatively or aggressively, or even both at once, as in cooperating for defense. How the potential, or potentials, develop depends on which wolf is fed—that is, on how individuals are raised, how they are taught to respond, and what circumstances they find themselves managing.

Some individuals are beyond the reach of appeals to perform in a socially defined "good" way. An extreme is found among psychopathic sadists. They get their only real pleasure in life from hurting people, and they spend their time looking for opportunities. One cannot appeal to their "human" side. They are often charming, and may promise anything and seem to be reformed, but in reality they almost never change. They are rare, but they have a disproportionately large effect on society, because they often become mass murderers and sometimes become heads of state. About 1 percent of humans show psychopathic traits (Kiehl and Buckholtz 2010; Taylor 2021). This is a condition that is notoriously hard to treat. Leaders are much more likely than the general public to show such traits, since psychopaths are highly attracted to wealth and power, and have no compunctions about using any and all methods to get those. Psychopaths are notoriously hungry for power and control, and they often get it. CEOs have a higher psychopathy rate than any other job category; lawyers and media people rank high (Dutton 2013). Nurses, teachers, therapists, craftspeople, and other service occupations rank lowest.

Many systems have been proposed for describing evil in individuals. A "dark triad" of narcissism, psychopathy, and Machiavellianism has been recognized for some time as common among strongman leaders (Jones and Paulhus 2017). Up to 12 percent of corporate leaders show at least some psychopathy (Taylor 2021, citing a large literature).

Far more common are people who are more humane, and can manage ordinary human relationships, but are still far enough toward the bad wolf to be hungry for power, and prone to use it murderously and brutally. At this writing, about forty nations worldwide are headed by such people, and they occur in almost every government. Such people are also hard to change. In fact, for the average human, it is easy to bring out the 50 percent that is good (the "divine spark" of Quaker thought), but exceedingly difficult to change the 50 percent that is not—in other words, to increase the good at the expense of the bad. This is notoriously frustrating to psychotherapists. It is conventional wisdom among them that the deepest and most important defenses are the hardest to change, since they are overlearned and have been used by default countless times in the past. They lead to broadly defensive behavior that may color all an individual's life (see, again, Baumeister 1997; Beck 1999). Counter-messages against their failed but seductive messages must be reiterated. A similar fifty/fifty break shows itself in movie viewing. Feel-good movies like *It's a Wonderful Life* are ever popular. Also popular are extremely sadistic books, films and video games. Their wide sale and viewing are proof of both fascination and repulsion.

Goodness is gentle and local, and almost always felt and directed toward members of one's own family and reference group. Evil is usually expressed through hostility and is directed at structural opponent groups and at anyone believed to be a threat. The extreme sensitivity of humans to the slightest sign of disrespect or dislike by their reference-group members keeps most people in a constant state of insecurity; they imagine slights and resent those. It takes considerable self-confidence not to be thus trapped. Scapegoating structural-opponent group members is the almost inevitable result of such offense-taking.

Also, the fifty/fifty split shows why societies can drift along, little changed, for centuries. The efforts to improve are balanced or neutralized by complaining, and defensiveness about change. Progress depends on lucky inventions and hopeful, prosperous, confident times. Conversely, increasing disunion and corruption often lead to feedback loops—vicious spirals—that bring down dynasties and rulers (Turchin and Zefedov 2009). Most nations have a history of cycling between good times and collapse.

Human nature is revealed by what people see as "abnormal." Everywhere, people have a strong sense of the deep difference of individuals on the autistic spectrum: those who want to be nice but lack ability to understand others intuitively (Baron-Cohen 2011). This can be quite disturbing and even frightening to many people. Sociopaths—those with full understanding and intuitive insight and ability to relate, but no social conscience—are often liked and admired at first, but when they show their true colors, they are less popular. Borderline personality is associated with failure of empathy and erratic behavior (Baron-Cohen 2011); borderline individuals tend to flash into anger, making themselves as disproportionately disliked as sociopaths are disproportionately accepted. Psychopaths and highly aggressive people are seen as even more abnormal and disturbing. Humans intuitively recognize that someone who is solely devoted to self-advancement through hurting others is simply not a normal human.

Most people are intensely aware of others' sociability, and expect accommodation, sensitivity to others, desire to "get along," and empathy. This involves intuitively understanding others and their feelings (autistic people lack this but sociopaths have it), as well as considering and caring about others' feelings (autistic people have this but sociopaths and psychopaths lack it; Baron-Cohen 2011; Denworth 2017).

Latest among comprehensive schemes is one developed by Morton Moshagen and collaborators. They have recently postulated a unitary D-factor for the "dark" side of humanity: egoism, Machiavellianism, moral disengagement, narcissism, psychological entitlement, psychopathy, sadism, self-interest, spitefulness. They find that these traits are correlated in individuals they test (Kaufman 2018; Moshagen et al. 2018). This probably explains evil leaders. It does not explain why whole populations suddenly turn murderous, as the Germans did under Hitler. Duplicity and major lying are at the core of such transformations (Jones and Paulhus 2017), and are basic to fascism, including modern American right-wing politics. However, lying is not an adequate explanation. People are all too prone to turn suddenly and violently evil toward potentially rival groups in their own societies, and toward "enemy" neighbors, even without lies.

Paul Slovic and collaborators (2020) found strong correlations in the United States between approving of war if US troops are threatened, giving the death penalty to arch-criminals, supporting gun owners, and punishing illegal immigrants condignly. Of course, this is conservative Republican orthodoxy. It is no surprise that the positions were also correlated with anti-abortion sentiment. Even so, the correlation of the defensive group of stances is reasonable, and surely not confined to the United States.

The range of humans from good to bad is apparently universal. There are records of both extremes, and everything in between, in most societies large enough to show normal human variation. Most ordinary humans are in the middle somewhere. They also vary over time and gender. Young males are notoriously the most violent members of society, a fact that seems universal not only among humans but among all mammals, but this is partly because they have the strength and agility to manage it and still escape (see Collins 2008). The topic is, however, highly complex, with young males in human societies being sometimes extremely peaceful (as, in our experience, among the Maya of Quintana Roo) and sometimes famously warlike (as among some Native American groups in past centuries). Differences are explained and analyzed in detail in a major set of collected studies (Gutmann 2021; Gutmann et al. 2021).

Widely known is the enormous variation in conflict among and within societies (Falk and Hildebolt 2017). The Semai and Temiar of Malaysia fear conflict, anger, and disruption, and suppress those feelings almost totally, thus being a nonviolent society (Dentan 1979, 2008; Robarchek and Robarchek 1998). By contrast, some societies have become so violent that they have not survived; the death rate was too high to keep them viable. Among surviving societies, outliers include the highlanders of Papua New Guinea (Falk and Hildebolt 2017), and, until recently, the Waorani and some neighbors in the Upper Amazon (Robarchek and Robarchek 1998), among whom murder may have caused up to a third of deaths. The vast majority of societies are somewhere in between, with violent death rates averaging perhaps one per thousand per year. The violent death rate in the long twentieth century has been high. There have been long periods of peace in most nations, but at least some war or genocide in almost all, and constant war in some. The United States has been at war almost continually during the entire period.

This widespread variation has led to speculation and debate on the abundance, and even existence, of war in early times. Writers like Steven Pinker (2011) find war common in small-scale societies, but their examples of extremely warlike societies are agricultural ones (such as the highland New Guineans and the Waorani), often disturbed by recent settler conflicts (Ferguson 2015, 2021). Nonagricultural societies, however, show almost as large differences, such as between the historic "fighting Cheyennes" (Grinnell 1915) and the more peaceful Californian groups—though even they had some early warfare (Jones and Klar 2007). Archaeology reveals major conflicts long before outside contact, from the Columbia Plateau of the United States (Harrod and Tyler 2016) to Kenya (Lahr et al. 2016).

General discussions of war before modern times find group conflict to be almost universal. Whether they count it as "war" depends on definition: do local violent raids and small-scale conquests count (LeBlanc and Register 2002), or must there be a formal polity that can formally declare war (Kelly 2000)? In the latter case, wars exist only among states, by definition, but almost all authorities agree that war between groups like the Northwest Coast nations, the highland Papua New Guinea groups, and the Plains Native Americans should count as war. Their conflicts were organized, often openly declared, and to varying degrees formalized and rule-governed (Keeley 1996; Turney-High 1949).

The variation in countries like Norway and China over even short time periods can be extremely high. Within a few centuries, Norway changed from the home of merciless Viking raiders to one of the most peaceful societies on earth. China has oscillated from peace to chaos, depending on dynastic cycles (E. N. Anderson 2019). The same people, under different conditions of threat, stress, and insecurity, may be absolutely peaceful or utterly violent. Individuals may act very differently if serving on the front lines of a violent war as opposed to tending the children back home.

Killing is usually a group matter. Most violent deaths take place in war, bandit raids, and genocide. Other things being equal, or even fairly unequal, the larger the group population the larger the conflicts and the more the deaths (Oka 2017)—but, on the whole, the fewer the wars (Pinker 2011). Overall, there is a tendency for violence to escalate as polities got larger, up to the complex chiefdom and early state level, and then to reduce, as states get better control of their citizens (Turchin 2018; Turchin and Zefedov 2009). Many of the rest are suicide bombings and other group-based activities. Many murders—perhaps most, worldwide—are gang activities, thus also group-based rather than individual. Finally, most individual murders are for social reasons, such as avenging social slights and infidelities. Cold-blooded murder for gain or from mental derangement is extremely rare by comparison.

Homicide rates in nations today vary from around 1 (in much of east Asia and Europe) to as high as 100 per 100,000 people per year. Rates are currently over 90 in Honduras, and well over 50 in Venezuela. The US murder rate is 5.8 per 100,000 as of 2020. Suicide rates long fluctuated around 12, but have been rising recently, reaching 13 by 2017 and going even higher since. Also, the high rates of opioid deaths include many voluntary overdoses not counted in suicide figures. Suicide rates in major US cities range from 6 per 100,000 in New York to 18 in Portland (Silva, Saiyed, De Maio and Benjamins 2021:104). Inner cities in the United States have murder rates up to 100 times as high as the more peaceful suburbs of those same cities. (This excludes police killings.) Seattle and San Jose have murder rates of 3 per 100,000; Detroit and Baltimore have rates of 37, more than 12 times as high (Silva, Saiyed, and Benjamins 2021:126). Modern medicine saves many lives that would have been lost from wounds even twenty years ago, so the murder rate is lowered, relative to past figures, by the higher rates of survival.

Recall also Collins's figures for domestic violence, which is far commoner than other types. It is usually less serious, but, even so, murder by family member is by far the commonest type of murder, and domestic violence is one of the commonest causes of death in young women. "Globally as many as 38% of all murders of women are committed by intimate partners" and violence against women by intimate partners affects from 22 percent of women in Europe to 32 percent in Africa and the Middle East (World Health Organization 2021). This contrasts with the rarity of killing in battle. Collins (2008:44–133) stresses the striking rarity of actually firing weapons at the enemy in a war. Battles are infrequent, and only a small percentage of soldiers fire at the enemy, estimated at 10–20 percent (Collins 2008:52–53, rounded). Descriptions of what he calls "forward panic" and of genocide show much higher rates of killing, but still the killing is episodic, under orders, and not done by most of those detailed for the task. Moreover, killers are usually traumatized by the event, if they are close enough to see the face of the enemy or sense the impact. Killing from a distance is easier, and so is killing from behind; there is a reason why executioners in the old days bound their victims' eyes and struck their heads off from above and behind them. In short, people do not like to kill each other, and do not willingly do it. Even assault and ordinary barroom fights are rather uncommon. Children are perpetrators and victims of frequent violence, but it is usually of a minor sort, though murder by family members remains a frequent cause of child death (Collins 2008).

Collins (2008:186–187) points out that nonviolent crimes are much more common than violent ones, with murder especially rare. Aggravated assault is more common than actual murder, with rates around 6 to 12 per 1000 people per year. Severe domestic abuse of children occurs in 2 to 4 percent of families (the rate is probably higher now). Alcohol is involved in about 25 percent of murders (Collins 2008:266), with aggravated assault comparable. Alcohol notoriously disinhibits fights, or provides excuses (drunken comportment includes feistiness), but does not literally cause them.

Collins also points out that bullying is common in the United States and many other societies. It is, however, rare in many others, from the Semai to the speakers of Yucatec Maya. It can be stopped by damping down conflict and regarding bully behavior as dishonorable and contemptible; bullies act for respect and status (Collins 2008). Eliminating bullying and cutthroat competition for status and prestige would go far to eliminate violence everywhere.

Millions of deaths a year ensue from sheer carelessness—driving, guns, etc. Many of these come from simple error, often due to simplifying heuristics that allow quick action but lead to mistakes (Gigerenzer 2007; Kahneman 2011). Cultural blinders and oversimplification lie behind many of these heuristics. Millions more come from tobacco, drugs, alcohol, and pollution—corporate killing, not counted as murder, but not well-intentioned. Millions more arise from personal conflict, often over "honor." Millions die from social policies that guarantee many deaths without actually being labeled as violent. Finally, millions occur in war. Rather few come from sheer sadistic evil.

One would think, from the above, that violence is culturally constructed to the point that nothing is "normal" to humans. This is not correct. Variation is large, but most societies fall into a broadly consistent pattern. The majority of well-documented societies, over history, have had a few murders per hundred thousand people per year, a war every generation or so, and countless minor fights in between (see, e.g., Collins 2008; Pinker 2011). This indicates broad consistency of humans in response to perceived threats, especially threats to their control of themselves, their lives, and their families. The record of mass killing during war is similar: it is not consistent, but is widespread and common enough to be a near-universal pattern (Kiernan 2007; Shaw 2003).

Variation is structured by political type. Until recently, societies were either small-scale hunting-gathering or horticultural groups, or agrarian states led by a king (or queen, or emperor, or qan . . .) and practicing a large amount of war and raid. A few societies, very often basically pastoral ones like the Mongol and Turkic hordes, have been chronically violent. Settler colonial societies are usually violent toward groups they are replacing. Some agrarian societies, such as traditional China, have tended to be extremely peaceful for long periods, but then violent during dynastic transitions and other break-downs. All such matters are strongly cyclic (Turchin and Zefedov 2009).

Individuals vary in how reactive they are to anger, with innate mammalian aggressiveness mattering as well as culture. They also differ in how fearful they are. A highly angry coward will not fight, unless armed and up against good odds. A highly courageous but not particularly aggressive person will not fight, either. Such an individual will find better ways to prevail in life unless in an actual war or equivalent. It follows that war and genocide are usually started by the most violent and least inhibited persons, a point of obvious importance. People follow orders, if often grudgingly. When the orders are given by Hitler, Stalin, or their like, tremendous bloodshed ensues. Preventing such people from getting power is more important than we real-ized (Taylor 2021).

Impressionistically, it seems that students of violence in general (such as Alvarez and Bachman 2016; Baumeister 1997; Collins 2008) emphasize the rarity of actual face-to-face deadly force and even of any killing, while geno-cide scholars (Anderson and Anderson 2013, Kiernan 2007, Rummel 1998, and many others) see a great deal of violence, with some extreme cases in which whole populations rise up and massacre neighbors, friends, anyone (as in Rwanda in 1994). There is something of a "glass half full, glass half empty" problem here. Certainly, humans are not innately violent and mur-derous, like Thomas Hobbes's "savages," but humans are not peaceable and gentle either (as seen by, e.g., Bregman 2020). There is also no evidence for the huge reduction in violence over time alleged by Steven Pinker in *The Better Angels of Our Nature* (2011). Early times were apparently not so vio-lent as he alleges, though evidence is imperfect. Pinker stacked his case by describing the most violent societies known to anthropology and implying or stating directly that they are typical of our past; actually, at least a few of them have become violent in historic times, because of settler encroachment (Fry 2013). The remote past remains a closed book, but almost certainly was not violent at that level. Conversely, modern times are certainly not as peace-ful as he says. Genocide and structural violence are pervasive; he wrote them largely out of his book.

THE PROBLEMS OF SOCIABILITY

Humans are unique among animals in their propensity for huge and violent conflicts. These often begins at very local levels. Much is caught by the classic proverb "I against my brother, my brother and I against our cousin, my cousin, brother and I against our village, and our village against the world!" (See Voorhees et al. 2020; the proverb is widely known in the Middle East and Mediterranean). Much violence is indeed within the family and neighborhood. For the last five thousand years, most violence has taken place above the village level, in local or wide-scale wars and genocides, but the most pervasive violence is still within the immediate group. Being hyper social and aggressive, people are prone to take offense at even the tiniest suggestion of social downjudging or losing social place or danger of it. They are also prone to form coalitions. They form coalitions most easily and strongly when they act for defense. Bloc hatred is universal and deep.

Coalitions, however, are fluid. They can fall apart into competing blocs. Treachery is common. Suspicion is constant, and security hard to find. Add to this the universal mammalian fact that serious fear must take precedence over everything else, and one sees that humans live a life of social worry. Moreover, especially in modern society, people have crosscutting loyalties: family, religion, nation, political ideology, class, even amusements. This is one clear difference between people and other animals. When in conflict, they tend to identify with the strongest group that will have them, which makes obvious sense. This often forces a choice between a powerful but small elite and a large but weakened mass. People recognize that meanness signals a tendency to treachery and betrayal, but a fair face may do so equally well, so people tend to suspicion.

In many small-scale societies, ostracism meant death. It is now less serious, but still frightening. Loss of power, control, prestige, and standing are only slightly less so. People are scared of direct attack, physical or not. They are scared of betrayal, especially of being abandoned by their groupmates in the face of such attack. They are scared of losing control over their lives, especially of losing it to other people. All these and other social fears drive resistance, anger, and ultimately hatred if they are channeled by an evil leader. They also serve like other fears to preoccupy people and prevent them from focusing on advancing the good. Students of violence (Alvarez and Bachman 2016; Collins 2008; etc.) stress fear as lying behind a great deal of that behavior.

This being so, it makes sense for humans to support the stronger side if they can reasonably do it. Thus, people tend to rally behind the rich and powerful, even if those individuals are exploiting them shamelessly. Politics reveals a chronic problem for revolutionaries: people usually prefer to support the establishment. They identify upward. In American politics, Republicans usually win (ninety-six years holding the presidency since the party began, to the Democrats' sixty-four in the same period, as of this writing). This is especially common among self-consciously "traditional" citizens; even the least affluent of them usually favor the rich, and often despise other less-affluent persons. Democrats win when the rich stumble in a major way, as in 1929 and 2008, discrediting the powerful and leaving the world open for a union of the less powerful. There is also, and not only in the United States, a tendency to get tired of any group in power for very long, so parties tend to alternate, though there are spectacular exceptions, such as Japan, where the Liberal Democrats (center-right in spite of the name) have ruled almost continuously since democracy began there.

Also, given a choice of elites to identify with and follow, people naturally tend to follow the ones most like themselves. Southerners follow southern leaders, urban liberals follow urban liberals, Republicans follow Republicans, Democrats follow Democrats, and so on. Naturally, this leads to disliking the followers of the rival elites. Identifying up, and following leaders no matter where they lead, is the source of a huge amount of the world's evil. We will consider later the problems presented by "strongmen."

Randall Collins (2008) expresses skepticism about any search for motives: "Motives tend to emerge as the conflict heats up. . . . Motives are a category of folk cognition used by participants for explaining events to themselves, and by outsiders such as news reporters, lawyers, and officials . . . [but] multiple, shifting accounts of what the conflict is about are part of the texture of the action itself" (2008:337). Collins grounds violence in the drama of the moment: moods, cultural directives to defend honor or simply to fight to show off, interaction ritual involving escalation, and the "micro-sociology" of immediate encounters. He shows that a great deal of what passes for motives in court, the media, people's tales, and elsewhere is clearly invented ad hoc, often long after the fact. This well-known fact deconstructs Fiske and Rai's case for "virtuous violence" (Fiske and Rai 2014).

THREATS TO SOLIDARITY: WHY GOOD FAILS

Evil unites. Philosophers since the ancient Greeks, if not before, have observed that people unite most effectively against a common enemy. Since evil lives on, by, and for hate, it is naturally a powerful unifying force. Unifying good people is classically compared to herding cats, just as unifying people for evil is often compared to herding sheep to the slaughter. The astonishing unity of the free world against Russia's invasion of Ukraine stands in extremely dramatic contrast to the almost complete failure to respond in more than token fashion to the far greater danger of global climate change. Even the immediate threat of the COVID-19 pandemic inspired confused and fragmented responses.

By contrast, good divides. It makes everyone look to his or her immediate concerns. It values diversity. It tolerates dissent and encourages discussion. It meets divisiveness with civility. It respects individuals and their ways and opinions. It recognizes that helping the world involves everyone seeking in their own ways for solutions and improvements. It revels in moderation and abhors angry overstatement.

Thus, the best way to unite the good is to unite them against evil. Possibly second best is uniting them behind a noble ideal, but too many ideals are the "exclusionary ideologies" of genocide research (Harff 2012). Religious ideals can also unite, but except for highly scripted ones such as the Mennonites, Mormons, Salafis, and monastic movements, religious denominations are usually well supplied with difference and conflict. They dissolve easily into factions and "heresies."

Leaders and would-be leaders classically organize people through charisma, generosity, help to the weak, support to the frail, and other social goods. This leads to the feeling that the great Arab historian Ibn Khaldun called '*asabiyah:* social bonding and loyalty created by the generosity, competence, courage, and organizing skills of the leader and his more able followers. 'Asabiyah is necessary for any successful political movement, though few if any modern leaders can hope for the devotion of a Khaldunian Arab warrior, or expect followers as loyal as those of Shakespeare's King Henry rallying the troops before Agincourt.

Needs for sharing and security, desires for love and care, and successes of leadership and loyalty are organized by every successful society into institutions. These can be roughly divided into two sorts: values and structures. Values are the usual ones: mutual aid, tolerance, reasonableness, and so on. Structures are the forms of governance; Hobbes saw kingdoms as the only successful polities, but now we know that everything from the blissful anarchy of a hunting-gathering band to the complex democracy of a modern Western state can work. People at any level can choose between many possible forms of organization (Graeber and Wengrow 2021). All structures and systems have their life spans, however.

Everyday differences over desires, perceptions of insult or disrespect, and conflicts over control cause much strife. More serious are divided loyalties, which produce endless conflicts, often themes for tragedy. Greek tragedies often turn on a protagonist caught by conflicting loyalties, forced to choose in a context where any choice means death. Tensions between blood kin and marital kin are particularly common in drama. The conflict that has probably inspired the most literary activity is the timeless story of true love despite family opposition. It is immortalized in literature from *Romeo and Juliet* to countless folk ballads and stories around the world. Much of this literature turns on the ease with which such matters could have been resolved, had the contestants only talked it out with each other. In *Romeo and Juliet*, the tragedy forces them to do exactly that—too late for the unfortunate lovers.

An extremely revealing point about popular literature is its universal recursion to good guys vs. bad guys, the good guys almost always being "us" in some sense, the bad guys being "the others"—almost always a rival group, not strangers. Alternatively, from Sherlock Holmes to Superman, there were noble crime-fighters capturing an endless succession of vile criminals. Every culture has these stories.

Really great literature often shows the complexity of the real world; consider how Shakespeare's plays always have spokespersons for all sides. *The Tragedy of Julius Caesar* presents a flawed Caesar, an idealist if scoundrelly Cassius, and a conflicted and easily led Brutus. Really serious moral issues are resolved in comedies like *Measure for Measure* by such transparent deus ex machina endings that the intent is clearly to leave the audience with the moral question that the contrived ending does not really resolve. But such stories do not sell well to the masses. Simple good vs. bad keeps encouraging everyone to see themselves as shining heroes and to look for enemies everywhere else. A result is that conflicts like that between Democrats and Republicans in the United States have become mad Hollywood fever dreams. People reduce the most complex questions to partisan hate, in ways all too correctly anticipated with fear by such founding fathers as Madison and Hamilton (Hamilton et al. 1961). They tried hard to make such scenarios unlikely, but ultimately did not succeed.

Humans are particularly prone to take completely arbitrary and imaginary markers for group identification, and then kill with rabid violence over challenges to those. Flags, "race," trivial religious differences ("heresies"), ideological minutiae, arbitrary words that become identified as "dishonorable," different clothing colors, and countless other examples occur. Sports fan conflicts that get out of hand have caused wars, such as the five-day "soccer war" in 1969 between Honduras and El Salvador (Collins 2008:328).

The dynamics of rise and fall in dominance are particularly prone to produce violence. Formerly dominant groups that are losing their edge are extremely dangerous. Less-educated whites threatened by minority groups that are getting better educated and more fairly treated provide an example familiar in the United States and Europe. Traditional religious groups threatened by secularism are increasingly dangerous in the Middle East, India, the United States, and elsewhere. India, in fact, is fast collapsing into a Hindu-supremacist state where freedom of religion is no longer assured and persecution of non-Hindus is regular; the future of India as a secular democracy is in serious danger (Parth and Peterson 2022). The rapid worldwide rise in right-wing extremism in the twenty-first century tracks rising fear among such groups as inequality increases, limiting access to resources. Getting individually or socially better off seems more difficult; progress and change are increasingly seen as the enemy.

Violence is most often started by heads of state or by the large-scale enterprise rulers to protect and expand their power over their political bases. In former times, the leaders had to be minimally competent, since they had to organize and often fight in wars. Today, the leader is more and more apt to be someone like Hitler, Stalin, and Trump, someone who places themselves firmly above the law and even above truth, using the Big Lie technique, defying experts, and thus inevitably leading their countries into disasters—yet keeping the enthusiasm of their core supporters. They appeal, however, to the same timeless animal reasons for conflict: Hitler's "blood and soil" (Kiernan 2007), and dominance in hierarchy.

Studies like these seem to move between scales with reckless abandon. It is true that understanding war requires attention to emergent matters that do not appear in one-on-one conflict. However, the basics of conflict continue. All human conflict is, by definition, social, even if it is only a parent disciplining a child. The basics are the same at all scales: challenge, anger, overreaction, escalation, violence. The main emergent is conformity: the demonic "following orders" that turns decent humans into perpetrators of genocide. Yet even that appears at one-on-one levels. Violent people are conforming to cultural rules about reacting and attacking.

THE IMPACT OF CHILD-REARING

Babies almost immediately develop good emotions and behavior. They are born already reacting positively to their parents' voices. They soon display innate patterns of care-seeking and affection, to which adults respond (Tomasello 2016). They smile, touch, show delight at play, and cuddle. At first, they cry only because of actual discomfort or fear of abandonment. They fear falls, neglect, and strange disturbing experiences such as loud noises. Later they begin to show selfishness and defensiveness. By one and a half or two, they learn to feel and express personal wants, to have their own agendas, and above all to fear loss of control. This leads to protests at discipline, and soon to the "terrible twos," which come about when toddlers are required to learn limits. Babies also cry in sympathy with other crying babies, and toddlers help each other and react with real compassion to one another's hurts (Tomasello 2016). Absolutely key in human development is the period from two to five, when children test the limits of control over their little world. Parents and peers prune back extensions that are unacceptable to society. Sensitive, caring parents and normal children deal with this well. Children, and their parents too, learn to avoid selfishness, violence, and irrational anger and fear, without cutting off independence and self-reliance. Inept parents and neurologically different children may not be so lucky. At worst, aggressive and mean tendencies are not cut back; outgoing, warm, caring ones are.

The resulting unpleasantries are characteristic of three-year-old children's behavior. Some of these are fixed in behavior. It is difficult (if not impossible) to grow out of *all* babyish defense mechanisms. The stock phrases "disapproving," "sick and tired," "won't put up a minute longer," all key into this: they are mothers' phrases that get internalized and repeated in adulthood. Cowardly defensiveness is often a grown-up's response to being scolded by stern parents. The extreme patriarchy of fringe religious sects is surely related to much scolding by mothers.

Another inevitable part of infancy is deferring to and adulating authority, being weak, and having to develop independence and agency very slowly and gradually. Without doing so, deferring becomes cringing, weakness becomes cowardice, and obedience becomes mindless conformity. Conversely, parents, no matter how democratic, cannot avoid the need to control their children. Such control can easily be overextended into the wider society, even to oppressing the weak. When parents fall into such behavior, children rebel and become defiant, and that too can be overgeneralized and overextended in later life. Training for independence and self-reliance does not simply happen. It must be consciously directed. In former times, that was necessary, and was done. Today, too many people fall into the traps. Extension of normal family relationships can thus break for good or ill.

Recent studies confirm the good old Victorian diagnosis of the origins of bad behavior: bad seed (genetics), bad rearing, bad company (Baumeister 1997; Beck 1999; Belsky et al. 2020; Collins 2008; and other major references for evil). Genetics may be the least of these, but there is some genetic loading for psychopathy and other extreme conditions. Familial genes *not* passed on to the child may still greatly influence them, since they may shape the child-rearing behavior of the parents (Kong et al. 2018).

Punitive rearing with physical punishment and/or family violence and abusiveness establishes physicality over thinking, and violence over peace. Physical punishment has effects similar to those of outright abuse (Gershoff et al. 2018). Very early poverty and deprivation can lead to slight but real failures in brain development that cannot be corrected by later good nutrition and living arrangements (Mackes et al. 2020); and poverty in later life causes damages too (Mani et al. 2013). In fact, early-life mental problems are always difficult to fix (Starr 2018). Conversely, family life with caretaking parents and a nurturant, supportive family leads to care, responsibility, and helping.

The key is teaching children from the beginning that defensiveness can be a serious problem, and teaching them how to deal with attacks, threats, stresses, and fear without giving in to overemotional and excessively negative defense. Learning self-control is critical (Baumeister 1997; Belsky et al. 2020). They need to be taught how to deal with hateful lies and why such lies are so plausible. Parents who praise their children's accomplishments without being warm and loving can cause worry and defense—these are the "spoiled children" of legend. Warm, loving parents, even those who indulge their children, do not "spoil" them (Brummelman et al. 2015; Gopnik 2016).

Ideally, children learn to take people as they are, then deal with them reasonably and sensibly. The difference is strikingly clear when a troubled kid is in school. The bullies beat them up, the puritanical teachers made them stay after school or go to the principal's office. In such a situation, the child raises hell. The reasonable teachers deal with trouble by sympathetic cautioning and preemptive rule-setting. In the latter situation, the troubled kid rarely makes any trouble at all. Gopnik (2016) says: "If you want to think of an ideal context for children, it would probably mean more mud, livestock and relatives than we can usually give our children in an urban setting"; quoted in Winerman 2017).

We now know that humans are born with a great deal of moral equipment, some of which goes so far back in time that we share it with chimpanzees (de Waal 2005; Johnson 2014). However, moral instincts determine only very basic concerns. The rest of morality has to be explained as the development of self-conscious social codes. Children begin to work these out on their own. With inborn tendencies, parental guidance, and peer interaction, they work out playground codes by the age of four or five. These are common knowledge: Don't hurt other kids, care and share, be fair in dividing goodies, and so forth. Many people never advance beyond this, and a few never get even this far. A functional society requires rather more, but at least playground morality is valuable and indeed essential. It is also shared almost worldwide. It also explains why homeschooling and exclusive private schools can be very bad for a child who never gets gets the wide experience with humanity—unless special attention is paid to that, as good homeschoolers do.

Without playground morality as a foundation, humans would not come so universally to standards of duty, integrity, fairness, honesty, generosity, courage, self-sacrifice, responsibility, and respect—these all being universal in every human society (see, e.g., Brown 1991), though different societies may value some of these more and others less. Honesty is very highly valued in some societies and hardly valued in others, but every group on earth pays at least lip service to it. From playground morality we learn to manage certain tensions: individual rights vs social obligations, honesty vs politeness, active help vs simply not harming others, and so on. Mark Johnson (2014) has even developed a whole moral system from innatist perceptions. The child develops courage, based on innate tendencies to explore, adventure, love, and otherwise take risks. In so far as these are supported and praised, the child is literally "en-couraged." Cowardice is often shamed out of a child, mostly by peers. Both courage and cowardice are modeled by parents and peers. It takes tremendous courage to interact with people and to be a moral individual in society.

The best caregivers teach their children to cope competently and courageously with life's problems, but no child or adult ever fully loses the deep-buried memory of a time when every stress was an incomprehensible, unmanageable menace (Beck 1999). The worst caregivers subject their children to random brutalization; the children learn to cope by violence and cruelty. Life becomes a dialogue between strong, exploratory, confident, outgoing tendencies and scared, weak, abject ones. Roy Baumeister (1997, 2006) has pointed out that high self-esteem coupled with insecurity is more apt to lead to violence than low self-esteem. The proud and touchy are dangerous. People who have suffered bad treatment by others will often blame themselves, develop a confused self-esteem and self-image, and become touchy and defensive in consequence (Callan et al. 2014).

Prejudice and bias have a terrible effect on children in the targeted groups. Recent thorough, excellent studies report levels of trauma and stress in adolescents subjected to poor or biased treatment (Benner et al. 2018) and effects of growing up with racism on African Americans (Roberts et al. 2021). The effects are not good. George Bonanno (2004, 2021), among others, has demonstrated that trauma is well managed by most people, who are incredibly resilient, but some damage can always persist, and a sizable percentage of people, around a fourth, are seriously hurt. He found that flexibility was critical, with a sequence involving context sensitivity, repertoire of coping strategies, and feedback monitoring (which can be as simple as talking to yourself). Knowing options, keeping them open, and assessing them as they are deployed are keys to coping with tragedy or misfortune. This is progressively more difficult if one was raised in a harsh environment with few choices and much suffering.

Getting children from rival groups together can make them friends (White et al. 2021), but only if it is done with wisdom and care. Decades of school integration in the United States have failed to cure racism. Yugoslavia fell apart partly because of the failure of well-intentioned school integration and children's programs to dent ethnic hatreds there (Alexander and Christia 2011). More contact between rival groups often makes prejudice worse, not better (Kotzur and Wagner 2021). Managing such contact is critical: whether it means working together for a common goal, or merely being thrown together in a situation where conflict can be exacerbated. The best parenting can be derailed in "tween" and teenage years. Children at that age tend to conform to peers instead of elders (Harris 1998).

When the child finds a successful coping strategy, this becomes a deeply and vitally important and cherished part of their life. It is defended at all costs. Threats to it and criticisms of it are particularly deadly. If it is an immature and ultimately poor system, like abusive violence or denial, the person is stuck for life with it; it is very hard to change (Ellis 1962). Evil results when one's most deeply cherished coping mechanisms are challenged in such a way that they invoke further coping mechanisms that are often developments from the immature, weak, and frightened responses of childhood. This grows worse in proportion to how much of one's life, career, and inner self is tied up in the coping mechanism. This, among other things, explains the extreme behavior of religious fanatics. For people who are both personally weak and deeply religious, religion has been the great coping mechanism, best because it is most social and most deeply shared with the accepting social group. Many, when socially challenged, gravitate to extreme and exclusionary religious sects. In a world where bullying younger children was normal and expected, children routinely become bullies (see Baumeister 1997). Many keep it up into adulthood, where it usually became political. In a world where bullying is sharply checked, children avoid it.

Chapter 3

Histories

THE HISTORY OF HUMAN EVIL

The straightforward history of mass murder has been covered countless times. (*Blood and Soil* by Ben Kiernan [2007] stands out.) All that is needed here is to examine special topics that relate closely to the thesis of the present book. Ecology, religion, and politics are part of the ultimate backstory of evil, so their specific roles will be considered in this chapter.

For a million years, more or less, humans lived in small groups, rather fluid, structured largely by kinship but accepting nonkin as spouses or simply wanderers looking for a home. Larger polities emerged quite early, but the state—an institution with formal laws and an elite who had the right of enforcing them—developed a mere five thousand years ago. It arose from village-level societies that came together for reasons still obscure, but probably including war (for debates on the subject, see Graeber and Wengrow 2021, especially sections on the ancient Near East). The average state-level society throughout history consisted of tight local communities ruled by a king or equivalent. There were small republics, often city-states, and vast sprawling nomad polities led by charismatic heads like Genghis Khan, but most polities were dynastic kingdoms. Higher authority set general policies and started wars, but had limited power to manage on the ground; "Heaven is high and the emperor is far away," as the Chinese said.

These conditions in local communities forced personal and interpersonal responsibility, since local communities—from city wards to rural villages to ships at sea—had to manage themselves. Like the "average" human, good to people most of the time but hostile on occasion, the average society was an accommodation between peaceful everyday life and frequent violence from bandits and warbands and occasional invasion by enemies.

Civilization, when it emerged in the form of urban-centered societies with standing armies or equivalents, quickly fell into a pattern. There were small-scale local societies (villages, nomadic tribes, and so on) still governed by elders but tributary to the state. There were large plantations, mines, and (later) oil wells and the less-skilled forms of staple manufacturing, run by a powerful boss and worked by landless and often servile labor. There were skilled workforces of business operators, bureaucrats, scribes, priests, and other professionals. The ruler—king or military leader—would try to balance all these.

This threefold division is still with us. In general, the small-scale units—now farms and small towns—are conservative, but not hidebound. The rulers of servile-worked enterprises, from ancient Roman estates to nineteenth-century plantations, are extremely right-wing, because of felt need to manage a workforce controlled by force rather than wages. By contrast, professionals and many urbanites tend toward a morality captured by the French Revolution's slogan, *liberté, egalité, fraternité*—in modern garb, freedom, equality before the law, and tolerance. Educated Westerners now see this as obviously "right" and "moral," but the results of both voting and armed conflict, worldwide, show that people often prefer a strongman leader to democracy or the rule of law (Stanley 2020).

Elites in early times were usually elite by birth. A conquering ancestor started a chiefly, kingly, or patriarchal dynasty. Such nobles by inheritance had codes of conduct that damped down overreaction, though there were also "honor" codes that tended to make it worse. The damping-down codes have gone the way of traditional culture, leaving us with failed protections in that area. Hereditary privilege is alive and well today, but largely in "racial" group categories, not in dynasties. Individual elites today are more often defined by money or immediate political power. Traditional religions usually advocate leveling, but allow hierarchy, and the result is an enormous range, from the extreme egalitarianism of early Quakers to the extreme hierarchy of the Catholic church. Only Confucianism—more philosophy than religion—deals forthrightly with hierarchy and how to structure it and modify it to make it bearable and even beneficial. (China had vast abuses of power in early times, and has even worse ones now, but they were justified by Legalism and more recently Communism, not by Confucianism.)

Early social worlds broke apart in modern times, as autocrats got more and more ways to rule directly and cruelly, and as local communities fell apart and eventually collapsed. Robert Putnam described this process in Italy (Putnam 1993) and the United States (Putnam 2000). Some communities got deeply involved in trade, commerce, and knowledge, and thus into Enlightenment virtues of equality, solidarity, mutual responsibility, and civil discourse. The results include some of the worst conditions humans have ever experienced.

Slavery reached a peak of cruelty in the eighteenth and nineteenth centuries (see, e.g., Stedman 1988). Genocide peaked in the twentieth. Structural violence merged into deliberate campaigns of mass starvation (Howard-Hassman 2016). Conversely, the best conditions humans have ever known exist today in Scandinavia and some other small rich countries (consider the crude but significant measure of life expectancy, now well over eighty in these countries). Health and wealth beyond the dreams of ancient kings are routine today in such countries as Norway.

Modern politics takes off to a great extent from Locke and Kant. The more realistic, materialistic side of the Locke-Kant tradition led through the Enlightenment, the Founding Fathers, Marx, and other visionaries to modern liberal and left politics. The more Platonic-idealists side went toward conservatism—essentializing Tradition, Race, and other dubious entities. Classical conservatism likes hierarchy and fears change (Jost et al. 2003).

The Enlightenment is now giving way to expanding autocracy, at least in part because the world is filling up. There are no more frontiers to settle or new lands to raid for riches. War is more dangerous than ever, as nuclear warheads and drone-carried bombs multiply, so regimes have turned to genocide as the best way to unite people in a common cause. The age of interpolity war—basically from the earliest states up until 1900—has been replaced by the age of genocide. Even during World War II, an exceptionally bloody conflict, genocide caused a large percentage of the deaths.

Chinese dynasties were started by leading generals four times (Han, Sui, Tang, and Song); by extremely violent local leaders three times (Qin, Ming, communist); by foreign war bands and warrior peoples six times (Jin, Wei, Liao, Jin, Yuan, Qing). The violent extremists take over when there is general chaos and no way for a general to emerge easily. This pattern is repeated in Honduras, El Salvador, and elsewhere today. As usual, this scales down: Gangs get taken over by their worst members. It can then happen that the worst gang takes over the country.

It has been said that "God is always on the side of the heavier artillery"—a line variously misattributed but of unknown origin. (It once ended "bigger battalions.") Equally old, and equally misattributed, is the dubious wisdom "An army of sheep led by a lion does better than an army of lions led by a sheep." Both are wrong: the real success very often goes in the end to the more united and motivated side. Extreme cases are the success of a few small Native American groups at surviving and holding their land despite the might of genocidal governments. The Yaqui and Seri in Mexico and the Mapuche in Chile are examples. More recently, we have seen the Viet Cong and the Taliban resoundingly defeat the United States, and the resistance of Ukraine to Putin's troops. Not even God can reliably give victory to heavier artillery in the service of a vacillating and overextended power attacking highly committed local people.

Technology has changed importantly over time. Technology is, basically, rational action directed to inventing devices that can remove bottlenecks and blockages on satisfying wants and needs. The greatest technological achievements—the ones that really opened the world to humans—are all anonymous achievements of the distant past: fire, the bow and arrow, agriculture and domestication, writing, the wheel, urban planning, specified roles and functions in government, pottery, money, metallurgy, and the other classic markers of cultural evolution. Money is treated astonishingly differently in different cultures (Cohen et al. 2019), partly because it is a notional entity—a measure of value rather than a real thing (Graeber 2014). It is instantiated in coins and bills, but now that almost all the money in the United States consists only of electronic records, we are made aware that money is, ultimately, a social agreement.

Notably important technological innovations have been in communication. Writing, data storage from baked clay tablets to computers, printing, the telephone and its child the cellphone, radio, television, and social media have all been popular, spread fast, and been adopted widely. Radio, then TV, then cellphones all spread with incredible speed, faster than other technological improvements. Other important areas of innovation have been food production and storage, medicine, transportation, and urban planning including things like sanitation. Consideration of these takes us far from mass violence, but it is necessary to note that mass killings have become rapidly more common and deadly with inventions in improved communication, information processing, and organization. These make surveillance, discovery, control, and ultimately mass murder ever more easy and simple.

ECOLOGIES OF VIOLENCE

Violence, including structural violence, has an ecology. It necessarily occurs in particular economic arrangements, and some arrangements breed more violence than others. Food production and consumption, and their psychology, vary enormously across cultures (Rozin et al. 2019; Talhelm and Oishi 2019). Ecologies matter in the politics of good and evil. (Observations below are drawn from longer analysis in E. N. Anderson 2014.)

Paddy rice agriculture forces sustainability because otherwise it crashes in a very few years. Slash-and-burn also crashes if done badly, but the time is longer, thirty to fifty years. Wheat-livestock is less prone to encourage sustainability, since farmers can goose it for a long time with more and more fertilizer or rotation or the like without an immediate crash. Also, it can be extremely extensive (vs. intensive), allowing plantation agriculture with bonded labor to develop. One cannot do that easily with rice; farmers must be fairly independent, to maintain the irrigation works and fields. Rice farming with enslaved persons failed in the United States, to be replaced by cotton, an ideal crop for plantations using servile labor. Low-yield wheat agriculture forced Europe to go seafaring, first to get fish for food, then to make money. This led to the rise of science, partly because of needs in shipping, manufacturing, and commerce. Dependence on long-range voyaging and trade led to colonialism and conquest. The world is influenced everywhere by the wheat-and-livestock world that Europeans propagated.

Throughout history, a major predictor of reactionary politics and violent oppression has been giant plantation agriculture, in which the plantations are worked by servile labor. The labor force is paid starvation wages, replaced easily, terrorized into putting up with any treatment, and denied rights under law. Through most of history, the labor has been actually enslaved, but landless laborers on contracts that keep them in debt to the landlords serve quite as well.

Servile-worked estates go back to Babylonian temple lands, ancient Egyptian pharaonic fields, and (much later) slaveholding plantations in China. They dominated agriculture in the Roman Empire, especially in Byzantine times. Most farms were smallholdings, but the great estates dominated the agricultural landscape and above all the political landscape. They were owned by royalty, senators, and the very rich. The Byzantine Empire's notorious failure to accomplish much in its thousand-year reign (Gibbon 1995 [1776–1788]) was due at least in part to its dependence on the slave trade and on slave-worked large-scale agriculture.

Large estates worked by serfs then dominated Europe until modern times. Meanwhile, in China, large estates gave way increasingly to smallholder farms, and servile labor to yeoman farmers (E. N. Anderson 2019). China runs opposite to the West in these matters. Imperialism and colonialism drive ecological disaster wherever they occur. The track runs from Babylonia and Assyria to Rome to the Portuguese and Spanish empires to modern times. These gave us slavery and plantations and colonialism. Extremely consistent over time and space is the fact that rural and primary-production economies and communities are the most conservative, then heavy manufacturing ones, then light manufacturers, then skilled service industries. A disproportionate share of progress in freedom throughout history has come from trade-and-knowledge-based states.

Agrarian societies of the past were all apical—with kings or strongmen—and all had slavery or servile classes. The plantation owners, and others who controlled these unfortunates, were the leaders and drivers of hierarchic, repressive ideologies. This is still the case. Giant agribusiness interests have been supplemented by giant fossil fuel interests and other large-scale primary-production interests, from big dams to mining, but the core is still plantations, ranches, oil wells, and coal mines.

The political economy of hierarchically organized primary production is, in fact, the main source of the financial backing for right-wing politics. It is a world that naturally leads to workers being unpaid or underpaid and repressed, women kept "barefoot, pregnant and in the kitchen," freedom of opinion being outlawed, and respect for hierarchy being the highest virtue. The small-farming sector is always significantly more free; independent farm women do not easily reduce to baby-producing machines. Even the small-farm world remains more conservative than the urban one, in every modern society known to the present writer. Rural and semirural areas remain the stronghold of far-right voting.

Evil thus can come from sociopathic or psychopathic individuals, from dysfunctional families, and from involvement in bad company (gangs or the like), but once those are established, the great economic driver comes from particular socioeconomic formations that privilege hierarchically organized basic production. The extreme counter is the world of international or interpolity trade and communication; here, individual enterprise, creativity, adaptability, and learning are rewarded. Trade and commerce can be intensely reactionary too, but at least there is the possibility of better.

Ecology influences personality, though erratically and unpredictably. Herders tend to be more independent, freewheeling, and quick to arouse than farmers (Talhelm and Oishi 2019). Mountain people are notoriously more independent and hard to control than easily conquered valley-dwellers. South Chinese, used to the large-scale, tight cooperation of rice farming, are more cooperative and collectivist than north Chinese, who have small farms (Cohen and Kitayama 2019; Talhelm and Oishi 2019; in spite of criticism [Ruan et al. 2014] this finding seems to survive). ENA can add confirming notes from fieldwork in China: Hakka, Teochiu, and Akha, all small-scale hill farmers, are notably more independent than intensive rice-farmers, and the boat-dwelling fisherfolk are the most independent of all, a point well known among Cantonese (E. N. Anderson 2007).

Societies also vary from violent and murderous to peaceful and gentle. All geographic regions have the range, and the differences are loosely patterned. Groups that live in mountain areas between two large and powerful empires tend to be wild and hard to control. The Caucasus and the mountains separating Pakistan from Afghanistan provide examples, and the Scottish-English border once had that reputation. Peasant villages in agrarian empires tend to be peaceful, since the empire can crush them if they rebel. Trading cities and towns are relatively peaceful, since they must maintain peace to keep trade flourishing, but they still have an appreciable amount of crime, since there is considerable flow of wealth.

Beyond that, the economic grounding of hatred and fascism is rather poorly known, partly because there is surprisingly little consistent and definite emerging from existing research (see, e.g., Harff 2012; Mann 2004, 2005; Paxton 2005; Snyder 2015, for particularly good histories that make this point). All sorts of people became fascists in 1930s Europe, including many of the best poets and thinkers as well as captains of industry and street thugs. Outside of the link with plantation-style agriculture, there was an astonishingly broad coalition supporting fascist leaders. Today, there are clearer worldwide patterns of primary production and giant international firms vs. small-scale enterprises and service professions, but links need further study. Thus, in the end, emotional violence and systematic structural violence often come together, via ecologies of honor, exploitation, workforce control, and resource conflict.

RELIGION AS SOURCE OF VIOLENCE

Religion has developed a reputation as a source of bigotry and hatred. It has been the most common source of genocides and similar mass killings, over the longest time. Religious massacres go back very far in history, and have been abundant, especially in the western Eurasian world, during the last two thousand years. Yet religion has also done an enormous amount of good. Religions have mobilized literally billions of people in good service. Atheists are simply wrong in their frequent charge that religion is nothing but a source of evil. Over time, many religious organizations have proved easily bent to authoritarian positions and policies. Those policies, however, often prove to have been set by giant landed interests or other existing power systems, rather than emerging from the religions as such. It takes some effort to make Jesus's teachings of peace, love, sharing, and poverty into a justification for mass murder by elites, and the effort is rather more likely to be expended by conservative elites than by the masses.

In traditional societies, morality is generally taught in the broad context of religion, defined here as the collective representation of community (Durkheim 1995[1912]) in a sacralized form. Religion involves a god, a spirit realm, a pantheon, a real-world entity such as the sun or moon that is worshipped, or any similar divinized realm that has tremendous but generally invisible power. All human cultural groups, without exception, have such a system. In most of them it is highly elaborate, with ceremonies involving art, music, recitation of myths, special foods, and other showy and often costly means of revealing one's commitment and arousing it among others.

Group solidarity and following group rules and morals are greatly helped by such means.

The Seshat group of social historians find that moralistic religions—here meaning world religions as opposed to local traditions—follow development of military technology (Hoyer and Reddish 2019). Military technology allows states to expand, eventually taking over neighbors and forming empires. The "Axial Age" (800–200 CE) tracked the rise of iron weaponry, large-scale cavalry, improved archery, and other means of allowing war on a huge scale, with massed armies. Imperial wars cause moral stress and moral thought, as people observe the rise of powerful, rival states in multistate systems. The great world religions owe their status to empires (Hoyer and Reddish 2019): Zoroastrianism to the Achaemenid Persian empire, Buddhism to the Gupta Empire (traditionally to Ashoka, r. ca. 268–232 BCE, but his predecessors had already adopted it), Christianity to Constantine and his Roman followers, Islam to the Arab conquests of the 600s CE. China owes its Confucian-Daoist-Imperial synthesis to the Han Dynasty (206 BCE–220 CE). Han state intellectuals showed brilliance at devising a religious cover for expansionism (E. N. Anderson 2019).

States need more and more rationalized bureaucracies of priests, bureaucrats, statesmen, and professionals. These develop increasingly self-conscious and specific moral and ethical codes, featuring loyalty to one's state, ideals of peace but perceived necessity of war, and powerful patriarchal inheritance systems and thus narrow sexual morality.

The Axial Age (Hoyer and Reddish 2019; Jaspers 1953) was anticipated by many new religions and philosophies from earlier times, especially the monotheism of Akhenaten and the comprehensive religious philosophy of Zarathustra. The Axial ideas, according to Karl Jaspers, included egalitarianism, rationalism, comprehensive morality, restraints on government, and other modernizing ideas. Thinkers of those time started the balls rolling, by developing moralities and worldviews intended to be followed by all humans, or at least all those in positions of responsibility (Hoyer and Reddish 2019).

Rationalism (social construction of detached contemplation of the world), equality at particular social levels, and self-conscious morality and personal freedom appeared as a complex in the Mediterranean world, Persia, India, and China. Jaspers thought these were independent developments, but it seems highly unlikely that they were. The societies in question were known to be in contact by then, as we can see from rapid transfers of such technologies as bronze and iron metallurgy and grain cultivation. Significant evidence of intellectual contact range from widespread story lines to direct philosophical influences (Beckwith 2015).

Typical of Axial duality was the Zoroastrian opposition of "*asha* (goodness, order, and truth) and *druj* ('the lie,' considered to be female)" (Reddish and Bidmead 2019:128; see also Hoyer and Reddish 2019). Something like this was very widespread in the ancient world; both "Satan" and "devil" come from words for "the lie," in Hebrew and Greek respectively. (The Hebrew is *shaytan*; the Greek is *diabolos*, literally "thrown apart" from the truth.)

Jaspers sees mainly good things following from Axial ideas, but one concept fairly new at the time was to have pernicious results. This was the idea that things of the spirit were good, things of the flesh evil. Apparently beginning with Zoroastrianism and other Mesopotamian-Iranian teachings, this idea became wildly popular in late antiquity, spreading to India and eventually worldwide. It led to modern puritanism, and to much unnecessary mortification of the flesh. The idea of withdrawing from a world seen as hopelessly evil often accompanies this belief, but is more widespread, and can accompany more good-doing. Medieval monks and Chinese hermits could be mere sloths, renouncing the world and living on charity, but at other times they were the centers of help and care in their communities. Similarly, in South Asia and East Asia, renouncing what Chinese Buddhists called the "red dust" allowed either lazing or dedication.

Extreme puritanism leads to anhedonia (inability to enjoy anything), accidia (extreme boredom, seen as a sin in medieval times), and wide-flung intolerance. The puritanical sects of Christianity and Islam are infamously prone to terrorism, violence, and prejudice. Puritans feel themselves entitled to special consideration because of their moral superiority. This is as often true of left-wing and right-wing political activists as much as for religious puritans; there is a strong component of puritanism in extreme politics on both sides.

The Axial Age was followed around 1–100 CE with a further worldwide period of brilliance, innovation, and progress that extended as far as Mexico and Peru. Perhaps the warm, favorable climate of the period mattered. Then in 1100–1300, and even a bit after that in Europe, there was another Axial-like Age: a period of brilliant religious, philosophical, and technical progress in China, the Near East, southern Europe, and large parts of Africa. Then the late sixteenth and early seventeenth centuries were a time of major scientific breakthroughs in Western Europe.

Conversely, difficult periods for morality sometimes overlapped those periods of progress. The Roman Empire instituted tyranny, corruption, and abuse while developing philosophy and literature. The Dark Ages followed, roughly 500–1000. The period from 1100 to 1500 was an age of persecuting witches and heretics. In the early Christian church, as it grew and thus allowed power to become more and more important, two kinds of problematic people were attracted: puritans and power-hungry political operators. Here as in other faiths. thinkers and good people were increasingly sidelined as organized religion developed.

There followed a succession of moral reforms in Christianity, lead-ing to radical movements such as the Quakers and Unitarians (Freeman 2009). Similar movements in other cultures are common, such as the Three Teachings movement in medieval China, which sought to combine the more communitarian and practical-altruistic sides of Confucianism, Buddhism, and Daoism.

All of this brings us to the point of this section. Religion often kills. Genocide before 1900 was almost always religious. Heresies and religious differences in the West provoked mass killing. So did cults and mass move-ments in the East, though religious massacres were much less frequent there than in the West. Not only does evil win, but good fails. Charles Freeman's and R. L. Moore's histories of Christianity (Freeman 2005, 2009; Moore 2012) show that few cared about feeding the hungry, curing the sick, or clothing the naked. The public controversies of the church were about whether Jesus was the Man-God or the God-Man, whether his union with God was *homoousia* or *homoiousia* (Gibbon 1995, vol. 3, p. 787), and how many angels could dance on the point of a pin. The main business of the church and its sects, much of the time, was increasing its wealth while identifying and killing "heretics." Many of these were people who protested the evils of high churchmen. Many were simply those who had wealth worth confiscating. Often, the "heresies" were not much more real than the fantasies of QAnon (Moore 2012).

Religion as representation of a real face-to-face or politically defined com-munity is necessarily special-interest and exclusionary. As collective repre-sentation of community (Durkheim 1995), it represents a defined group, often in opposition to other groups. It can thus become an exclusionary ideology. "Parochial" interests, complete with suspicion and enmity toward at least some outsiders, can arise. Even when self-consciously about "all humans" or "all beings," it is typically about the sect (not even the whole religion).

New movements with religion-like characteristics share the same prob-lems, often becoming notably more negative and exclusionary than most religious sects. Libertarianism, fascism, communism, nationalism, and other ideologies historically based on or drawing from religion are even more exclusionary than most religions. Benedict Anderson (1991) has shown how nationalists borrowed ideas wholesale from religion when designing their national appeals.

Ultimately, religion cannot be purely good. As a collective representation of the community, it represents the community's bad as well as its good. World religions break down into local sects that represent their own commu-nities. The only hope is in tolerance. The Hittites called their capital "the city of a thousand gods" (Hoyer and Reddish 2019:205). In such a city, the good might hope that their side of the community gets its due share. Conversely, religion can be the collective representation of the most evil people in the community, as it certainly is in many current sects.

A characteristic of extreme, intolerant religion everywhere is its repression of women (Margolis 2021). In general, the more narrow, closed-minded, and exclusionary is the religion, the more it represses them. This is a worldwide phenomenon, and deserves more attention. Part of it certainly comes from defensiveness: in high-conflict areas, women must be protected, and a combination of real defense and paranoid mindset leads to repression. Part of it comes from puritanism. The whole question of worldwide repression of women is highly relevant to mass killing, if only because extreme ideologies of every kind—not just religion—indulge in it. The phenomenon needs much better explanations than it has received. Neither genes nor economics make much headway in understanding it. (We must thus regretfully take it no further, awaiting better syntheses of available materials.)

It appears that the great triangle of primary-production interests, psychopathic leaders, and ordinary bigots is incomplete without the additional presence of an organized, emotionally appealing, socially respected system that can promote hate of the weak and adulation of the strong. Right-wing Christians served that purpose under Hitler and Mussolini, and later under Trump. Right-wing "Hindutva" extremists have done the same in India, as have extreme Salafis in Islam. Religion is not alone: Communist far-leftists in Communist countries, fascists in totalitarian countries, and radical nationalists everywhere have carried the same burdens. Every country seems to have an equivalent. It is a critical variable in turning ordinary defensiveness into rabid hate, and thus a key factor in producing mass violence.

The rise of hierarchies as society becomes more complex leads to further needs and problems. Chiefdoms and early states were, overall, the most violent of human social types (Turchin 2018; Whitehouse et al. 2019:398). This forced societies to develop increasingly effective ways of deterring oppression and violence. Human sacrifice, for example, was almost universal in early states, but rapidly declined and disappeared with time. They also developed bureaucracies, usually at least somewhat meritocratic rather than based purely on descent. The "Axial Age" reforms were part of this.

Basic was an ability to reflect on morality, analyze it, and generalize moral principles beyond one's own society, ideally to the whole world (Hoyer and Reddish 2019). This involved developing a moral high god, or, in China and elsewhere in eastern Asia, deified Heaven. This being emerged from a process of generalizing moral principles to all members of society, and thus developing the concept of a "rule of law." Widely in the Axial Age, a basis of morality was the Golden Rule, "do as you would be done by," or the Silver Rule, famously stated by Confucius and many others: "do not do to others what you would not like done to yourself." (It has taken the next 2,500 years to come up with the Platinum Rule, which the present authors phrase as "do what helps others even if you would not want it for yourself, and do not inflict on them that which you like but they do not.") Tierney and Baumeister (2019:65) point out the Silver Rule has an advantage in focusing on the negative: it is easier to identify and avoid things that people do not like than to find out and supply all they want.

Such moral principles did not usually extend far. All Axial Age societies, and all civilizations before the nineteenth century, practiced slavery, assigned women to lower social positions than men, and practiced offensive war. Most continued to have divine kings, even after the idea of secular kings restrained by law was established. (China managed to have both at once, by a heroic act of accommodating contradictions.) But the seed was sown: societies became more rationalized, more rule-based, less violent, and ultimately less unequal in assigned status (though more unequal in actual wealth). (These understandings are largely derived from Max Weber, at various removes; see Weber 1978, also E. N. Anderson 2019; Hoyer and Reddish 2019; Whitehouse et al. 2019.)

There is no evidence of any progress in general morality or in good versus evil. Reports of anthropologists studying the simplest societies return a complex and deeply thought morality (e.g., Brandt 1954; Ladd 1957). Such concerns seem genuinely wired into the human brain or into the basic structure of society. As we saw above (Curry et al. 2019), basic morality is strikingly similar in all recorded societies. This is true in part because the evils are also quite general. Greed for prestige, status, and wealth, and defensiveness about same, are fairly general in societies, though very small-scale ones are mercifully spared from having much to be greedy about. What has changed is the scope of morality. The Axial Age was particularly important in taking it from the small local group to the wide world. However, the "world religions" of today are largely the result of early empires. Constantine made Christianity widespread. The Guptas did the same for Buddhism. The wide-ranging Companions of the Prophet accomplished it for Islam. The other major religions have similar stories.

Religions and comparable totalizing ideologies show a loose cycling similar to Ibn Khaldun dynastic cycles, but usually running far longer. Idealistic, well-meaning people start them, attracting a mixed cult following. Then, if the religion succeeds, everyone joins on. Then, eventually, the religion may lose credibility, retaining only the diehards or—at worst—only the evil people who corrupted it.

INDIVIDUALISM AND VIOLENCE

Individualism deserves a brief note here, because it has been falsely blamed for violence or credited with reducing same. Neither is true; we can find no substantiated claim that it makes much difference one way or another. Individualist societies and collectivist ones alike commit war and genocide.

Individualism, in the usual modern sense, developed from Levantine and Greek seafaring and small farming. The counter was the hierarchic order that developed in running extensive plantation and livestock agriculture. From the Greeks on down, individualism and liberalism are broadly predictable from the relative amounts of international trade and mental work in a society. Joseph Henrich (2020) is wrong in thinking individualism began with the Christian church (Charles Freeman, review of Henrich 2020 on amazon.com). Almost every scholar of such matters agrees that the ancient Greeks really invented individualism and all that goes with it (see Hoyer and Reddish 2019). The Romans kept it up, to varying degrees. The Dark Ages maintained it in philosophically reduced form. The Arab-Persian world picked it up, then gave it back to Europe in the later medieval period. Then the Mongols ruined the Middle East but introduced Chinese ideas. These slowly penetrated Europe, contributing to the Renaissance, the Scientific Revolution, the Industrial Revolution, and modernization. In all cases individualism tracked long-range trade and commerce, dying in agrarian hierarchic systems.

China paralleled the West in all this: individualism rose in the Warring States Period with philosophic Daoism and with forms of Confucianism that put the duties of morality on the individual. The Han dynasty advanced more communal goals. Dark ages followed, but Middle Eastern influences from 400 onward led to more individualism from that quarter. Then the Mongols hurt China by introducing totalitarianism, from which China never recovered, thus missing the revolutions that transformed the West. Even so, individualism flourished in the later, more autocratic dynasties (Santangelo 2021). It combined with or interfaced with communalism in complex ways.

Henrich shows that the mercantile-urban-trading world goes with individualism, egalitarianism, and honesty. The agrarian-imperial world goes with landlordism, small ingrown communities, a frozen-crust elite, and frequent corruption. Agrarian societies are given to groupiness and conformity, and above all differentiation by birth—castes, hereditary classes, systemic ethnic separation. The tension remains crucial, within the United States today as well as among nations. Democracy and individualism have proved decidedly unpopular—not found in most of the world except insofar as the United States and Europe have propagated it. Individualism as liberty of conscience nearly died out for good when the Persians almost took Greece. If they had won, democracy might never have restarted.

Individualism has a mixed record in regard to good and bad. It allows the good to mobilize and act, but allows the rise of fascist leaders. The all-importance of individualism in American culture has been much described and much criticized over the decades (de Tocqueville 2002; Bellah et al 1996; Putnam 2000). It gave us democracy and personal freedom, but it also gives us the idea that bullying others is simply an expression of the bully's "individual rights." It appears to be irrelevant to understanding genocide and similar phenomena. They occur in both individualist and collectivist societies, just as they do in both rich and poor ones.

HISTORIC CYCLES OF VIOLENCE:
THE IBN KHALDUN MODEL

A great deal of human evil is cyclic, directly predictable from a society's place in long cycles of integration and decline. The ancient Greeks, such as Polybius, already thought in terms of historic cycles. They saw a typical evolution from democracy to autocracy to tyranny to collapse and the rise of democracy once more.

The greatest work was done by the fourteenth-century Arab historian Ibn Khaldun (1958). The basic Ibn Khaldun cycle is predictable. It starts with takeover of society by a marginal but charismatic leader. When a society weakens or breaks down, marginal people can rapidly form coalitions and take over. This calls for good leaders, who command *'asabiyah*—loyalty and social solidarity. Ibn Khaldun saw them as usually emerging from nomad societies, because nomads routinely practice the inventiveness, generosity, and military skill that are required. A charismatic leader arising in such society can assemble a troop who will conquer a larger but fatally declining state; Genghis Khan with his Mongols, as an extreme case. However, a disaffected general of the declining state can sometimes do this (as did the founder of the Han Dynasty in China), and very rarely an upstart from the common people (as did the founder of Ming).

A period of stability follows; sometimes a Golden Age, sometimes simply a period of balance between good and ill. Inevitably, as population and wealth grow, there is a gradual pulling apart of society by inequality, elite overproduction, growing selfishness and corruption, and growing tendency to enrich self at expense of system. Government gets bigger and more distant, and breaks up into increasingly distinct competing blocs, within which individuals compete—above all for power, the almost-necessarily zero-sum commodity. Peter Turchin (Turchin 2016; Turchin and Zefedov 2009) has greatly expanded the power and range of Ibn Khaldun's theory. (See also E. N. Anderson 2019 for more, including the point that C. S. Hollings's resilience cycle is an independent discovery of the same cycle, but generalized to all animal life. Richard Lachmann, 2020, has independently discovered the same general cycle, apparently with no knowledge of Ibn Khaldun or Turchin.)

Often, the start and middle part of a cycle are a time when trade, commerce, and intellectual activities flourish. Progress grows from nomadizing, seafaring, small farming, trade, and commerce. Innovators benefit the collectivity by removing bottlenecks in expanding systems. The flourishing of prosperity is thus uneven. Elites, traders, and innovators benefit disproportionately. Small farmers and remote rural families do not. This leads to increasing inequality.

As the cycle progresses, the rich elites are challenged by upstarts and become more and more conservative. Ultimately, increasing power goes to reactionary elements: classically "women and eunuchs" in Ibn Khaldun's view, and also in Chinese historical writing too. Landed aristocrats traditionally get the blame in Europe, and corrupt local rulers in India and elsewhere. The key economic alteration is from an outward-looking economy to a landlord-run, reactionary economy of plantations and rural primary production. Ibn Khaldun was aware of this. Inequality alone can drive the whole cycle. Ibn Khaldun stressed the degeneration of the elite, exposed to court culture, with its luxuries and intrigues. Above all, he saw that court elites fall into corruption—selling favors to those with money. The economic driver can shorten or stretch out a cycle, depending on how long it takes for landed interests and corrupt politicians to arise. Ibn Khaldun saw about one hundred years as typical, but cycles of varying lengths arise from various causes (Turchin 2016; Turchin and Zefedov 2009).

It is possible to predict Ibn Khaldun cycles from a single variable: the level of inequality in power in the polity. (In the real world, this is never the only problem, but it could theoretically do all the damage by itself.) After a certain point, the powerful are above the law. They cannot be restrained or brought to account. At that point, corruption becomes pervasive. Social solidarity breaks down. Most people become passive and alienated, taking themselves out of the social game. Also, the more reactionary interests gain more and more power, allying with the government and often corrupting it. At this point, the government begins to fail pervasively to do its job, whatever that may be in the given society. People expect and come to depend on certain services; these are no longer provided. When this occurs, an evil leader or group may arise. That individual will inevitably come into conflict with the whole system, work against the common interest, and bring the state down.

Often, in such cases, if a new emperor, or in modern times a dictator, takes over, he fails to use *'asabiyah* to bring the land together and create a successful new regime. Instead, he cracks down on dissent, and makes mistakes in trying to self-aggrandize and grab more relative power. To deal with this, he cracks down more, and a vicious cycle sets in. He faces military overextension, economic miscalculations, and environmental messes. Then the regime collapses. This process was brilliantly described by Ibn Khaldun, and Turchin and his associates have confirmed it. Such a lord of misrule will develop a base that includes the mean-spirited and the stupid, as well as toadies and sycophants who will aid and abet the dictator in making ever-worse decisions, as we saw with Trump in dealing with the COVID-19 crisis.

The final blow is often given by an accident that would have been absorbed easily by an intact state. The immediate causes of the falls of Chinese dynasties include child emperors who could not control the state (Han, Song, Qing), rebellions that would have been managed easily by a functional state (Tang), by climate worsening (Yuan), and so on. In all these cases, the Ibn Khaldun dynamics were the real determining factors; the child emperors and rebellions merely gave the opportunity to the forces of final destruction.

Chaotic weather has brought down many states (see, e.g., Brooke 2014; Parker 2013). Any disaster can do it. However, the blame goes not to the disaster, but to the rot that had long set in. When a great tree near our house, eight feet thick and over a hundred feet tall, blew down in a windstorm, we found it was riddled with decay—the interior too rotten to hold. Such is the way of states. The alienated masses lose their passivity and break out in violent rebellion. The immediate cause of breakdown is powerful interests that are above the law and profit from harming the general public interest. In Ibn Khaldun's day, and in the Chinese dynasties (E. N. Anderson 2019), it was the great feudal-type landlords and cooperating interests. Today, it is the military-industrial complex, the fossil fuels industry, and, as in those ancient days, the giant landed agricultural interests.

The cycle then begins again. With luck, the dictator is succeeded by peaceful return to order, as happened after Franco in Spain and Salazar in Portugal. Sometimes a minor revolution or major demonstration activity is all that is needed, as in Pinochet's Chile, and Argentina in the 1970s. Sometimes the chaos leads to real social breakdown, often solved by invasion and conquest. Hitler's Germany fell only through this means. The same befell the Khmer Rouge in Cambodia. In earlier times the fall of the Song and Ming Dynasties in China exemplify the pattern. At other times, generals or other military types may win out and suppress rebellion, as in the chaotic periods following the fall of the Qin, Sui, and Tang Dynasties in China.

Not infrequently, the final phase of an Ibn Khaldun cycle leads to collapse of the country into bandit gangs or criminal rings, as in the case of the Yuan and Ming Dynasties in China, and more recently in Somalia, Honduras, and elsewhere. At this point, the strongest gang may be the victor that unifies the country. This is a possible fate for the United States in the next few years.

In an Ibn Khaldun cycle, the first generation *must* achieve—they must fight to take over and consolidate their hold. The second *must* administer, and do it reasonably well, hence—with luck—Golden Ages. The third and subsequent ones can boodle. A smooth-running state, elite overproduction, and inertia allow this. Corruption and factions then bring the system down. What makes the timing unpredictable are the stochastic events that trigger meltdowns. There may be a rule of three: even a weak government can withstand two shocks, but not three. Climate change, COVID-19, and racist violence are now hitting the United States at the same time.

Since people are about half good and half bad, these Khaldun cycles run endlessly. There is no balance, such as would occur if people were primarily one or the other. The West went through cycles of freeing and reaction, with reaction gaining during the free periods and vice versa. There was a free trend around 1100–1300, with republics taking hold in much of Europe. Reaction started in the 1160s, thanks to the Catholic church (Moore 2012). This was followed by more freeing of persons and conscience in the Protestant Reformation, but that led in its turn to crackdown after 1500. A freeing trend gave us the Dutch Republic, the Treaty of Westphalia, and the Glorious Revolution. There was reaction in the early eighteenth century, leading to resurgent freedom in the American and French Revolutions and onward to more and more liberation movements in Latin America and elsewhere. This led to reaction and world colonialism till 1945; a huge wave of liberation until 1991; reaction after that, reaching to a flood tide in the 2010s and 2020s, with the rapid rise of fascism worldwide. These local, and now worldwide, cycles are shakily correlated with Ibn Khaldun cycles; they exist on a different and poorly understood clock.

THE TWO FACES OF ENLIGHTENMENT

From the early seventeenth century onward, people worldwide—first in Europe, later in America, and soon around the globe—saw increasing social conflict and decreasing welfare (Parker 2013). Beginning in central Europe, they began to work toward peace, to level down nobility, and to spread communitarian morals (Te Brake 2017). This led to the Enlightenment in the eighteenth century (Kant 1978, 2002). The now-classic virtues of "liberty, equality, unity" were exalted. So were science, rationality, progress, personal freedom, and personal responsibility. Revolutions were launched to bring them to social reality. By the end of the eighteenth century, slavery was widely condemned, for the first time in all history. By the end of the nineteenth, it was illegal worldwide. Slow but sure expansion of Enlightenment ideas occurred through the twentieth century, but then began to reverse.

Liberal democracies arose, based on Enlightenment principles, and often based—explicitly (as in the United States) or not—on ideas of human rights and mutual support. These worked to the extent that they included an idea that *my rights stop where yours start*, and an idea that *we are all in this together*. Unfortunately, the Enlightenment tended to flourish only because the economies of the "Enlightened" countries were supported by cynical and aggressive colonialism, plantation slavery, exploitation, and resource drawdown worldwide. The Enlightenment arose to a great extent as a reaction against these (as in the writings of Kant, e.g., 2002, and Mill), but it was also funded by them. It now appears uncomfortably possible that Enlightenment ideals cannot survive without these. The world has filled up; there are no more frontiers to settle or vulnerable people to conquer and enslave. Though economies continue to expand on paper, resources are rapidly being depleted, leading to increasing competition and hardship.

Children of the Enlightenment (in both good and evil ways), the founding fathers of the United States recognized the need to minimize raw power, using balance of powers between states and nation and between legislative, executive, and judicial branches. That should have been enough, but the founding fathers failed massively by allowing "property" to count; only males with property could vote. Slowly, reform ended this voting restriction, but unfortunately not the ability of wealth to corrupt all levels and branches. Ideally, the United States could have developed the only ideology that is not exclusionary. This would have happened if it had made consistent the *rule of law* and thus due process; fully rational and rationalized systems of governance; total equality before the law; full recourse; balance of powers; personal freedom. This set of principles was more or less spelled out in the Federalist Papers (Hamilton, Madison, and Jay 1961) and elsewhere, but never fully freed from the old devils of property and inequality, most notoriously in racist slavery and its modern descendant white supremacy. Honesty including full disclosure, public record, and scientific evidence was valued, but not written into basic law.

The Enlightenment produced a counterreaction in thinkers such as Nietzsche, who accepted the belief that humans are innately violent and aggressive, and saw some of the resulting behavior as noble and worthwhile. Freud agreed with the innate violence and greed, but saw it as needing control by the superego. Hitler took an extreme right-wing path from Nietzschean philosophy and idealized hatred and genocide as well as violence and aggression.

The Enlightenment is now under concerted attack in many countries. China never really got on board (except in Hong Kong and Taiwan), and is now extreme in repudiating it. Xi Jinping dismisses all such talk of freedom of conscience, individual rights, and voting as Western colonialist nonsense. Russia was engaged with Enlightenment ideas from their origin onward, but never really bought into the program, and under Putin has renounced it explicitly and thoroughly, agreeing with Xi that it is a Western imperialist idea. Poland, Hungary, Turkey, and several other countries have drifted away from it.

Enlightenment values peaked with the Civil Rights Movement in the United States, and have been under attack since by an increasingly extreme, vocal, and powerful right wing. Trump had as little regard for its values as Xi. The future is uncertain, but a repressive surveillance state like Xi's China is very likely in the United States. Such a state cannot survive long. Concentrating all real power and decision-making in one fallible man leads to mistakes that rapidly ramify through a locked-in, over-rationalized system, bringing it down. Moreover, the virulent anti-science and anti-intellectual component of anti-Enlightenment thought, from 1930s fascism to Putin and to the religious rulers of Iran and Afghanistan, means that science and education are dismantled, something not happening (so far) in China but well under way in Hungary, India, Poland, Russia, Turkey, and elsewhere, and rapidly advancing in the United States during and since Trump's tenure.

NATIONALISM AS A HISTORIC FACTOR IN VIOLENCE

Nationalism, a major force since the development of the modern nation-state in the Treaty of Westphalia (1648) and after, has a mixed record. It has sometimes served as a way to marshal majorities against minorities, thus contributing to prejudice that has frequently led to hatred and genocide. Hitler played this card in Germany, to be followed by other fascists. Recently, this majoritarian nationalism has sparked genocide in Serbia, Russia, and elsewhere. It has led to extreme and vicious divisionary politics in India and China. The classic *divide et impera*, "divide and rule," of the ancient Romans is always a formidably successful dodge.

Conversely, the American idea of *e pluribus unum*—"from the many, one"—has led to creating strong nations from disparate groups. Even the relatively ethnically homogeneous realm of modern Japan was forged from a conflicting mess of regions, social categories, and ethnic Japanese vs. Koreans. Taiwan self-consciously unified, creating a modern democracy from what was a contentious set of mainlander elites, mainlander non-elites, and Taiwanese, all often at each other's throats (as ENA was able to observe directly in the 1960s and 1970s). New Zealand has been quite successful in creating a nation of white settlers and Indigenous Maori; continuing problems are being seriously addressed without recent destructive conflict (again, our observations confirm received wisdom). Fewer problems were faced by less diverse countries from Scandinavia, Ireland, and the Netherlands to Costa Rica, but even they had class and ethnic tensions that required nation-building. These countries are now the most successful the world has ever known, in terms of making a good living for most people. Health statistics say it all: these countries have the highest life expectancies and lowest infant and maternal mortality ever recorded, anywhere. Even Costa Rica's is ahead of that of the United States.

The countries with divisive politics are moving in the other direction, with the United States rapidly declining in life expectancy and maternal health, a decline tracking the exacerbation of ethnic and class tensions in recent years. Countries that self-consciously unite in nation-building are not necessarily utopias. Saudi Arabia and other Arab states have managed it by merciless repression. But combined with democracy and serious efforts to level up the disadvantaged, a self-conscious policy of *e pluribus unum* passes the alternatives.

Chapter 4

Performing and Projecting Evil

CONFORMING TO EVIL

All too commonly, evil is done because it is socially valued. People conform, but they tend to want to achieve and get status, and that means to be even more conformist than others. This is good when helping others is valued, but not at all good when prestige and power go to the most violent and rapacious, as was the case throughout a large part of human history.

People act badly when ordered to do so, as documented extensively in our book *Conforming to Genocide: The Wolf You Feed* (Anderson and Anderson 2020). Philip Zimbardo's experiments in this regard are notorious. He assigned some Stanford students to be prisoners, others to be jailers. The jailers so quickly started seriously mistreating the prisoners that the experiment had to be stopped within a week, but it left psychological scars on the participants that lasted for years (Zimbardo 2008). Zimbardo's experiment has been criticized on ethical grounds (e.g., Haslam et al. 2019; Le Texier 2019), and indeed led to changes in ethics that make it impossible to repeat today, but further research coming as close as possible to replication have shown that people are even more prone to get out of hand in such situations than Zimbardo originally concluded (Anderson and Anderson 2020; Zimbardo 2008). It is clear that creating factions, deliberately or inadvertently, is the easiest and quickest way to make people turn evil and guarantee that they act that way (Zimbardo 2008).

Stanley Milgram, in similar research, told subjects to give increasingly powerful electric shocks to victims (Milgram 1963, 1974); the shocks were purely fictional, but the experiments led to such dreadful findings that they too are now ruled out by generally agreed morality (enforced by human subjects review committees and similar institutions). They have been confirmed recently under more rigorous and morally vetted conditions (Burger 2009).

A recent study shows that the human brain responds with less empathy, regard, and guilt when acting under orders. Subjects gave each other small electric shocks for money or under orders. Subjects would give each other more shocks with less compassion when acting under orders. The difference was clear on brain scans, with the centers of social empathy and compassion lighting up considerably less in the under-orders condition (Netherlands Institute for Neuroscience 2020, citing Caspar et al. 2020).

This requires playing up society's fears, frustrations, challenges, and stresses, and wadding all up into hatred. In traditional societies, where rulers actually had to fight and manage wars, they could not afford to thin out their workforce too much, so genocide was rare and interpolity war was common. A problem commonly stressed in society, and thus done out of conformity, is the tendency to personalize everything, while failing to see structural and systematic reasons for trouble. People then go after the people they see as bad, and do much damage without accomplishing anything, since the system remains unchanged and merely re-creates "bad" people to serve it. Slavery was not relieved by trying to make slaveowners "better." The whole system had to go. We are now seeing that the same is true of the "war on drugs" and for-profit prisons.

China performed a long-running experiment with moral suasion by adhering for 2,500 years to Confucius's teachings that making rulers moral would solve society's problems and bring peace. Rulers soon realized that moral training was indeed vitally important, but that a firm structure of laws had to be in place also. The tension between moral suasion and firm law led to back-and-forth swings in Chinese history, with excesses in either direction leading to disorder (E. N. Anderson 2019).

STATUS, POWER, AND WEALTH

Evil often follows from desire for the Max Weber's classic trio of social motivators: Status, power, and wealth. There is more to social value than status, however. Status is only one part of social personhood, along with affection, respect, acceptance, validation, standing, approbation, and other social goods. Most people value these things highly, usually above all else. Fear of losing them gets translated onto wider arena, by displacement and projection, and lies behind a great deal of far larger-scale tragedies. Control of family members, often out of fear of their alienating their affection, is a classic driver of domestic violence (B. Anderson et al. 2004; Collins 2008). It is also a driver of belief in the evil nostrums of politicians, right-wing preachers, and other sowers of discord. It is certainly a major factor in genocide, which always involves a perceived need by a majority to "control" a minority to the point of extermination. Defending one's sense of control may, in fact, be the major factor behind evil, a point that deserves further study.

Power is only one part of control, the other parts being self-control and security. "Power tends to corrupt, and absolute power corrupts absolutely," as Lord Acton famously wrote in a letter in 1887. The line was adapted by Rudolph Rummel in the opening line of his classic work *Death by Government* (1994:1) as "Power kills, and absolute Power kills absolutely." Almost everyone who has power abuses it, even if only "for your own good" (Miller 1990). Social power not only corrupts, even the competition for it corrupts. Control of one's life, on the other hand, does not; the contrast was studied by A. Cislak et al. (2018). Competition for status often gets uglier than competition for power, because people see status as easier and safer to compete for (Hays et al. 2015).

The commonest evil motivated by desire for wealth is simple: stronger take from weaker. In the old days of Vikings and Mongols, the strong looted, raped, killed, or enslaved the weak. Today, the strong pollute, use their political power to cut off the starving and sick, and invoke wars to bankroll their munitions companies. None of this is as simple as it was in Viking times, however. Personality, social norms for cutthroat competition and bullying, and constant minor conflict lie behind it. It requires those contexts to flourish.

Conflict is probably most often over resources—land and loot—but resource conflicts are also the easiest to resolve, because rational material self-interest can intervene to stop people losing control. Conflicts over power are more emotional and deadly, especially when a group is desperately trying to protect its power and privilege in the face of rising challenges. Wealth and resources can be multiplied indefinitely, and the best way to get them is usually to cooperate with others in raising everyone's level. Power, at least within hierarchies, is different: it is achieved at the expense of others, and there is less and less room at the top. There can be only one supreme leader, only a few top officials, and thus on down the scale; only the bottom is fully open. Rising in a hierarchy involves increasingly sharp competition.

Conflicts over "honor," prestige, and social place are particularly hard to treat. Conflicts over control of imagined groups—"heretics," "races," "ethnic identities," and the like, all the "imagined communities" of Benedict Anderson (1991)—are typically the worst of all, often leading to complete loss of even the pretense of rationality and self-control. They are the conflicts that leave tens of millions dead for no identifiable material reason, as in genocides.

The reasons for war and genocide are usually complex, with war being invoked only when several reasons come together. These include desire for land and loot, desire for prestige and power, and simple loyalties and hatreds. Hatred of the enemy leads to mass murder, including indiscriminate killing of civilians, something universal in war (Kiernan 2007; Shaw 2003). Under these conditions, evil is often all too pleasurable. Humans take horrible satisfaction in killing their enemies, often by fiendish tortures. Mass killing is universal not only in war but also in settler genocides, when a powerful group displaces a weak one from its territory. Genocide has also been a standard way to dispose of a too-visible minority, especially if it is seen by the majority as somehow challenging majority dominance.

An all-too-typical progress of conflict begins when powerful individuals or groups—up to and including nation-states—are selfish or inconsiderate, get called out and challenged for it, and then become furious because of the loss of face thus entailed. This leads to escalating conflict. It also leads to consideration of bullying. Bullies get together, dominate, attract groupies, and persecute the weak (Collins 2008; Hymel and Swearer 2015). Any society has a certain number of bullies, many of whom are sociopaths, psychopaths, and violent aggressors. They take over when there is no strong pressure from both ideology and immediate need. They are supported by bully groupies, the persons who are weak but follow and adulate bullies as a source of indirect strength. (Collins 2008:156–65 has a whole bullying taxonomy). Such people are often smug, defiant, and nasty, with a general attitude of opposition to what is usually considered socially good. Hitler's Nazis frequently exhibited this behavior. Trump's more violent followers are recent classic examples.

The anarchists from Thomas Paine onward were right about power and status, rather than wealth, being the main source of evil. They saw disproportionate and unequal power as the real problem. People rarely unite and fight over mere money or other mobile resources. They fight over land, over sacred matters, and over power. They fight because of nostalgia for a better past, when they had more power, and fear of a worse future. The founding fathers of the United States were aware of this, but with the exception of Paine they stopped short of advocating anarchy. Seeing structure as necessary to society, they advocated balancing and equalizing powers to keep powerful individuals under control.

The conclusion can only be that saving the world is a matter of evening out power. Indeed it must be balanced, and people must be made to feel in control and hopeful. The anarchists were wrong in thinking it could simply be abolished. It cannot be eliminated. It can only be spread around. No society can exist without power and control being major issues. The founding fathers, among many polities, were wise in having three branches to balance each other, with each branch subdivided in different ways. If one acts bad the other two can gang up on it. Unfortunately, their system has proved inadequate, given modern ways of lying and corrupting. Giant firms got powerful enough to coopt all branches of government. The founding fathers were uncomfortably aware that such things could happen (they read their

Adam Smith) but they seem not to have known what to do about it. Balance of power is necessary first of all, to make sure that every power is checked by counterpower with interest in maintaining that counter. Three branches of government are necessary to prevent deadlock. We must now figure out how to deal with rampant corruption and authoritarianism even in theoretically power-balanced governments.

LIMITED GOOD AND ZERO-SUM GAMES

Feeding into this is zero-sum gaming. Traditional agrarian societies had strict limits on their resources and their ability to increase those, and thus were basically zero-sum economies In the Middle Ages, the economy expanded at a glacial pace, if at all. Good was limited, population was usually expanding, and one could get seriously better off only at another's expense. To religious thinkers, this limited economy was "the world" and "the red dust"; monasteries, nunneries, and hermitages were the only escape. This led to certain mindsets: honor culture (Uskul et al. 2019), a tendency to avoid rocking the boat, and other adaptations to hard limits.

One of the very worst problems of humanity is what ENA's graduate adviser George Foster called "the image of limited good" (Foster 1961, 1965). He based his conclusions on work with nonaffluent people in Mexico. A farmer in Mexico may actually have few chances, and come to see good as strictly limited. Foster found that people overgeneralize the economic zero-sum game: we can get social standing, respect, and even love only by taking them away from others. Thus, life, beyond getting an ordinary minimal livelihood, is fierce competition. We can advance by sheer luck, so societies with a strong "limited good" belief have their treasure tales and stories of lotteries won (as Foster showed). Usually, however, in the limited-good view, wealth comes from at the expense of others.

The great triumph of economic and social science over the last three hundred years was showing convincingly that we can all advance by working together to improve everyone's lot—playing positive-sum instead of zero-sum games. Unfortunately, too few are convinced. Even liberals sometimes talk as if the rich *must* pay workers badly to thrive. Yet, we have a positive-sum world: economies can expand, power can be shared more and more widely and equally, and status can rise open-endedly by doing good. Yet people still have a default zero-sum mindset (Boyer 2018). The point was also made some time ago by Lester Thurow, in *The Zero-Sum Society* (1980). Today, international surveys show that richer countries have less of it, poorer more, but all are prone (Różycka-Tran et al. 2015).

Citing research, Charles Koch, the major funder of the far right in the United States for a generation, says this: "about two-thirds of people think that most others see the world through a zero-sum lens. They also overwhelmingly assume that most people believe that one person's success means another person's loss" (Koch 2020:245). Attacking people, as rivals, becomes a way of life. Koch's book involves some apology for his own past. He has realized the problems with the zero-sum view.

Competitive team sports, and the modern world's obsession with them, greatly increase the zero-sum mentality. People learn to think that there are always winners and losers, and for every winning team there must be a losing one. A billionaire CEO like Koch knows that limited-good thinking is about power, not about profit. He knows, and states in his book, that he can pay workers more and treat them better and get more productivity that way. When the rich go out of their way to pay their workers starvation wages and treat them like dust, as so many billionaire CEOs do, it is about showing off power and control in a world of zero-sum gaming. The rich know money does not exist; it is a fiction (Graeber 2014). It is power and control that are real. Money is one measure of that, rather than a "thing in itself."

Control over other people is often a negative-sum game: it is accomplished by harming them at the expense of the controller. Sometimes this is necessary: society must spend money on policing, to keep criminals under control. The hopeful movements to eliminate police or guards have, alas, never worked in societies larger than a few hundred people. More deadly serious for society is control for evil reasons: domestic violence, government repression, ship captains flogging their crews, plantation owners using enslaved workers, bosses oppressing workers instead of paying them well, and all the other ways humans control each other. At some point, zero-sum crosses over into negative-sum: the powerful are harming themselves by harming the weak even more.

Whatever certain historians may claim, slavery, fascism, wife beating, and Orwellian tactics have never helped a society. The human and opportunity costs are both unsupportable. The profits of the southern plantation owners were nothing compared to what would have accrued if the Africans had been left to do free labor at home and the slavers compelled to do honest work themselves. The success of the North and of free societies everywhere, as opposed to the endless intractable poverty of slave societies and their successors, shows this clearly (see, e.g., Mintz 1985; Stedman 1988). The southern United States is still far worse off than the North, with slavery as a key explanation. It created a society of oppressed workers and parasitic, cruel elites that persists and self-replicates despite change and modernization.

It thus appears that the real underlying reason for the zero-sum and negative-sum mentality is fear of losing control of others. It is now the source of much, very possibly most, of the world's suffering. The limited-good view creates weakness and fear, and thus defensiveness. Then cowardly defensiveness leads to hatred and bigotry. It also leads to exaggerated offense-taking, and thus the "honor" game. It leads to everything from looting to callous business practices. All these are most often displaced onto weaker groups. People recognize that being "nice" (in the culturally appropriate way) is socially obligatory, and is thus not much of an investment. They therefore assume, often with good reason, that even the mildest nasty crack or cutting remark displays serious hostility. They thus react very strongly, often violently. When zero-sum crosses into negative-sum, all society loses, and the resulting economic woes cause even worse political reactions. The resulting downward spiral seems part of many Ibn Khaldun–type collapses.

Many Trump voters must have known that Trump could not do anything but hurt the economy and American society, but they were willing to harm themselves and their own interests simply to harm rival groups even more. Only immediate and condign social sanctions can stop such negative-sum gaming. Much of individual and group rivalry, competition for wealth, intolerance, and defense of "entitlement" comes from this. Those who resent having to be civil to "lower" people, or who take offense at the poor simply for existing, reveal this mindset.

Most people know they cannot get away with open outrageous selfishness, but they constantly try to push the limits just a little—to take just one, cheat just a bit, and give themselves the benefit of the doubt. The level to which people do this varies enormously from person to person. Common experience shows that some people are incredibly virtuous and almost never play weasel games; a few cheat every time they can. Most people are conscientious but imperfect. Conscience does restrain them. Also, in every society on earth, people enforce rough-and-ready sociability on each other. Everyday social rules discourage open selfishness and unfairness. People defend their rights, and often police others.

COMPETITIVE CONTROL: "GREED"

It is in the context of limited good that we can understand "greed." Greed is here taken to mean desire for getting wealth at inordinate cost to other people—competitors or victims. It is about getting power and prestige (status, standing) from wealth taken from others by predatory means. Those who simply want more resources are more prone to cooperate and be reasonable, because making everything better for everybody is the best, or at least safest, way to ensure profits. Adam Smith (1910 [1776]) was right: society depends on people being a bit "selfish" and a bit favoring to their families and communities. Too common, however, is competition for control. As William Wordsworth penned in his poem "Rob Roy's Grave": "The good old rule sufficeth them, the simple plan, Let him take who has the power, and let him keep who can."

The most deadly form of greed today is corporate profiting from others' deaths. Selling tobacco is the extreme case; smoking was estimated to cause 25 percent of all deaths, worldwide, in the late twentieth century (WHO). Drugs (legal and illegal), alcohol, pollution, munitions and arms, and agricultural chemicals take a toll. All are controlled by large corporations (not always legal ones).

Minor, but pernicious, self-indulgence occurs when people take lavish care of themselves and their families while neglecting the community. They may simply see no better option. They may fear poverty and failure, like the classic "miser." A chronic part of this is "entitlement": one's group is naturally superior, or at least higher in the hierarchy, so it deserves more. This includes the negative (narcissist) form of entitlement: the narcissist feels more sensitive or more hurt, so claims to need and deserve more (Beck 1999).

This ideation feeds the whole impulse to fight one's way up the hierarchy, but, above all, it lies behind prejudice and bigotry. It is probably necessary to them. It is made enormously worse by insecurity: if one's place on the hierarchy and one's sense of entitlement are threatened, one normally reacts with high emotion, exactly the sort of overdriven negative emotion that leads to hatred and prejudicial behavior. Brooding and ruminating on this fear is still worse. This is clear in the autobiography and other writings of Hitler, and to some extent in writings of other classic strongmen from Stalin, who murdered many of his early supporters, to Trump with his endless tweets about betrayal by subordinates.

Greed often stems from excessive desire, or need, or social pressure to get more wealth, power, and prestige *now* and let the future and the wider community worry about themselves. It comes from cowardice in many cases. Misers are afraid of losing their fortunes, and hypercompetitive moneymakers often fight the world out of fear of the same. People then try to fix the social damage by conformity. Society loses; the rich spend on houses, yachts, and gems to conform and impress, rather than investing in anything potentially valuable to the world. On a lesser plane, many householders, stuck in a faceless suburb with little sense of community, spend their spare money on endless fixing up of their houses, simply for lack of any better outlet for it. Spending it on the community would be better for all, and many house-owners even know it, but good options are not there.

Selfish greed must be distinguished from trade-offs between necessary self- and family care and general good-doing, and contexts for various changing levels of balancing these. That makes selfish greed insidiously difficult to distinguish from normal self-interest. Public greed is shown in callousness, seen in denying health care to the poor, or displacing minority communities to build facilities benefiting majorities, or failing to supply food in a famine.

There are those who do not even rise to the level of selfish greed. They limit themselves far short of success by negativity and hate. They spend their time worrying, complaining, and angering. They are limited by their ability to get along with people and with everyday problems. They then fail at fairness, do poorly in the world, and blame others more and more. They become easy targets for hateful leaders mobilizing general resentment. They become the shock troops of genocide.

FRUSTRATION AND DEFENSE OF HONOR

Frustration, of any sort, frequently feeds the bad wolf. People brood on their frustrations, and often act out their resulting anger. John Dollard developed the frustration-aggression hypothesis in the 1930s (Dollard et al. 1939). It has been variously supported and attacked since. It does not usually hold (Collins 2008; Kruglanski et al. 2019). In fact, frustrated people usually talk out their problems, or swallow their annoyance, or figure out rational ways to deal with the frustrations in question (such as actually reading the instructions—notoriously a last-ditch recourse). Often, those who can lose to anger and violence under frustrating stress are often those who come from rough backgrounds and difficult environments (Atherton et al. 2020), but often they are not.

Social Dominance Orientation is a psychological concept explored by Bob Altemeyer, often in collaboration with politicians who have real-world experience with it (Dean and Altemeyer 2020; Duckitt and Sibley 2009). Altemeyer has constructed measures of how much individuals desire social dominance, notably but not only political power. It is a part of Social Dominance Theory, a comprehensive theory of how attitudes of social dominance play across a wide range of personality traits and individual behaviors (see Sidanius et al. 2017, esp. 153–57). An interesting insight from social dominance theory is the importance of distinctive markers for minority groups: veiling for Muslim women, language use by Native Americans, and the like. These are frequently banned or discouraged by racist majorities, so they become loci of control and resistance (Kachanoff, Kteily, et al. 2020). Such restrictions, like all racism, harm the recipients psychologically (Kachanoff, Taylor, et al. 2019). Social Dominance Orientation is also part of, or closely related to, authoritarianism (Costello et al. 2022).

Social construction of social dominance is clearest in "honor cultures" (or "honor societies"), as described by Richard Nisbett and others (Nisbett

and Cohen 1996). These societies arise in violent areas, often mountain-
ous border zones or frontiers. They tend to have extremely high levels of
violence, as individuals jockey for power and status in a world where that
comes from defending one's public image—"honor"—by that means (Collins
2008:229–30). Moreover, they cause a particular problem, since they encourage defiance, overreaction to challenge, and displacement. Bullies in honor
cultures love to provoke weaker people into starting a fight, simply to be able
to crush them and win respect. This is a universal technique in rough bars, and
well known to schoolyard bullies, but it is certainly common in international
politics as well.

Pontus Leander and coworkers report: "When thwarted goals increase
endorsement of violence, it may not always reflect antisocial tendencies or
some breakdown of self-regulation per se; such responses can also reflect an
active process of self-regulation, whose purpose is to comply with the norms
of one's social environment" (Leander et al. 2020:249). As Leander and colleagues found, working-class American males are expected to fight when their
honor is directly challenged. (This is less true now than in our Midwestern
youth, but it is still common.) This derives from the old British Isles pattern,
seen in many Scottish ballads and Elizabethan plays. Leander and colleagues
found that the way one phrases the case can make more educated people pro-
or anti-war, and we know how easy it is to use social pressure to get young
people to become gangsters, suicide bombers, or soldiers. In such cultures,
is not true that controlling violence is "competent, good, praiseworthy, and
deserving of respect" (Leander et al. 2020:250; see also Collins 2008:229–30
and elsewhere). Quite the reverse: violence is respected, if "honor" is at issue.

Much of this behavior was clearly copied from kings' treatment of subjects. In general, a risk factor for developing violent cultures is inequality.
It is particularly pernicious when it disempowers ordinary people and local
communities, because it then devastates self-efficacy and personal and community responsibility.

Worldwide, there is a significant correlation of honor cultures—high on
personal touchiness—with pastoral and nomadic cultures, as Nisbett and
Cohen pointed out. There is also a correlation with mountains marginal to
densely settled lowlands. Appalachia is an obvious US example, though
Nisbett and Cohen refer to the South as a whole. Similarly, the mountains
of Pakistan and Afghanistan are much in the news recently. One can add the
Caucasus, the Balkans, the mountains of southern Italy (the Mafia is endemic
to mountain towns in western Sicily), and quite a few other such areas. Latin
American cultures are often "honor cultures" too (Gul, Cross, and Uskul
2021), but to varying degrees; Mexicans are aware that there is a huge gra-
dient from the machismo of much of the north to friendly tranquility in the

south. Middle Eastern cultures are typically "honor cultures," thanks to desert and mountain traditions.

The common theme is that these are regions intrinsically hard to control, but fairly densely populated by independent people. Conflict over resources, including above all personal respect, is inevitable and hard to resolve (Nisbett and Cohen 1996). Cultures of honor display considerably higher levels of violence, notably including within-family and within-neighborhood violence, relative to "cultures of dignity" like the middle-class US norm (Gul, Cross, and Uskul 2021), or ordinary agrarian regimes. This presents a challenge for social order, including policing (especially if the police are from the honor culture themselves; see Collins 2008) and psychological treatment (Gul, Cross, and Uskul 2021).

Norms and frustrations interact in genocide: "threats to perceived control . . . increase some of the insidious normative influence effects studied in the wake of the Holocaust, including the bystander effect and obedience to authority" (Leander et al. 2020:250). In general, where power is valued, showing power by the most direct method—violence—is valued as a prerogative of the powerful; violence can be highly self-affirming for that reason alone, especially where culturally normal (Leander et al. 2020:251). In short, "people often look to their social environment when their personal goals are thwarted" (Leander et al. 2020:251), and use whatever cultural model best fits their perceived situation; "increased endorsement of violence mainly occurs among goal-thwarted individuals whose social networks are likely to normatively prescribe violence" (Leander et al. 2020:265).

The violent cultural model noted by Leander and colleagues prevailed in Midwestern families in our youth: parents disciplined their children by spanking or beating, and the children carried that lesson forward by bullying weaker children. Fights among young males were expected, with the strongest fighter getting respect. Among upper-middle-class and upper-class families, an occasional alternative or supplement was the puritanical model: thin-lipped, supercilious disapproval of unconventional or disruptive or simply "different" behavior. This was backed up by very strict and often arbitrary standards—rigid enforcement of old-fashioned manners, dress codes, moral behavior, and the like.

In short, in many societies, especially those used to fighting, it is positively noble and virtuous to confront enemies, even imagined or weaker ones, and weak to negotiate or discuss things civilly. This lies behind the confrontational rhetoric that has gone so far out of control in the world today. People conclude it is better to play negative-sum games than to play positive-sum ones, as long as there is a thin rag of "ideology" to pull over the hatred. Obviously, violent and disorganized times bring out more violence. Long-continued anarchy normalizes it, giving us the Vikings, the tribal societies of the Afghan mountains, the mountain peoples of Papua New Guinea, and other chronically violent groups. In these societies, violence and murder were not considered evil or wrong, so long as they were "honorable." Thus, culture alone can create violence, without individual psychodynamics being necessary. In fact, in most such societies, violence is largely among young men, and concentrated among those who are aggressive but fragile—the brittle self-confidence described at length by Baumeister (1997). His descriptions fit honor killers better than any others; he discusses honor violence at length.

All this can change, and does change when social control becomes routine. The rise of states ended Viking raiding. These cultural models have a history: violence comes from violence; puritanism from socially unstable societies where violence is controlled but upward or downward mobility are easy. Reasonable models appear when people feel secure and able to control their lives (Bandura 1982, 1986). With adulthood, individuals learn that everybody has a mix—violent in some situations, rigid in others, reasonable in still others. Of course, which model is invoked in which situation depends on what has worked before, on what is culturally standardized and available, and on individual personality. Life is more complex than in grade school, making patterns harder to tease out. The complexity of such systems makes resolution difficult (Prime et al. 2020).

DISCOUNTING: SOME LIVES MATTER LESS

A division into "worthy" and "unworthy" is basic to group hatred. It is an important key to evil. Tracy Kidder's summary of Paul Farmer's premise applies: "The idea that some lives matter less is the root of all that's wrong with the world" (Kidder 2009:294). Hating the poor for being poor, hating weak and disabled people for their disabilities, and failing even to consider the unfortunates who find themselves in the way of a dam or military base, reminds us that Kidder and Farmer have an important perception.

However, Kidder's formulation has one major problem. As noted above, Randall Collins and many others (B. Anderson et al. 2004) document the very high rate of domestic violence: brutality against the people who matter *most* in one's life. They are subjects of violence specifically because they can devastate the spouses or parents or other agents who are abusing them. The issue is more a matter of deserving. Batterers think their spouses and children deserve to be beaten and abused, however much they may matter.

Basic to humans is love for family and close friends, then rapid fading to complete disregard for remote and unknown people. Children must be told to "think of the starving masses" far away, because they do not automatically care for them. Humans range from those who do not care even about their families (sociopaths and psychopaths) to people who truly do love and help the world, such as the many who have served selflessly and devotedly in the most appalling situations, from war-torn Afghanistan to refugee camps in Cambodia.

Discounting often goes far beyond mere disregard (as we may disregard those starving masses). Spouse abusers and child abusers may love the victim but still think the victim is not worthy of good treatment. Typical of humanity is extreme solidarity and devotion to one's immediate family, and by extension to family-like groups, sometimes whole religious sects (Swann et al. 2014). However, this is not the whole story. Crimes of passion, including in-family murders, are extremely common, not because the victims matter less but because they matter so much. Controlling them, even to the point of death, is existentially important to the killer.

Hatred often involves obsessive focus on the hated individuals or groups. Revolutions, in fact, are specifically directed at those who matter more, at least in the wider society's hierarchy. They are considered all-important and all-powerful. They must be eliminated. Kidder's generalization applies largely to killing through callousness and irresponsibility, and to warfare against groups considered to be merely in the way rather than worthy enemies. Carey et al. (2021) argue that thinking some matter *more* may be a better way of phrasing the issue (cf. Stiglitz 2019; Stiglitz et al. 2019).

It is more accurate to restate the view as distinguishing between the worthy and the unworthy. Some people and environments are worthy of being helped, protected, and preserved. Others are not worthy of consideration, or not worthy of protection, or not worthy of life. This allows us to deal with such facts as Nazi hatred of Jews whether the Jews were seen as powerful ("running the banks") or powerless, and the Maoist hatred of all elites. Much group hatred is of that sort; minorities who get power are hated all the more for it. Successful political parties are more hated by their opponents than insignificant ones.

People generally support their ingroup, but usually do not want to harm outgroups unless convinced to do it by fighting or by propaganda. Left to themselves, they will help or be neutral (Aalerding et al. 2018). However, they attribute bad motives to "the others," and thus think low of them (Shin and Niv 2021). In war or chaos, people become slowly accustomed to harming the enemy, and come to act in ways they would not normally imagine doing (Anderson and Anderson 2017, 2020; Baumeister 1997). Millions of "good Germans" found their initial acts in war and genocide to be utterly repulsive, but soon habituated and sometimes came to enjoy killing. Such habituation can involve weakening of left frontal lobe neural responses that lead to preventing and avoiding harm (Han et al. 2021). Perpetrators of evil thus come to think of it as routine or see it as something they were ordered to do. They are sometimes surprised when victims express horror at what is being done to them (Baumeister 1997).

OTHERING

Groups sometimes come into competition for resources. Big groups and highly solidary groups have the advantage over smaller or less united ones. It is notorious that even the most arbitrary differences can make people into opposing groups. Teachers used to demonstrate this by sorting students out into those that showed up with one shirt color vs another, or other completely arbitrary differences, and making them into competing teams. This was so horribly effective at making enemies that it is now regarded as unethical. Also, psychologists have found that it is strikingly difficult to find neutral matters that do not already have pejorative connotations (Hong and Ratner 2021). Shirt colors are already matters of bias and dislike among certain people.

Rothschild et al. (2012) showed that people routinely scapegoat, either to displace blame or reduce guilt while also increasing control. We have long known that people known to be of "mixed race" tend to get classified in the least prestigious race, a phenomenon called "hypodescent" (Ho et al. 2011). People even dislike those who are conspicuously virtuous (Parks and Stone 2010), partly from envy, but partly just because they are "different."

Negative feelings toward strange groups may be rooted in the human bio-logical heritage. Chimpanzees and even macaques fear and reject outgroup members while showing liking toward in-group members (Mahajan et al. 2011). Humans, and even monkeys, can overcome these feelings to vary-ing degrees, but they are hard to eliminate. Othering—labeling a group as "other" in the sense of dangerously different—follows from this (De Dreu et al. 2016). On the other hand, and contrary to a widespread myth, humans do not normally fear, hate, or cause trouble to strangers, though they may show surprise and even some fear at "different-looking" and "different-sounding" people. The authors of this book have traveled all over the world, worked in field situations in dozens of countries, and been well received everywhere except in a few places where outsiders had routinely caused trouble.

The real basis of othering is rivalry. The word is derived from Latin *rivus*, "riverbank," with reference to the competition for irrigation water in ancient Italy; it is familiar also from other dryland societies. Long-term rival groups become *structural opponent groups*, defining each other by their competition or by the subjection of one to the other. White people and Black people in the United States are in this relationship. They naturally assume antagonism, and tend to think of the other as the main opponent group (Roberts et al. 2021; Roberts and Rizzo 2021). This is the case even though we usually realize that almost all Black people, and many white people, are actually mixed. A "Black" person can be lighter than a "white" person (Gilchrist 2006). Specific prejudice changes sharply at the US borders with Canada and Mexico. Suddenly, Native Americans become the most visible structural opponent group, sometimes to the near erasure of Black people, who were until recently "invisible" in Mexico (Bonfil Batalla 1996). Someone who is "Black" in the United States is likely to be "mestizo" in Mexico.

Human society being as complex as it is, an individual is always a member of several crosscutting groups. A young Moroccan Muslim in Paris can identify as French, Moroccan, Maliki Muslim (the traditional, peaceful, relatively liberal Islam of Morocco), Salafi (the intolerant, extremist Islam of the terrorists), a soccer player, a restaurant worker, or a member of yet other groups. If he shifts his reference group from Maliki to Salafi, this may turn him from model citizen to terrorist. Another characteristic of human groups is relations of inclusion, as in the aforementioned saying "I against my brother." Genghis Khan was the master of assembling vast armies of the basis of wider and wider inclusion, up to legendary descent of all Mongol and related peoples from an ancestral gray wolf. After his death the Mongol Empire fell apart by the reverse process, with descent groups cleaving away.

Change over time can steadily reduce the power of one group and increase the power of another. This can produce major tensions. In the United States today, several identifiable groups are facing changes that scare them. Most obvious is the fossil fuel industry, and its allies such as chemical-intensive agribusiness and the plastics industry. Long associated with misery, depression, and devastation of psyches and communities (Obschonka et al. 2018), the fossil fuel industry is now heating the planet into collapse.

Conversely, groups seeing themselves on the "right side of history" become empowered. They compete with dominant groups and with the Establishment. The labor movement, youth movements, rising regional powers, and other traditionally "down" groups that see themselves getting better off invoke "revolutions of rising expectations." They are more prone to hate upward—to go after the elites and rulers. The groups fearing decline and displacement are prone to hate downward, attacking the poor and the less-advantaged minorities. The predicted trajectory of the group is more apt to structure rivalry than is actual deprivation.

Hierarchy and inequality predict othering and prejudice well. A leading scholar of prejudice, Nour Kteily, and his research group made people react in more prejudiced or less prejudiced ways according to whether the researchers stressed hierarchy or equality in experimental materials (Lucas and Kteily 2018). An experiment in Germany found that ordinary Germans were negatively judgmental of a woman in a hijab. They would judge nonconforming behavior by such a person more negatively than they judged the same behavior by the same woman when she was not so dressed. Yet, happily, an altruistic act by a hijab-wearer dispelled negative thinking (Choi et al 2019).

In either case, the triumph of one coalition over another ends in bloodshed. Europe from 1914 to 1945 saw a whole range of extremist "othering" movements, from fascism to Stalinism, all wishing to obliterate each other. Genocide became standard politics. The outbreak of nationalism and militarism in the First World War started this, leading to reactionary politics in the 1920s, which in turn led to the Great Depression, and that in its own turn led to extreme hatred and eventually World War II. After that, the world moved toward peace, sanity, and liberation, with colonialism virtually ending, before another brief cycle of reaction set in during the 1970s. Then liberation (especially the fall of the Soviet Union) and reaction alternated, until a new, long, and continuing period of reaction set in after 2000.

PREJUDICE

Prejudice of one sort or another is almost universal among humans. Since Gordon Allport's classic *The Nature of Prejudice* (1954), scholars have known it is widespread, pernicious, and hard to cure. Most people do not realize how prejudiced they are, until their attention is forcibly directed to it by some social event. The range among individuals is, however, enormous. Some are almost free of it, while others, like Hitler and his Nazis, have lives dominated by hatred of almost every conceivable group other than their own (Bergh and Akrami 2016). People can even be prejudiced against their own group (and thus dislike themselves). This is a fate sadly common among overweight people (Bergh et al. 2016). Some women and minority-group members absorb the wider society's low opinions, leading to depression and other griefs.

Many theories of prejudice exist, ranging from society-based to individual-based, but all converging on the major fact: people everywhere tend to dislike rival or threatening groups (Maitner et al. 2017; Sibley and Barlow 2017). Everything from a rather shakily defined "authoritarian personality" to bad parenting has been invoked (Duckitt 2001 provides a review of theories). Notable are a combination of right-wing authoritarianism and social dominance orientation (Dean and Altemeyer 2020; Duckitt and Sibley 2009). These, together, lead to "competition-driven power, dominance, and superiority" and "threat-driven collective security and social control" (Duckitt and Sibley 2017:212). They comprise the psychological basis of fascist and authoritarian regimes. Left-wingers can be as prejudiced as right-wingers, but the basic definition of "conservatism" includes a hierarchic view of the world, while "liberals" are supposed to be egalitarian, so, to the degree this holds true, prejudice comes easier to conservatives (Costello et al. 2022). Thomas Costello and coworkers, in a paper that represents a major advance in studies of authoritarianism, found that both left-wing and right-wing authoritarians shared general intolerance, closed-mindedness, and top-down thinking (following leaders). (There are so few left-wing authoritarians in the United States that some scholars had concluded they were a mythical beast, but Costello found some old-time dogmatic Marxists, extreme "woke" individuals, and similar thinkers, largely in other countries.) Their "'heart' of authoritarianism" consists of "preference for social uniformity, prejudice toward different others, willingness to wield group authority to coerce behavior, cognitive rigidity, aggression and punitiveness toward perceived enemies, outsized concern for hierarchy, and moral absolutism." Left-wing radicals were more prone to antihierarchical aggression and anticonventional thinking, and were more cognitively open, but were more negative in general.

All these psychological factors have their value in predicting individual behavior, but they turn out to have little value in predicting war, civil strife, or genocide (Anderson and Anderson 2013, 2020; Harff 2012; Hinton 2021; Nyseth Brehm 2017; Rummel 1994). Wars have happened at fairly frequent intervals in almost all societies. Long-peaceful societies like Qing China and Tokugawa Japan can suddenly dissolve into pervasive violence when the dynasty weakens. Genocide happens in famously peaceful societies like Cambodia and Rwanda. It happens in societies without any special history of authoritarianism, such as the United States and Australia. The rate of authoritarian personalities, if there is such a category, is probably about comparable worldwide. Bigotry and hatred are so common and well-distributed worldwide that if they predicted violence, all societies would be destroyed. Personality, culture, and situation interact in such complex ways that in one situation all but the most saintly are devils, whereas in another all but the most demonic are saintly, or at least civil. The shift from one state to another can be incredibly rapid.

DEHUMANIZATION

Prejudice includes dehumanization and infrahumanization (Leyens et al. 2007). Virtually every scholar of genocide, and many scholars of war and of violence in general, has remarked on the use of terms like "rats," "cockroaches," and "vermin" to describe victims. Sometimes victims are described as "machinelike" or "lacking human feelings" rather than being animalized (Kteily et al. 2016). People appear to be so reluctant to kill each other that they have to see the others as less than human to make mass murder bearable.

The problem comes when it becomes clear that mass murderers have not really dehumanized their victims, but see them as "human, all too human" (in the words of Nietzsche, 1911). They know exactly how to torture and humiliate them most effectively (Baumeister 1997). Also, the "others" may be regarded as human but of a lower order of humanity (Enock et al. 2021). Thus, many psychologists call this infrahumanization as opposed to dehumanization (Castano 2012; Leyens et al. 2007). Markowitz and Slovic (2020) differentiate the two, reserving the latter for extreme denial of human qualities and feelings to the victims.

Rats and cockroaches are simply killed, in the most quick and inconspicuous way possible. Genocide and mass murder, by contrast, invariably involve rape, torture, humiliation, and other systematic and carefully thought-out cruelty. All that depends on knowing that the victims are fully human and feel exactly the way the torturer would under similar circumstances. Nobody bothers to humiliate a cockroach. Thus, "dehumanization" is a complex figure of speech—not literal, but not mere metaphor either. It is as if there is some essential humanity that is replaced by some characteristics of a cockroach, leaving the person to suffer as a human would, despite the cockroach-like quality.

David Livingstone Smith (2011, 2020, 2021) has become the philosopher of dehumanization. Smith is quite aware of the fact that nobody really treats their victims the way they treat rats and cockroaches. His major book *Making Monsters* (2021) considers anti-Semitism in Europe, especially under the Nazis, and repression of African Americans, especially under slavery. He refutes the argument that it is merely a manner of speaking by citing huge amounts of literature from both places seriously alleging that the victimized groups are literally inhuman and subhuman. (They could be stronger [Black people] or craftier [Jews] than ordinary people, so long as they are "inferior" in other ways.) Smith reports that Jews were considered by the Nazis to be fiendishly clever, and even racist Americans in slavery days in the south admitted that African Americans were clever and "tricky," often outwitting their masters.

Many southern Americans, in particular, have seen Black people in about the way anthropologists see Homo erectus: human in some sense, but a lesser species. Much of the rhetoric goes back to the centuries when "blood" carried the "essence" of personhood, as in Spain, where the "blue blood" of nobles contrasted with ordinary red blood and, worse, with the evil corrupt blood of anyone with Jewish ancestry, however long converted to Christianity.

Smith points out that one Morgan Godwyn in 1680 already pointed out that racists could not really believe Black people were subhuman, because they frequently promote enslaved men to be overseers, organizers, military commanders, and other highly demanding and responsible positions. Also, many well-to-do white males had long and close sexual relations with African American women (recall Thomas Jefferson). Moreover, Africans were routinely converted to Christianity, proving that the owners and other racists knew perfectly well that Africans were teachable, and understood them to have souls, despite frequent rhetorical denial.

Throughout the book, Smith cites countless rhetorical extremes and countless horrific acts. Always, those acts are worse than anything anyone would do to an actual rat or cockroach. (He also, on p. 242, points out that rats are not really all that bad.) Smith concludes that it is possible to compartmentalize. People can believe that "the others" are human and yet subhuman. It is well known to psychologists that humans can hold two opposite views at once, carefully avoiding internal comparison of their ideas.

Smith deals strictly with the cognitive side of dehumanization—what people actually think about kinds, species, differences. He is relatively quiet about the emotional side. Yet most of the quotes he cites show nothing like normal rational thought. They show hatred gone to the point of literal madness—the point at which people cannot think rationally, and engage in raving. Some of the Nazi rhetoric about the Jews even caused Hitler to silence the writers. Clearly, dehumanization starts with hatred. The groups are hated, then demonized or bestialized.

Other cultures and subcultures do things differently. "Others" may be called monsters, fiends, or devils. Working-class Americans use nether body parts and body excretions: anyone disliked is a prick, asshole, or shit. Other cultures, including Mexican and Cantonese, do the same. Mexicans may call someone an animal, but real insults are more anatomical: *pendejo* (prick) or worse. Cantonese do not usually animalize; a vile person is a *leun* or *chat* (prick), *sifat* (asshole), and so forth. Traditionally, Chinese tended to call vile people "barbarians" or "ghosts," or both, as in the famous Cantonese expletive *faan kuai lou* ("foreign ghost person," often translated "foreign devil"). Other cultures use still other slanders and insults. Many traditional small-scale societies simply use the name of a neighboring group, thinking that is as bad as an insult can get.

In short, hatred can use anything disliked or disgusting; animals are merely one convenient target. Hatred can lead to horrific treatment even without degrading, as in many (probably most) cases of sadistic killing and of domestic violence. The horrors inflicted on Jewish and Black people are often inflicted on the bigots' own group members, including their wives, husbands, partners, children, often without any name-calling. (It is astonishing to find how many famous bigots were also violent family-member abusers.) What matters is the hate.

People also use animal metaphors to praise people: men are lions, women are foxes. Descent from noble animals is high praise, rather than putdown.

The Turkic peoples boast of descent from a gray wolf; the Mongols, from a gray wolf and a fallow doe. Australian Aboriginals have their totemic animals, North American Natives their animal spirit guardians.

Believing that some humans are literally inhuman is often motivated belief in patent nonsense. People hate themselves into believing the worst about "the others." Hate is the motive; cognition allows it to make a mad sort of sense. The commonest of these motivated beliefs—one documented very widely—is not dehumanization, but is the mistake made by Hobbes and Freud: that people are basically selfish, out for what they can get, and innately prone to "the warre of each against all," in Hobbes's famous phrase. Hobbes was aware that people are really more social than that, but many who espouse his view are much less nuanced.

Melissa Pavetitch and Sofia Stathi (2021) studied the flip side of dehumanizing: thinking the very best of "our" group. "We" are brave, virtuous, pure, and better than those others. The universally documented negative stereotype of "the others" is that they are selfish, greedy, scheming, lazy, and dirty—the traits supposedly typical of rats, cockroaches, and so forth. "We," of course, are the opposite. Religion adds that "we" are chosen and blessed, while "they" are damned. This allows us to excuse our uncomfortably obvious similarities to the "others"; yes, we are all visibly greedy, lazy, and so on, but "we" are blessed, and they are not. This perception has allowed religion to be the great home of extreme exclusionary beliefs.

Quite different, and more like genuine literal dehumanization, is the common practice of condemning vast numbers of faceless humans to death simply by not doing anything for them in cases of need. The Irish potato famine is a famous case. So are evictions of whole communities for the purpose of building dams and reservoirs; almost nobody ever bothers to compensate the refugees adequately (Scudder 2005). The Trump administration's, and later Republican states,' callous condemnation of hundreds of thousands of Americans to death by COVID-19 simply to keep the economy open is another case in point. This involves genuine disregard of the victims as human, or even as visible. They are simply erased.

ENA read Smith's book just after reading Rutger Bregman's *HumanKind* (2020), a cheery work that shows—correctly enough—that most humans are perfectly decent and pleasant most of the time. It is hard to see these books as describing the same species. To dehumanize a bit, it is like reading a book about bunnies and then a book about crocodiles. To maintain our other animal metaphor, Bregman knows only the good wolf, though he does provide excellent rules for being good to people, thus implying that he knows people are not always good and can be made better and treated better. Even so, Bregman's world has no place for the psychopaths who take over nations and whip their citizenry into a frenzy of murder and cruelty. Bregman mistakenly assumes that humans are domesticated, like dogs, and even calls us *Homo puppy*. In fact, humans are not domesticated by any scientific definition. They have not deliberately selected themselves for anything in particular, nor have they evolved tranquil behavior or its correlates. If humans have selected themselves for anything, it is hatred and cruelty, since group warfare is universal in history and has caused countless deaths (Bowles 2006; Turchin 2016). Humans are, in fact, by far the most menacing animal; no other species commits genocide, enslaves its own species, or indulges in pointless mass murder. Bregman tells of the good wolf, as if it ruled alone. David Smith tells a very great deal about what feeds the evil wolf, and something about what to do about it.

There are at least four levels of dehumanization or infrahumanization. First comes simple disregard because nothing can be done, leading to disregard of remote tragedies. Next comes callousness when not much is possible. This often leads to callousness about people who could be helped, but are left to suffer. Finally, dehumanization reaches the level of Smith's book: active bigotry and prejudice, leading to "cockroach"-naming and ultimately genocide. Only the last two are of real concern.

Dehumanization includes the less well-known problem of demeaning. Juliana Schroeder and Nicholas Epley (2020) argue that psychological needs are as basic as food and water. They find that people tend to think other people do not really have those needs, at least not to the same extent that "I" do. The farther the person in question is from "me," the less he or she shares "my" deep psychological needs. People even think they have more of the negative psychological traits, such as jealousy and nervousness, than others. Manifestations of demeaning include infrahumanization, stereotyping, and mind perception—"my" perception of others' minds, and inferences about same. All these involve stereotyping others as less sensitive.

Nour Kteily and colleagues have been researching dehumanization for decades. They find that open, public dehumanizing rhetoric goes with more violence and torture than the subtle kinds, and that various stereotypes besides "rats and cockroaches" occur. Lions, robots, and other dubious creatures are brought into play (Kteily and Bruneau 2017; Kteily, Bruneau, et al. 2015; Kteily, Hodson and Bruneau 2016). Unsurprisingly, teachers who dehumanize students do not teach effectively (Bruneau et al. 2019). Black children in the United States are not only dehumanized but often not seen as children (Goff et al. 2014), hence the tendency to try in court and legally punish even subteen Black children as adults when white children are not so treated until eighteen or older.

This leads to at least four different types of scorn for the "others": cognitively thinking some groups are dumber but not doing anything much about it; thinking anyone socially low deserves it (belief in a just world [Lerner 1980]). This is often caused by self-justification, insecurity, or just doing your job. This can lead to indifference, callousness, and ultimately *bureaupathy*: causing the poor or weak or disadvantaged to die, simply because it is easy and safe. Permitting polluting factories, building big dams that displace thousands without resettlement, and other such projects are sources of many of the world's unnecessary deaths, but are not counted in the genocide rolls (Anderson and Anderson 2020). Another curse is fear of competition, and thus the tendency to hate the weaker competitors and curry favor with the stronger ones.

HATRED

Hate has two very different forms: hate based on personal experience of dealing with real enemies, and social hate, learned from the wider society and targeted at "the other"—usually a vague, menacing, undefined, ill-known mass of people.

People often invent new "minorities" to hate. Medieval churchmen and rulers invented heresies whenever they needed an excuse to crack down on people they did not like. R. L. Moore has shown how the church and local lords turned random deviants into whole organized—but imaginary—movements. They often then using the "heresy" as an excuse to take over land (Moore 2012; see also Gibbon 1995 [1776–1788]).

One massacred heresy was the Catharist one. Its teachings were unclear, but the orthodox agreed that the teachings were wrong. By the mid-1200s the Catharists were indeed somewhat organized, but they never were more than a folk movement of asceticism and puritanism; they were not an organized church, merely a movement within Catholicism. Still, they presented enough of a threat to the venal and power-abusing church hierarchies to bring down savage repression on themselves. A peak was the siege of Béziers in 1209, which led to the famous advice by Arnaud Amalric, the religious advisor, to Simon de Montfort, the conqueror: "Kill them all; God will recognize his own"—or, in modern American idiomatic speech, "Kill 'em all and let God sort 'em out." This was recorded by one Caesarius a decade or so later (Coulton 1910:241; Morris2012:248).

People hate other groups because those groups are perceived as rivals or fold breakers, but the *alleged* reasons for hatred always involve dishonest negative stereotyping of the groups. The minority in question is claimed to be violent, treacherous, unable to control emotions, abusive, and weak, but also "uppity." Rich minorities are alleged to be stingy and dishonest. Poor ones are said to be dirty, stupid, promiscuous, and rude. They are compared to everybody's least favorite animals. These stereotypes recur over and over in accounts of persecution and genocide. They also occur when a group is working itself up to attack and loot another group; people usually feel bad about robbing groups they respect. The victimized group has to be perceived as unworthy and as deserving of being robbed. Another problem is personalizing: seeing bad acts by minority members as due to that group's natural badness, rather than—for instance—desperation due to poverty and oppression. People tend to be especially afraid of local minorities, especially those dispersed in society, like Jews in Hitler's Germany.

An extreme case has been presented recently by the widespread stereotyping of Muslims as murderous terrorists, even though the billion and a half Muslims of the world have produced only a few thousand terrorists. The stereotyping is usually done by Christians, who ignore the fact that Christians have been carpet-bombing Muslim societies practically "into the Stone Age" for years. George W. Bush's Iraq war, started by a barefaced lie about Iraq's alleged "weapons of mass destruction," killed far more people than Muslim terrorists have done.

Which group an individual hates is determined by culture and society. Evil people, especially evil leaders, try to make themselves the reference people for support groups in stress, and their groups the "good" reference groups. Hitler made himself and his Nazis the go-to people for dealing with stress in 1930s Germany. The Hutu leadership did the same in Rwanda in 1994. Good people get trapped in more and more evil, by following society at such times.

The more innocent, naive, and uneducated people are, the more easily they are fooled by public lies. The more mean-spirited and spiteful people are, the more easily they convince themselves to hate and to believe hateful stories. The unfortunate abundance of people who are both naive and mean-spirited guarantees a vast following for any charismatic leader of genocide or aggressive war.

MOTIVATED BELIEF AND EXTREMIST IDEOLOGY

Bias involves motivated belief (Tomasello 2018): people believe what they want to believe. In this case, the problem is motivated beliefs about the inhumanity of "the others." This leads to irrational overreaction to minor slights and problems. This in turn allows the lies to build up into exclusionary ideology. Extreme and vitriolic speech ("hate speech," a loose term), accompanying exclusionary ideologies, has become a worldwide phenomenon, "ricocheting across different parts of the world" (Udupa, Gagliardone and Hervik 2021:11). It is most often deployed against minorities, but also against liberals, conservatives, communists, fascists, and anyone else visible.

Migrants are often the victims of especially vicious campaigns. Amplified by social media and extremist governments, it has fallen into a worldwide feedback loop, a vicious spiral of more and more extreme misrepresentations and violent language (Udupa, Gagliardone and Hervik 2021).

Once that is in place, unfair justice, selective rights, and oppression follow. Forgiveness of the weak is rare. The rule of law is first made dependent on position in the hierarchy, and then breaks down completely, with the rulers above the law, and the poor below it—subject to arbitrary expropriation and killing. This creates a situation in which the most amoral and cruel become the leaders, and the masses become more and more beaten down—reduced to cowardly defensiveness, shown by hopeless conformity (as in Orwell's *1984*) or gang violence.

As society becomes more dependent on lies, it becomes increasingly expedient to the leaders to destroy science, education, and free inquiry. The press is muzzled. Schools become propaganda outlets. Any intellectualism is suspect. This is exactly the progression so well known in the history of Hitler's Germany, Mussolini's Italy, Stalin's USSR, Xi Jinping's China, and many other places, going back to the shadowy rulers of ancient Assyria. It relies on the frailties of human nature.

HATE TURNS TO VIOLENCE

Feeling out of control of one's life is a disturbingly good predictor of prejudice and hatred (Kofta et al. 2020; they studied anti-Semitism but the finding is general). For one thing, hurt people feel out of control, and anger makes them feel more in control, so the hurt-to-anger progression is common (Lemay et al. 2012). Especially at risk of falling into irrational hatred are people of a dominant majority who are not doing well, are not in good control of their lives, and yet feel strong entitlement simply because of their majority status. It need not even be a majority doing the oppressing; weak males are notoriously threatened by successful women, and the white minority held South Africa in chains for decades.

Hitler was perhaps the master of this game, but it was ancient long before his time. Recently, Donald Trump and Fox News have been the world's leaders in this, though there is competition. Resentful Muslims have rallied to the Salafist cause. Desperate farmers in Asia backed Communist leaders. Largely rural and less-educated voters from Brazil to Russia have repeatedly voted in fascist regimes. In all cases, the right-wing votership is overwhelmingly members of a majority (according to their ideas) that feel themselves threatened by modernity and globalization: the rural and small-town voters, the less educated, the less successful, the de-industrialized, and those who make a living from sunsetting industries. Hitler too drew by far the most support from rural areas (Simon 2021).

One can vaguely classify revolutions into "revolutions of rising expectations," often Communist or socialist, and revolutions by those feeling left behind and peripheralized, including many fascist and religious movements. Recently, the latter have been the worst. The worst violence is often done by governments suppressing revolutions, as in Syria recently.

Overall, since 1980, most dramatic political changes in the world have been rightward shifts. The fate of the USSR and East Europe is a particularly instructive case. Russia has gone fascist under the former communist leader Putin (the similarity of the communist and fascist regimes is striking, but not surprising). Poland and Hungary have elected extreme right-wing governments. Most of the former SSRs are still autocratic but without communist ideals. By contrast, only the Baltics and Georgia, and in so far as possible the Ukraine, shifted liberal. Outside that universe, liberal-ward changes are uncommon everywhere. The world's votership and power elites have shifted sharply to the right. Conflicts occur when powerful right-wing leaders attack weak democratic nations. Russia invaded and took over parts of Georgia in 2008 and of Ukraine in 2014, then attacked Ukraine itself in 2022.

Those who believe they are embattled on all sides, or trapped in a Hobbesian "war of each against all," will naturally be defensive. This is much stronger in groups; a group believing itself embattled will be extremely reactive, often genocidal. A group believing itself entitled will react with extremism when its members feel challenged by the rise of other groups. This is most visible in majorities that see minorities rising in society, but it is far from unknown among the minorities themselves. The temptation for a minority to hate a structural opponent majority is hard to resist, even for those who know that only tolerance and egalitarianism can help them in the end.

Fear of women and gender-nonconforming persons is common among males, especially self-consciously heterosexual males, who are often so neurotic about "gays" that they are often suspected of being latent homosexuals themselves (a point made by Freudians, at least speculatively, and neither confirmed nor refuted by science). Deflection, displacement, and projection are great: they allow people to displace antagonism from loved ones, and from actual scary enemies. Often the actual hurts come from loved ones, but they are usually considered taboo for antagonistic reactions, especially violence. Hence the whole scapegoat concept. Racism is a typical case. Steven Roberts and Michael Rizzo have recently identified six bases of American racism (Roberts and Rizzo 2021:475) (See Figure 4.1).

Obviously, these apply to any prejudice, whether racial, religious, gender-related, or other. The authors point out that no one starts out being racist. Again, this applies to any prejudice. Recall that the "races" of American popular discourse have nothing to do with biology, and in fact they change with almost every census. Many societies worldwide have had no skin color bias. Most have had some form of prejudice—if not racial, then religious, linguistic, or other—but some have almost totally avoided such group judgments. In short, fear of a rival or potentially rival group produces hatred. Feelings of entitlement for "my" group make it worse.

PUTTING IT ALL TOGETHER

The stage is set for a full theory of why people deliberately harm each other out of all proportion to what would be needed for self-defense, group defense, maintaining order, preserving health (like Aristotle's surgeons), and the public good. We need a theory that will comprehensively include domestic violence, aggressive war, looting, genocide, callous displacement of poor people for the benefit of the rich, poisoning millions with dangerous chemicals (as through pollution or tobacco huckstering), and other clear wrongs. (The following depends heavily on Baumeister 1997, Beck 1999, Collins 2008, Staub 2011, and Waller 2016.)

The progression from ordinary life to evil is usually through anger, then personal hate, then group hate, then real bigotry, then bullying, then exclusionist ideology and ideologues, and finally strongman leadership and its usual end in genocide. These have a backstory, and our sources, especially Baumeister and Beck, agree that it very often lies in weakness and insecurity caused by harsh, judgmental, or otherwise problematical child-rearing and early life.

Much anger is simple and fully appropriate reaction to real threat—the classic "fight, flight, freeze." This is not evil by the definition of the present book. The problem is judging how much to react to threat. Reasonable reactions are a necessary part of life. Overreaction is inevitable, since underreacting in an uncertain situation would be dangerous. The real danger is overreaction to minor or imagined threats or from displacement of anger and hate onto innocent targets. Overreaction almost always comes from excessive fear, often from a sense of weakness and inadequacy. All our sources agree on that. It can be personal, in brittle and aggressive people (Baumeister 1997), or cultural, in "honor cultures." Displacement is usually due to cultural and social pressures: individuals are strongly sanctioned against threatening their immediate loved ones and peers, but encouraged to be hateful and cruel toward minorities, or the poor, or animals, or other inappropriate targets.

The result is unprovoked or inadequately justified violent aggression, or narrowly selfish competition. These two are often combined, as in classic Viking or Mongol raiding, colonial wars, and drug gangsterism. In anthropological terms, racism, religious bigotry, and other kinds of hateful prejudice are cultural constructions of cowardly displacement. The honor syndrome (basic to, but not confined to, "honor cultures") is a cultural construction of defensiveness based on fear of social disdain or disapproval in unstable cultures where that can result in violence and death. Both are thus different kinds of fear-based defensiveness.

Killing also comes from sheer desire for wealth, as in drug gang operations, Mafia shakedowns, and other ordinary crime. Even there, however, defensiveness enters; such criminal operations are hotbeds of honor culture, as Mafia rules show. Historically, the Mafia grew out of Sicilian hill towns' honor cultures in unsettled times, not out of crime rings per se.

However, this does not explain war, genocide, and other mass killing. It does not explain the sheer callousness of bureaucrats who let millions starve, or CEOs who let thousands die from poisons and pollution released by their companies. In these cases, the people active in such pursuits do it under orders, or powerful social pressure, rather than because they are directly motivated. People do it because it is human to conform. People depend so heavily on their social groups that they may do anything the group and its leaders require. Cultural traditions often require a man—very rarely a woman—to prove himself through violence, in cultures ranging from medieval Europe to Genghis Khan's Mongolia. Strongman leaders from Emperor Wu of Han to Hitler demand their subjects die in millions for them, and the subjects do so, most of them willingly and without protest. Culture and leaders similarly encourage competition for wealth in societies like medieval Venice and Genoa and the modern United States.

In honor cultures, individuals, especially men, are expected to work themselves up into anger and violence when challenged. Other cultures (the Semai are the extreme) damp such behavior down. They are either outright pacifist, or given to reasonable moderation, like ancient Greeks and middle-class European and American liberals. Evil leaders take advantage of the human tendency of challenged individuals to work themselves up into a fury by deliberately dwelling on angry reactions. Working up hate vs. damping it down emerges as a critical issue.

Simple conformity explains nothing about the real basis of evil, though, because the evil behaviors must be started by someone. Someone must invoke the violence or start the cynical pursuit of gain. Cultural traditions all started at some point, most of them fairly recently by historical standards, and thus must be explained. One obvious wellspring, beyond simple defensiveness and its cultural constructions, is simple competition gone out of control.

However, in all those cases, we are forced to inquire why some go all out to kill rivals and loot their goods, while others practice peace and good works. Even the Mongol hordes did not mobilize everybody; someone had to stay home and herd the sheep. The most important for our purposes are the coping mechanisms that people learn to assess and deal with threat, stress, and fear. Since people learn their major coping mechanisms as young children, they carry childish defense mechanisms into adulthood. The key to evil, then, is a set of childish defense mechanisms that perceive high levels of threat, respond with high levels of fear, and cope by violence or by grasping for others' wealth. Cowardly defensiveness is a direct and clear predictor of everything from bullying to miserliness. Translated into cultural patterns, it lies behind genocide, looting, and other evils that depend on the strong robbing or killing the weak for no acceptable reason. In violent situations it leads to violence; in peacetime it may more often take the forms of cheating, unfair competition, lobbying for special favors, and other dubious techniques of enrichment at public expense. In traditional days, kings and emperors killed their political opponents and warred against lootable neighbors; that was at least courageous. Today's tyrants war against their own helpless and innocent minorities.

Finally, there are situations in which even the strongest and most courageous are forced into aggressive fighting and seizing property. This is clearest in borderland situations, as we have seen. It also occurs in situations of social breakdown or deregulation, such as the cyclic collapses of China's imperial dynasties, the wild frontier of the United States in the nineteenth century, and the inner city of Rio de Janeiro. Strong young men do what is necessary, though most women and the very old and young can stay out of the conflicts. Innate and learned levels of aggressiveness matter even in those situations.

Chapter 5

Evil into Politics

EVIL LEADERS

Hierarchies are necessary to society, but they can be maintained by mutual duties and respect, and can allow bottom dogs to work their way upward and sometimes win (Boehm 1999; Sapolsky 2017). The more conservative ones model traditions as the Way Things Are, making Adam Smith–style positive-sum gaming difficult.

One problem throughout history, but especially during the last one hundred years, is the ability of the worst human beings to rise to the top. Evil leaders, "strongmen" in the view of Ruth Ben-Ghiat (2020a, 2020b), are a distinct and identifiable set of people. They are little changed from ancient Greek demagogues and medieval war-band leaders. Frank Dikötter, in *How to Be a Dictator* (2019), has described the type memorably (see also Anderson and Anderson 2020).

Bill Eddy, an expert on such individuals, calls them High-Conflict Personalities (Eddy 2019). They demonstrate narcissism and sociopathy (some would say psychopathy), and often other dubious traits. Ben-Ghiat and Dikötter both point out that a significant trait shared by most of them is open womanizing—not just ordinary skirt-chasing, but open, boastful seduction and even rape or quasi-rape of women, often much younger ones. Hitler was an odd exception, but Berlusconi, Gaddafi, the Philippines' Duterte, and Donald Trump are flamboyant examples, studied in Ruth Ben-Ghiat's book *Strongmen*. This trait is shared with many ordinary bullies and bad actors, including crime bosses.

They are characterized by tremendous drive for success and admiration, tremendous combativeness, and a tendency to see the world in black and white, with the "white" being anything that aids and supports them and the "black" being almost everything else—especially anything that opposes them and their interests. The color terms are further appropriate in that they are almost all racists (though admittedly not all are white; many, indeed, have hated whites). Eddy, Dikötter, and Ben-Ghiat all see the media as fueling such people. Their highly polarized and emotionalized style fits the media's affection for stories of that sort.

The British psychologist Steve Taylor (2021) has argued that such strongmen, including Donald Trump, tend toward the psychopathic and narcissistic end of the human continuum in such traits. They exhibit the "dark triad" of those two traits plus Machiavellianism. They lack empathy and compassion, and tend to hubris and cruelty. Taylor reports that the Polish psychologist Andrzej Lobaczewsky coined the term "pathocracy" for rule by such people (he had suffered under both Hitler and Polish Communism). Taylor advocates somehow preventing such people from getting public power, but admits this is difficult at best.

Insight into the strongman mentality is provided by a study of Stewart Rhodes, founder and longtime leader of the Oath Keepers, a neofascist militia active in violent confrontations in the United States. An intelligent, educated man, he was drawn to more and more extreme right-wing politics. He moved farther and farther into the Montana woods, taking his wife and children with him, keeping them isolated, and treating them in an increasingly abusive manner, until they left him. A bully to neighbors and followers, he carried a gun at all times and threatened his family with it (Wilber 2021). The pattern of increasing extremism, increasing abuse, and increasingly aggressive leadership of an extremist group is characteristic of more famous strongmen, and from Rhodes's abusive behavior we can understand better the more successful examples of the breed.

Eddy sees a classic course in behavior: the high-conflict leader invents a fantasy crisis, designates Targets of Blame (fantasy enemies), and sets himself up—he is almost always male—as a fantasy hero. He creates an idealized, narcissistic image of himself as the one unbeatable fearless leader who can stop the enemy. These enemies are always minorities, usually already-unpopular ones. The targets often shift, though particularly salient structural opponent groups—the Jews in Germany, Black people in the United States, and counterparts in other fascist countries—are attacked all the time. Otherwise, consistency and follow-through are not concepts in the minds of such leaders; they follow the soundbites and the TV coverage. Eddy tells us what to do: never believe the fantasies; oppose the claims with cool, sober, but constantly repeated facts. Do not oppose with emotion or overstatement; that is playing the high-conflict game. The high-conflict leaders and their followers are already the masters of that game.

Evil leaders cannot arise in a vacuum. They must be backed by criminals or shady interests. They draw on lazy or incompetent people threatened by more energetic and competent ones. Above all, they are backed in modern societies by dinosaur interests: corporations directly threatened by progress or peace.

The great ability of evil leaders—the story of their success—is that they can flip people from feeding their good wolves to feeding their bad ones. They can make a model citizen into a suicide bomber or a genocidal mass murderer. If humans did not have both wolves within them, they could not turn bad, but they require substantial social pressure to turn from good to evil. Some individuals behave badly all their lives, but most do not. They are murderous only when led to it by social pressure from leaders and peers.

All genocides and most wars of aggression involve an escalating series of more and more outrageous and hateful exaggerations and outright lies, told by the government and promoted through any and all available media. This technique is as old as history, but was truly perfected by Joseph Goebbels under Hitler. Strongmen since have copied him. Without these lie campaigns, only a small percentage of humanity is hateful enough to want war and genocide. The more extreme and pervasive the lies, the more people get sucked into the nightmarish views of the world that these lies perpetrate.

An inept evil leader will get the 10 percent of humanity who are genuinely bad actors behind him. A successful liar will add the next 10 percent. Increasing the extremism and pervasiveness of lies will involve more and more, though the truly good will probably never be on board. Trump perfected the Big Lie technique, going beyond Joseph Goebbels: "The number of documented falsehoods he [Trump] uttered as president increased from 5.9 a day in 2017 to an average of 22 a day in 2019, for a total of 16,241 in his first three years in office" (Ben-Ghiat 2020a:116). The *Washington Post* logged 30,573 falsehoods stated by Trump during the total time of his presidency.

Basic to the appeal of evil leaders is widespread free-floating frustration and resentment. These usually originate from ordinary life and close contacts, but are easily mobilized and directed against victims, usually minorities. Evil leaders have such resentments in great abundance. They are typically insecure; their notorious tendency to become more and more punitive and violent as they spend more time in office is at least partly due to their increasing insecurity as their power grows (Ben-Ghiat 2020a; Dikötter 2019; Mooijman et al. 2015).

This leads to ambiguity about power among revolutionaries. They are reacting to bullying and bureaupathy, but they often want power to get revenge rather than democratic equalization of power. This leads to the depressing cycle noted by many thinkers: the revolutionaries win and institute a regime even more repressive than the former one. This has been noted, for instance, for Russia and China after Communist takeover, and now Russia appears headed for even more autocratic rule, while China under Xi Jinping has become more repressive than under other post-Mao leaders. Iran became even more repressive after the displacement of the Shah by the Shi'a theocracy. ENA remember talking to one Iranian radical shortly before the revolution. Asked what he would do if he won, he replied: "We'll do to them what they did to us." Which, indeed, happened, to Iran's loss.

Ben-Ghiat's book *Strongmen* (Ben-Ghiat 2020a) provides deep accounts of several such individuals, from outright fascists like Mussolini and Hitler to right-wing demagogues like Italy's Berlusconi and Libya's Gaddafi, with side references to Pinochet, Putin, Mobutu, and others. She pays particular attention to Donald Trump, the latest in the depressing roll of would-be tyrants. To those who have studied the rise of such leaders, it seems highly likely that if Trump had succeeded in getting a second term by dubious means, he would have instituted mass killing. She chronicles the ties between many of these people: ex-Nazis tutored Pinochet, and international hookups of torturers and subverters of democracy propagated through the dark web (the shady or illegal side of the Internet). The personalities of strongmen remain constantly interesting. There is a whole book dedicated to various theories of how Hitler went wrong (Rosenbaum 2014).

The backing of Big Oil is obtrusively evident in many of these cases: Gaddafi, Putin, Trump, and others. "All twenty-first-century authoritarians suppress climate change science, lest that discourage the plunder of national resources that generates profits for them and their allies" (Ben-Ghiat 2020a:96). All had the support of primary-production export-oriented industries, the interests that bleed their own countries for the benefit of international shareholders.

Corruption is inevitable in such regimes; in fact, the leaders were often installed by shady interests. "As in other countries, the rise of authoritarianism in America has meant the end of accountability and ethical standards in government" (Ben-Ghiat 2020a:162). The strongman always "proclaims law-and-order rule, yet enables lawlessness. . . . The strongman's trick is to seem exceptional and yet to embody the national everyman, with all of his endearing flaws. . . . The familiarity of these personages, marketed by their personality cults and populist ideologies as 'one of us,' is also why many people don't see them as dangerous early on" (Ben-Ghiat 2020a:251–52).

Ben-Ghiat has further written that strongmen win "at moments of transition, when traditional parties and political systems no longer seem adequate." They get "an improbable mix of supporters." A strongman can be "whatever his followers need him to be at that moment. It's no accident that modern personality cults first developed in the 1920s, along with the Hollywood star system, since they share an important quality of celebrity: The object of fascination must seem accessible but also be remote and untouchable. In the political sphere, this translates into leaders who are acclaimed both as men of the people and as men above all other men" (Ben-Ghiat 2020b). She points out that evil leaders often come from communications fields: Berlusconi the TV magnate, Trump the reality-show star. She sees them as often "weak and paranoid" men who try to appear macho.

There is, however, no real pattern to when strongmen arise. In premodern times, they emerged at the collapse of empires, often starting new empires of their own. Caesar, Tamerlane, Zhu Yuanzhang (who founded the Ming Dynasty), Hideyoshi in sixteenth-century Japan, and other bare-fisted adventurers of agrarian imperial days fit the pattern. In Europe, fascism grew after loss in war or collapse of country, as fascism did in Germany and Austria after the collapse of the German and Austro-Hungarian empires in World War I. This did not apply to Japan, Turkey, Thailand, Brazil, or other non-European powers. Racism, anti-immigrant sentiments, religious reaction, and economic woes are among the drivers in these and other countries (Arzheimer 2017). Sometimes a coup or an invader puts a strongman in office. The most widespread theme is the tendency of rural people and traditionally religious people to be twin pillars of support, often with recourse to misogynist and heterosexist rhetoric in the religions as well as to their promotion of believers as chosen and entitled.

Fascists or "authoritarian populists" have recently won at the ballot box, in reasonably free if not totally fair elections, in Brazil, Hungary, India, Philippines, Poland, Turkey, the United States, and to varying degrees in many other countries. The correlation is not with bad times; many of these victories took place during very good times, economically and socially. The common theme was that fascism won over democratic governments that seemed to be dithering over crime, corruption, terrorism, or immigration. People wanted a change. Trump, always indiscriminate in condemnation, pushed all buttons. Others concentrated on one or another: immigration in Hungary, secularization in Turkey, drug crime in the Philippines, and so on. More classic issues of gender hierarchy, control of society, and similar matters played a part, but the common theme of election rhetoric in all these cases—from Hitler and Mussolini onward—is one of disorder, especially illegal and highly visible disorder. Many people, worldwide, react to that by abandoning the Enlightenment and democracy, and putting their trust in a strongman.

There is common ground in most of these elections, and in other rightward shifts, such as the Taliban victory in Afghanistan and the shift of Xi Jinping from Communism to something very much like fascism. Power-hungry politicians mobilize rural, small-town, and ideologically traditional voters; they are funded by fossil fuel corporations and large agribusiness interests (possibly not in the Taliban case; they were funded from Pakistan). Xi Jinping in China was not elected in a general election; he took over by getting the Chinese Communist Party to support him. The nature of his opposition is not clear, but he was quick to crack down on dissent of all kinds, promote a highly tendentious and dishonest view of Chinese history (with extremist Communism idealized). He began genocide of minorities. This allows us to speculate that he has right-wing backing by giant primary-production interests, in opposition to an inferred opposition that supported diversity, small-scale enterprise, flexibility, and social and economic openness. Xi is very close in actual politics to Trump and to Brazil's Bolsonaro. He has long abandoned actual Marxist or Maoist socialism.

FASCISM

Hermann Goering, as quoted in *Nuremberg Diary* by Gustave M. Gilbert (1947), said: "Voice or no voice, the people can always be brought to the bidding of the leaders. That is easy. All you have to do is tell them they are being attacked and then denounce the pacifists for lack of patriotism and exposing the country to danger. It works the same way in any country."

The twentieth century saw the rise of fascism and authoritarian Stalinist Communism. The term "fascism" was coined by Benito Mussolini, who set the general tone of the movement, though he began as a working-class socialist. Fascism soon reached its apotheosis in Adolf Hitler, who has tended to be taken as the incarnation of fascist politics. He was the most successful, but using him and his behavior to define the movement is not adequate. One must also consider Mussolini and such avowed fascist leaders as Generalissimo Franco of Spain.

At the same time, Communism rose, initially offering hope to the oppressed, but very soon following fascism into dictatorship and oppression. Stalin and Hitler notoriously learned from each other. They were allied until Hitler turned on the USSR. The excesses of Stalin and Mao Zedong need no introduction. Communism has morphed into a form of fascism under Xi Jinping. A few countries, such as Cuba, maintained a milder form, closer to what Marx intended, but still autocratic.

One would have thought communism and its problems are too well known in the United States to need further notice, but that seems not to be the case. The Republicans have been labeling civil rights, economic stimuli, and even social distancing during COVID-19 as "communist." Suffice it to say that communism was defined by Marx and Engels as government control of the means of production, and distribution such that everyone gets what he or she needs. This has rarely been tried above the local-commune level. The USSR and China quickly regressed to very different systems, much more like fascism than like Marx's ideals. Providing roads, bridges, and minimal welfare is not only not communism, it is not even socialism; every state government from ancient Egypt and Babylon onward has done that much.

The appeal of fascism and communism continues to amaze. Deeply instructive, and extremely disturbing, is contemplating the enthusiastic reception of fascism and communism among the aesthetes and high intellectuals of the early twentieth century. These were the best-educated people the world has ever known, in terms of traditional liberal arts. They absorbed far more literature, art, and philosophy in college than students do today. Yet Ezra Pound and Martin Heidegger were lifelong Nazi supporters. H. L. Mencken was not much better. T. S. Eliot, e. e., cummings, Carl Jung, W. B. Yeats, and many others flirted with fascism in its early years, though most became disillusioned. On the communist side, there were at least equal numbers of intellectuals who flirted with that dubious ideology. It is necessary only to mention Stalin's love of good classical music. Mao Zedong was a good poet and prose stylist. Indeed, art is no protector of humanity.

Americans remain amazingly ignorant about fascism and its powerful effects on the United States ever since the 1920s (for this and what follows, see Mann 2004, 2005; Paxton 2004; Snyder 2015, 2017, 2018). Fascism was always maintained by outrageous lies, and the more extreme and outrageous the lies and rhetoric, the better. A sort of Darwinian selection leads to the most effective lies taking over. Such lies are not mere untruths; they are inflammatory statements directed at the most "wronged," downward-bound, or alienated people. Fascists since Goebbels have been aware that strategic lying is successful even if the liar knows it will be instantly refuted, because just getting it out there and getting discourse on the issue started can be quite enough. Also, Goebbels's insistence that a lie repeated often enough becomes "truth"—or at least generally believed—has been proved repeatedly, though largely of lies that appealed to motivated belief.

In the economy, fascism consists of Hitler's "national socialism" (of which the term "Nazi" is an abbreviation): Government fusion with giant firms to dominate the economy and control workers as well as production and distribution. In Germany, the firms were preexisting corporations such as I. G., Farben and Volkswagen. In the United States, Trump appointed executives from giant oil and munitions corporations to all possible major government positions, probably copying Hitler, whose works he had studied. Other countries have done the same, often bending state or "parastatal" corporations to the purpose. Either way, this is socialism from the top: government control of production by controlling giant interests rather than by nationalizing all enterprises. It can, however, also be called capitalism, since the firms remain dominated by CEOs and CFOs rather than by outright government employees. This corporativist component is diagnostic of the movement, and European fascism took it as defining. The opposition of "capitalism" and "socialism," so religiously pursued by Americans, is thus reduced to nonsense. They are most effective, and most horrible, when combined into one top-down system.

Often the justification of the whole system is not explained; it is just taken as a given. Only the smarter fascists bother to justify this via "nature" or God. Hitler justified his scheme as "natural," on the theory that big animals eat little ones, but did not go into much more detail. (Classic studies of Hitler's regime and its economic organization include Franz Neumann's *Behemoth*, 1944, an analysis written when Hitler was still in power. Neumann followed it up with the idealistic work *The Democratic and Authoritarian State*, 1957, which held up a model of open, transparent, debate-conscious government in opposition to fascism and Stalinism.)

With this goes a basic fascist worldview. The dominant theme is a feeling of pervasive persecution by "Jews," "liberals," and any and every other conspicuous group that can be considered as opposition. This view has much in common with the weak, insecure defensiveness noted in previous chapters. The real opposition to fascism lies in self-confidence, modesty, hope, indifference to power, and feeling one can cope with change. Fascism, both the hyperaggressive form and the greedy and selfish form, is cowardice with power, elaborated into a worldview.

Recently, more and more countries have voted for fascist governments, or installed them by coup or civil war. People tend to ally with the strong against the weak. Only in serious cases, where they can get overwhelming support, do they ally with the weak against the strong. Of all significant social movements, only the labor movement managed this for any length of time. Rural regions, and historically conservative ones, back fascism. So do extreme nationalists, to the point that fascism is sometimes equated incorrectly with hyper nationalism. A striking number of the world's major countries have had at least one episode of fascism in the last one hundred years.

Jason Stanley's excellent book *How Fascism Works* discusses several identifying features. He sees it as clearly the ideology of Trump, and of Bolsonaro in Brazil, Modi in India, Orbán in Hungary (who makes no secret of it), Erdoğan in Turkey, and others. For Stanley, fascism starts with mythification of a golden past, when families were patriarchal, violence was adulated, hierarchies were strong, and everyone was happy (Stanley 2020:3–23). Stanley then discusses propaganda, including the Big Lie and its relatives. He identifies anti-intellectualism, including anti-science, alternative facts, and the rest, as a major characteristic of fascism. (To pick a Spanish example: "'Death to the Intelligentsia' became a Falangist rallying cry; Franco equated scientists with enemies of the state"; Ehrlich 2022:335.) He then focuses on the most obvious fascist behavior: hatred of minorities and women. Sections on hierarchy, law, and sex follow. Fascists not only persecute minorities; their repression and sequestering of women is a major part of their agenda. Stanley identifies groups like Taliban as more fascist than Islamic.

Fascism seeks authoritarian leadership of a state. It begins as a movement wanting authoritarian control, like Mussolini's original "fascist" movement. Above all, and truly diagnostic, is reliance on the Big Lie technique. Ideally, the regime can repress all truth, as China has eliminated the Tiananmen Square incident from all public knowledge or record. Failing that, the regime may drench the media with so many lies, "alternative facts," conspiracy theories, and even genuine but confusing facts that everyone loses track of what is true (Stanley 2020:56–77). The party members are forced to repeat these lies as absolute truth. They allow no dissent or discussion. Often, the people also are required to believe the Big Lies, or claim they do, especially the lies about minority ethnic and religious groups.

Fascists are experts at seeking out what the most bigoted and hateful people want to hear. Leaders marshal bigots for the cause by giving them exactly what they want to hear. This appeals especially to those already suspicious of minorities, expecting the worst motives from them (Ames and Fiske 2015). Minorities and immigrants are evil and scheming, women are polluting and "hysterical," the powers that be are our benevolent protectors, law and order is our only hope, the purpose of government is military and police protection rather than personal welfare. Such hearers indulge in motivated social cognition (Jost et al. 2003). They believe what they want to believe, especially since it is said by "strong leaders." They want to believe it because it deals with their gut fears and their sense of entitlement.

Fascist groups base their ideology on racism and/or religious bigotry. Indeed, this is often taken as definitive, but it is inadequate to define fascism, since many other movements marshal hatred. Fascists, however, make hatred more central, sometimes not even pretending to offer much else. Forced eventually to behave accordingly, they all commit genocide if they are in power for long. The nonexistence of the "races" of Nazi and white supremacist ideology merely encourages racists to use the concepts even more (Sussman 2014).

Fascist movements idealize force and violence, both military and civilian (Mann 2004, 2005; Paxton 2004; Snyder 2015, 2017, 2018; Stanley 2020). They glorify physical strength and devalue those they consider "weak," including women and especially LGBTQ+ persons. Often, such movements scare followers into hating minorities by claiming the minorities rape the women of the majority or dominant culture. This is clearly a tactic of blaming the enemy for one's own vices, for fascists who get power for any length of time invariably indulge in mass killing, through war or genocide, and in mass rape. Rape as a systematic and organized tactic to terrorize and torture the enemy—men as well as women—was particularly salient in the cases of Afghanistan, India, Rwanda, Serbia, and many other places during fascistic and genocidal periods. An extreme and harrowing account of systematic violent rape over decades in Turkey is provided in *The Thirty-Year Genocide* (Morris and Ze'evi 2019; here it is blamed on "Muslims" in general, which was not the case; the specific rulers of the time organized it; see Akçam 2012). Extensive rape is present in all documented genocides and all well-documented wars of any size. The fascist glorification of strength, obsession with controlling women, and hatred of homosexuality has not escaped Freudian analysis, with no proofs of connection, but many arguments made.

Fascists promise all sorts of things, fail to deliver, blame their enemies, and get into a loop of more and more blame and persecution. Of course, most political movements do some of this, but fascists add their economic order, wide-flung hatreds, and the Big Lie technique, among other distinctive things. The leader is a "strongman." He demands loyalty. He and his high command are above the law and above ordinary considerations of truth. Conversely, the poor and minorities are beneath the law, fair game for police or even laypersons to abuse or even kill (Stanley 2020:78–126).

Stanley also observes that fascists share the general conservative opposition to labor unions, to welfare systems, and dislike of cities for their dirt, ethnic variety, and unpredictable politics, although not a marker of fascism. Lawrence Britt has a fuller definition of fascism (Britt, 2003), emphasizing sexism, corporate power, and repression of arts (Britt, 2003).

Timothy Snyder has listed a wider range of characteristics of "tyranny" (Snyder 2017), which he finds clearly expressed in the leading evil regimes of today: Duterte's Philippines, Brazil under Bolsonaro, Trump's administration in America, the Chinese communist dictatorship, and others. In 2021 he listed ways his book *On Tyranny* was fulfilled in the political reality of the 2017–2021 period (Snyder 2021).

All politicians manipulate facts and nonfacts to their own ends, but fascists—generally following Goebbels—use the more systematic Big Lie technique. Almost all scholars of fascism emphasize this. Four types of lies dominate politics. First, and by far the most important, is the idea that our group is God's people, the others are barely human if at all, and we must repress or even get rid of them. The basic idea that "we" are special and entitled, while our structural opponents are low and undeserving, derives originally from religion. It was re-spun by nationalism with the rise of the nation-state (Benedict Anderson 1991). It is also characteristic of sociopaths and psychopaths, who believe that they as individuals are special and entitled, and can deal with other people accordingly. It survives as the basic foundational myth of modern fascism, seen in white supremacy, anti-Semitism, hatred of "other" genders, and many other forms. Fascist politicians immediately gravitate to this lie as their major ongoing talking point. Hitler's

"German people," Mao's "true communists," and Trump's "MAGA people" and (interchangeably) "real Americans" are from the same root.

Second come cynical, motivated lies by big firms: tobacco, fossil fuels, chemicals, agribusiness, and the like. Munitions firms are notorious for spreading misinformation to encourage war and thus increase profits. Third is pseudoscience based on ignorance and fear, such as antivaccination propaganda. Fourth comes the opposition to self-improvement that comes from the need to deny that "I have a problem." In personal life, this extends from refusal to deal with really life-threatening problems like epidemics, substance abuse, refusal to exercise, and refusal to deal with mental issues. In politics, it takes the form of denying that the country needs economic measures, infrastructure improvements, better education, and other improvements. Fascists are masters of combining these four types of lies.

Some fascists were much milder than Hitler and his followers. Franco in Spain and Salazar in Portugal did not invest so heavily in the Big Lie or in massacre of minorities, though they used both on occasion. Borderline fascists like Pinochet in Chile, Ferdinand Marcos in the Philippines, and Saddam Hussein in Iraq picked up some of the behaviors, notably militarism and murderous repression of opposition, but were not classic wielders of the Big Lie. Still less fascistic are simple military dictators, who abound everywhere in every age. These satisfy the criteria of autocracy, brutal repression, economic bossism, right-wing rhetoric, and so forth, and usually repress women, traditional rival ethnic groups, and LBGTQ+ persons, but do not indulge in Big Lies or in indiscriminate anti-minority campaigns. By these and all other standards, Donald Trump is well over into the classic fascist zone, and has dragged the Republican Party into it (see, e.g., Snyder 2018, 2021).

Military dictatorship and authoritarian populism are (by definition) less totally committed to Big Lies, and they may downplay the racism and bigotry. They do not necessarily glorify personal strength. They simply involve either a military junta or charismatic right-wing leaders who take over and institute a reign of harsh discipline or outright terror. They often commit politicide—elimination of political rivals and potential rivals—but rarely full genocide. Currently, Egypt's Sisi and the postcommunist bosses of Central Asia are examples. Such regimes can turn fascist, or even drift in and out of fascism. They may thus be difficult or impossible to classify. One cannot expect clear categories in real-world politics.

Authoritarian socialism differs in actually nationalizing at least some means of production, and cracking down on mass killing economic elites as well as political rivals, rather than ethnic or religious groups. Extreme communist states have killed many types of groups, indiscriminately. All these forms can blend into each other.

Brazil, India, Hungary, and Turkey have certainly gone from democratic to fascist in recent years, as noted by Stanley (2020). The Philippines under Duterte is more authoritarian populist than fascist. Honduras (until late 2021) and El Salvador, in spite of repression and murder, seem more like drug-gang states than like fascist ones. Poland is close to fascism, but seems more like a right-wing religious state. The same could be said of Iran. Afghanistan, however, has gone full fascist with the Taliban: their genocidal treatment of minorities, their extreme repression of women, their chronic dishonesty, and many other traits are diagnostic of fascism but explicitly forbidden by Islam. Their opposition to education and knowledge is not strictly forbidden by Islam, but strongly discouraged; by contrast, it is basic to fascism (Stanley 2020:36–56).

A major conclusion of Stanley and others is that fascism successfully structures politics along ethnic and religious lines, as opposed to class lines (Stanley 2020:156–85). This is clearly the most important thing that has happened in the United States in the last thirty years. Stanley notes the decline of labor unions as part of this. Crushing labor unions, and breaking up labor solidarity in general, has been done by bosses since firms began, and from the nineteenth century onward they learned to do it by "playing the race card." This began in the American South, where poor whites were set against free Blacks even before the Civil War, and on a mass scale after it. The imaginary "races" push out the very real issues of class, pay, and working conditions as ways to organize, or disorganize, labor. A side effect has been the devastation of community; people turn inward, often bounding their world at the edges of their nuclear families or of their "racial" communities.

Fascism and other ideological-authoritarian regimes are not efficient; they do not respond well to crises or changes. They tend to lose support of those who would vote if they could. They need heavy financial support. In understanding the success of totalitarian regimes, one must follow the money as well as chronicle the ideology and the repressive measures.

TERRORISM

Terrorism, here, means small-scale action to cause fear and destabilize ordinary society. The term has been used for everything from aggressive war to social harassment, but restricting it to the grassroots violence of small groups and lone wolves provides us with a single, specific type of behavior that has its own literature and set of explanations. Of course, all war involves terror, but if the term is used broadly there will have to be a new term for the small-scale variety.

Terrorism, thus defined (with some elasticity), has been thoroughly surveyed by Erica Chenoweth and Pamela Moore in *The Politics of Terror* (2018). They consider it from many points of view: strategic, organizational, psychological, structural, and others. They find very few specific conclusions that have high generality; there is not much in common between the nineteenth-century anarchists, the modern Islamic State, the Weathermen, Aum Shinrikyo, and various other extreme causes. By definition, all these are small and marginal movements, attracting disaffected people. They are often majority members disillusioned with majority politics. Psychological factors from paranoia to revenge, and even novelty-seeking, are examined by Chenoweth and Moore (2018:98–106) and found wanting; terrorists are a wide range of people, and often strikingly "normal." More useful is examining open or covert state-level backing, all too common and often poorly hidden. More useful also are examining moral disengagement (Bandura 2016), displacement, abrogation of responsibility, dehumanization of victims, and blaming victims even if clearly innocent bystanders.

Arie Kruglanski, Jocelyn Bélanger, and Rohan Gunaratna have written a detailed and thorough work, *The Three Pillars of Radicalization: Needs, Narratives, and Networks* (2019). (See also Kruglanski et al. 2017), on how people change from ordinary peaceful individuals to Islamic terrorists. They include considerable comparative material on Tamil Hindu terrorists in Sri Lanka, anti-government terrorists in the United States, and other suicidal fighters for the cause; their model is intended to be general, not confined to Muslim terrorists.

The need most relevant are not needs for material goods, but the need for significance—what some psychologists would call meaning in life, or self-efficacy. It involves finding security in acceptance by their group for deeds and beliefs held significant. Also critical are needs for recognition, admiration, respect, and belonging. Terrorist groups provide these when other venues do not. The "narratives" of their title are coherent stories of what it means to be a good Muslim, a hero of the movement, and a self-realized and valued member of the cause. Cultural models are translated into personal stories through action. An important backup is a felt need for closure: a sense that life is under control, or at least that one's narrative is known, coherent, and decided.

The networks are the terrorist networks that flourish worldwide and are carefully cultivated by extremists. They confirm Scott Atran's findings (Atran 2010, 2019), and those of Bélanger et al. (2014), that poverty, lack of education, stress, mental illness, and other supposed causative factors have little or no correlation with terrorism. Terrorists are often well-educated, professional people. Atran details many cases of such individuals who were radicalized by family tragedies in repressive regimes, influences from friends and mentors, and other personal factors. Similarly, although they evoked Western references to Freud on humanity's "primitive urges of aggression and sex" (p. 55), those urges are no more primitive than the desire for peace, order, and tranquility, and are just as socially constructed in humans (Anderson and Anderson 2020; Sapolsky 2017). Atran has further contributed an important editorial in *Science* (Atran 2021), noting that experts were not in the least surprised by the Taliban's instant takeover of Afghanistan once the United States began to withdraw. He stresses their unity and dedication, especially as given by religion. Others have stressed the corruption and sloth of the Afghan government, and the total failure of the United States to make it a reasonable alternative to the Taliban in the eyes of most Afghans. In general, it appears that most persons knowledgeable about Afghanistan (including ENA, who has experience there) knew what was in store.

In fact, Muslim terrorists are apt to be middle class or higher (see esp. pp. 65–72), and are a good cross-section of the world population, not especially prone to mental troubles. Thus: "A major challenge in understanding extremism is to explain why *some* individuals support and enact behaviors that most *others* eschew or reject" (p. 41). They note that in war—and we may add, in genocide—many people, including the best, bravest, and most socially valuable, become violent, murderous, and destructive. Clearly, terrorists and soldiers need a "particularly intense commitment to goals those behaviors serve. . . . Through their propaganda and rhetoric, radical organization attempt to induce in individuals a motivational imbalance of this kind through appeals to values these persons hold sacred—such as honor, dignity, or duty" (p. 41). The great need met by serving against the enemy is significance: It represents a *"quest for significance"*—including "desire to matter, to be someone, to have respect" (p. 42, their italics). It is part of a *"struggle for recognition"* (p. 43, their italics).

Very often, quite ordinary people whose families have been killed by repressive governments will turn to suicide bombing in vengeance and in the more desperate need to kill self and take enemies along (p. 45, and elsewhere; see Atran 2010). They also act to avoid shame and disrespect, especially if they have committed themselves. Islamic radical leaders are expert at leading recruits along until they become more and more committed, and then they are too ashamed to back out. All this is "rational" in some sense (p. 75), but only by the definition of "rational" that holds any conscious decision is, by definition, a "rational choice."

Their rather complex model (p. 57) is based on individual needs for social recognition and honor, narratives of jihad and revenge, and networks of radicalized Muslim activists. Here social network theory and social movement theory enter, proving far more useful than individual-based explanations (pp. 78–86). Recruitment of Islamic terrorists is almost always through family and friendship links or through social media—radical but slick websites and pages recruit lonely, resentful, often emotionally vulnerable young Muslims (pp. 72, 78–80). Radicalization of recruits involves highlighting their grievances, especially oppression and personal harm and loss. Radicals provide a supportive group that promises a way out. A vicious cycle develops: more discussion and contact mean more extreme attitudes and more hatred. Terrorist leaders will also distort the truth in predictable ways, act outrageously to provoke a government overreaction, seek out ways to provide maximal outrage by one or a few acts, and otherwise take full advantage of weaknesses in the public security system. An overly repressive government overreacts and produces violence; an overly tolerant or weak one acts too late.

Fortunately, Kruglanski et al. (2017) report ways out. Successful programs provide some degree of financial security but concentrate much more on reprogramming captured terrorists and would-be terrorists. Authentic Muslim teachers explain to them the real teachings of Islam, including the highly explicit and unequivocal commands in the Quran against killing innocent and unarmed people even in jihad. Similar reprogramming was done with Tamil Hindu extremists in Sri Lanka with considerable success. The most important aspect of rehabilitation programs, however, is connecting the individuals in question with more normal and reasonable networks—not necessarily politically neutral ones, but at least peaceful ones that encourage people to live productive and helping lives rather than blowing themselves up.

All modern people are aware of the ways that social media encourage more and more extreme views via dedicated websites, Twitter feeds, chat rooms, and simple back-and-forth dialogue. Monitoring a wide range of political dialogues on social media reveals a consistent pattern of mutual reinforcement of extremism. Individuals tune out alternative views and talk each other into more intense positions. Any ill-meaning leader can take advantage of this with great ease.

In all these ways, terrorism is similar to genocide. The difference is that terrorists are usually few. When the Islamic State seized power in northern Iraq and eastern Syria, it immediately turned to genocide, virtually exterminating the Yazidi and killing large numbers of Shi'a Muslims and other groups held to be infidels. It seems that the main difference between terrorism and genocide is the number of people controlled by the leaders. Similarly, the civil war in Yemen pitted the extremist Shi'a Houthis against the equally extreme Wahhabist regime of Saudi Arabia, and the result was a total bloodbath where no civilian was safe—no child, woman, or elder. Thus, the motives for terrorism go far to explain the motives for genocide. The main difference is that terrorists must be actively recruited into networks and integrated into extreme, deviant social groups. Genociders are usually "good citizens":

Hitler's infamous "good Germans," the good Hutu in Rwanda, Mao's Red Guards. The social pressures are nationwide. Tremendous willpower is required to resist.

GENOCIDE

For many of us, the ultimate form of evil is genocide. It has led to between 160 and 200 million deaths since 1900, not counting deliberate starvation, displacement, and ecocide. Saucier and Akers (2018) provide a magnificent review of these totals and of the mindset behind them. Most of what follows reprises our earlier books (Anderson and Anderson 2013, 2017, 2020) but with new material.

The term was created by Rafael Lemkin just after World War II, to describe what Hitler and others had done. Lemkin was a tireless activist against genocide, eventually convincing the United Nations to develop a formal definition of it, eventually ratified by almost every nation. (See Figure 5.1). The core of the definition, now enshrined in international law, is that it involves killing of peaceful people who have done no harm or at least no harm that would excuse extermination (Jones 2011; Totten and Bartrop 2008), simply because they are members of an ethnic or religious group or similar social category. It is normally used for a government killing its own subjects. On the other hand, some scholars of mass murder use it to include all mass killing of civilians (Kiernan 2007; Shaw 2003, 2013), in which case it becomes virtually synonymous with war, since all wars produce "collateral damage." In international law, such killings are "crimes against humanity," not "genocide," but sanctioned equally.

Others have regarded slavery as genocidal, not only because of the clearly genocidal wars often incited to supply enslaved persons, but because it is so fatal to the people and cultures involved (Hinton 2021). This, like interpolity war, is beyond Lemkin's model. Also, the Convention excludes simple political killing, though large-scale massacre of political opponents and their families and associates, is as old as nation-states and as widespread. Such killing is now termed "politicide." Rudolph Rummel counted it as genocide in his books (1994, 1998), and following him we have also (Anderson and Anderson 2013, 2020). In the modern world, though not before 1900, they are predicted by the same factors. Before 1900, genocides were usually religious (extermination of "unbelievers" or "heretics"), while politicides were common, even routine, in agrarian empires, especially at the beginnings of dynasties.

Jeffrey Bachman, in an excellent review of the relevant literature, argues that war *is* genocide (Bachman 2020). This, however, would force us to coin a new term for Lemkin's concept. This latter is a horribly real and now very common fact of political life, and deserves analysis as a specific, named phenomenon. (Particularly good histories, describing antecedent events, include Akçam 2012; Charny 2016; Hinton 2005; Madley 2016; Tatz and Higgins 2016.)

Massacres—large-scale, often indiscriminate killings—have taken place since the beginning of time in almost all societies. Genocide is different in that it is systematic and official: bureaucratized massacre. It may be brief, but it may go on for years, unlike massacres. As such, it occurred in methodical religious repression in many societies throughout the history of civilization. The systematic exterminations of Jews and "heretics" in medieval Europe are prime examples. However, it was rather rare in nonreligious contexts until the last two or three hundred years. It became a standard tool of government during and since the Turkish genocides of the 1895–1925 period (Akçam 2012; Anderson and Anderson 2013; Morris and Ze'evi 2019, but that work blames Muslims in general for what was actually a coldly calculated government campaign in a previously quite tolerant polity).

Forced acculturation of whole groups to destroy their culture is also included within the definition. This includes forced schooling to destroy ethnicity, as in the case of Native Americans in most of North America over time. Usually, however, the term is reserved for attempted extermination with appreciable mass killing. Genocide scholars have recently realized that ecocide can be genocide, as when an entire ethnic group's livelihood is destroyed by big dams, agricultural settlement, or other megaprojects (Crook and Short 2021). States notoriously use famine and starvation for genocide, often enough to allow several large books to recount that history (Cameron 2018; Howard-Hassmann 2016; Sen 1982).

For decades after World War II, genocide was considered a crime peculiar to the darkest days of Hitler and Stalin, with possible extension to Mao and a few others, and thus was generally explained by the personalities of those individuals and the peculiar histories of the times. However, by the 1990s, genocide had become so common, widespread, and even routine that it had obviously become a regular tool of governments, not an aberration. Moreover, recognition was dawning that the behavior of powerful settlers to conquered minorities was often well within the United Nations definition, and the treatment of Native Americans, Australian Aboriginals, and similar displaced and long-disenfranchised colonial victims was duly added to genocide studies. This creates the category of settler genocides, which—unlike other genocides—are not associated with authoritarianism. Solid democracies from the United States (Madley 2016) to Australia committed settler genocides on a large scale during their settlement periods. However, such genocides are almost always against people who are not officially "citizens."

Thus, explanation of genocide as a general tool of statecraft began. One early attempt was Rudolph Rummel's memorable opening statement in his book *Death by Government*: "Power kills; absolute Power kills absolutely" (Rummel 1994:1). Rummel found that absolute power was always associated with large-scale terrorist murder, and in the twentieth century always with genocide. The link has held fairly well, but there is much more to say. Ben Kiernan titled his study of all mass murder with Hitler's own explanation: *Blood and Soil* (Kiernan 2007). Kiernan found that line to be quite adequate: genocide is about inherited identity (which is learned, not genetic as Hitler thought) and about taking land from the victims. It thus includes settler genocides, unlike Rummel's books. However, Kiernan's position does not tell us enough about genocide by the narrower definition: extermination of harmless, peaceful citizens or subjects simply because they hold a particular ethnic or religious identity.

By 2012, conflict scholars had narrowed the explanations down. Barbara Harff (2012) finally came up with a full predictive model. Harff confirmed Rummel's insight. Contrary to many theorists, she found that genocide is not associated with hard times or declining fortunes. The Great Depression may have made Hitler genocidal, but it had the opposite effects in the United Kingdom and the United States, making society more inclusive and progressive. Her new finding was that totalitarian regimes commit genocide when challenged. This normally happens in two cases: when they take over and consolidate control, or when they feel threatened by popular movements, local rebellions, or other unrest at times when the totalitarian regimes have a weak hold.

She identified quite different risk factors: prior genocide by the regime, open discrimination and bias in the regime and its leaders, ideology of the elite, general violence and instability in the country's recent history, and, most interesting and important, "exclusionary ideologies." These are ideologies that radically cut the "unworthy" from the "worthy," highlight defensive narrowness, and come down with extreme punishment on both nonmembers and nonconforming members. Communism and fascism are the most obvious. Extreme religious movements like right-wing Christianity and Islamic Wahhabism are also clear and evident. Racist and hyper nationalist movements have also sparked huge genocides, like those of Turkey in 1895–1925 and Rwanda in 1994. These movements all turn murderous when they can, and if they seize power in a nation they are almost sure to be followed by genocide.

She also found that genocides follow a fairly straightforward program: when an authoritarian leader takes over, or when a previously less totalitarian leader seizes total power, a consolidation genocide almost always takes place.

Thereafter, any major crisis—whether real or imagined by the leader—leads to another genocide.

This model has been fully confirmed, extended, and developed since, by ourselves (Anderson and Anderson 2013, 2020) and in a brilliant article by Hollie Nyseth Brehm (2017; see also Nyseth Brehm 2020). Unfortunately, thanks to conservatism on the part of governments and relative isolation of many genocide scholars, this highly predictive model has been neglected. The ongoing genocides in China, for instance, were predictable, and international action could have been taken. Genocidal treatment of Native Americans in Brazil is ramping up. Many situations in the world today are clearly pre-genocidal, lacking only a completely authoritarian government or a crisis to call out the demonization of minorities.

Students of settler genocides have added the point that governments need not be totalitarian if the victims are noncitizens who are in the position of conquered subjects being deprived of their land. Genocide of Indigenous people largely stopped in the United States, Canada, and Australia when the Indigenous people gained full citizenship, though cultural oppression (sometimes termed cultural genocide) continued. In other words, totalitarian power is likely to be asserted, and abused, against any noncitizen group. Democracies function only for their officially recognized citizens. We have recently seen this confirmed by Trump's full-fascist treatment of undocumented immigrants; they were routinely confined to literal cages and denied any rights, even to lifesaving medical care. This was against international law, but no enforcement of that law was possible at the time.

Alexander Hinton, leading anthropological scholar of genocide, has developed the idea of "cumulative radicalization," in which hate-based killings start slowly and move upward in steps to full-scale genocide (Hinton 2021:67–68). It "emerges from a historical backdrop and unfolds over time" (Hinton 2021:69). He also provides a different list of risk factors: Instability, past violence, lack of safeguards, motivation, capacity, weak buffering, enabling environment, and triggers (Hinton 2021:138). A major problem with this list is that it would predict genocide in every sizable state on earth, whenever government weakens. In fact, those risk factors do predict mass violence, but it is usually banditry, gangsterism, and civil unrest. Occasionally war or civil war ensues, but only under some circumstances—those listed by Harff—does it lead to genocide.

A further model by Gregory Stanton (2013) provides a closer look at the stages of ongoing genocide. Stanton looks closer at the actual events, from identifying a group, usually a minority, to labeling them as stigmatized, and on to violence. His insight is a valuable complement to the Harff model. It is easily found on the website of his group Genocide Watch, a resource that should be used by all interested persons.[1]

Genocide is usually based on hate, without any rational justification (for the psychology of genocide, see Newman 2020). The hate usually derives from insecurity and fear. Settler genocides involve the added impetus of taking land, extinguishing Indigenous title by exterminating the Indigenous individuals. Control is also a major factor. Genocide leaders demonstrate the control need gone mad, or at least to extreme levels, and the public that follows them is easily lured into terror and destruction by appeals to their safety in face of "dangerous" minorities.

Genocide always includes not only murder but also systematic rape of women and sometimes boys, systematic torture, humiliation, cruelty, cultural and religious repression, and every other instrument of harm that human evil can devise. A worldwide hookup of surveillance experts, torturers, mercenary soldiers, and perpetrators of genocide on the dark web keeps the perpetrators in touch, stimulated, and aware of new techniques of torture and mass terror.

Genocides range enormously in extent (for details see Anderson and Anderson 2013, 2020; Rummel 1998). Hitler's classic and defining genocide was not only enormous, involving millions of people all over Europe, but was indiscriminate: almost any identifiable minority was slated for extinction, from Jews to handicapped persons to modern artists. Mao and Stalin were equally murderous and almost as broad in their hates. The Cambodian genocide eliminated a higher percentage of the population than did any other genocide; it was slightly more narrowly targeted, involving only educated or upper-class Cambodians, mostly Khmer but including minorities generally. At the other end, the fascist genocides of Mussolini, Franco, and Salazar were much smaller and more narrowly targeted.

Other things being equal, the more extreme and exclusionary the rhetoric, the worse the killings. This has been true for Communism and fascism. However, genocide by religious extremists has not been clearly correlated with the level of religious extremism. Right-wing Islam has been genocidal in Afghanistan, Iran, and elsewhere, but confined itself to politicides in Saudi Arabia and the Gulf states. In contrast, much more moderate Islam was associated with the first great modern genocide, the long campaign by Turkish leaders (especially the Young Turks during the World War I years) against almost everyone not self-consciously Muslim Turk. Extremist sectarian Christianity was involved in genocide in Guatemala under Efraín Ríos Montt and in several other mass killings worldwide, but were not the leaders in the great genocides of Europe in the twentieth century. Buddhist genocides of non-Buddhists, as in Myanmar and Sri Lanka, have been carried out in societies that devoutly preach, but do not follow, the nonviolence and compassion central to Buddhism.

One depressing realization is that in all ongoing wars and genocides, all types of people join in with enthusiasm in continuing campaigns of rape, torture, looting, and murder (Kiernan 2007; Shaw 2003, 2013). Repression of minority communities in the dying Turkish empire went on for thirty years, with continuing butchery (Morris and Ze'evi 2019; Travis 2019). The United States settler genocide against Native Americans went on, intermittently and locally, for much of the eighteenth and all of the nineteenth centuries; Benjamin Madley's thorough account of massacres and violence in California (Madley 2016) is illustrative (see also Cameron et al. 2015). The same general story held in Australia (Moses 2004). Similar stories can be told of every genocide. In all cases, many people did not join in, but vast numbers did, without the slightest excuse. People can enjoy murdering each other just as they enjoy football and soccer games. Genghis Khan's idea of the good is far from unique to him. Despite Genghis, however, rape in these situations is not for pleasure or reproduction. It is done against all genders and ages, often quite indifferently, and is strictly a matter of violent humiliation and damage. Mass rape and looting are most typical of violent young men in warlike societies and situations, but are surprisingly common in any social breakdown. A particularly harrowing recent account, giving details of outrages and the enormous psychological damage occasioned, is Jan Ilhan Kizilhan's account of the Islamic State's genocidal campaign of mass murder, rape, and sexual enslavement in attempted genocide of the Yazidi minority in Iraq (Kizilhan 2022). Similar stories from Nazi Germany and other genocides abound in the literature.

Genocide is rampant today, with huge campaigns of murder and cultural destruction against Tibetans and Uyghurs (Roberts 2020) in China, Rohingya in Burma, various groups in eastern Congo (Prunier 2011), and elsewhere. Politicide grades into gang murders in Honduras, Brazil, and other Latin American countries.

CORPORATE FUNDING OF SOCIAL CONFLICT

Fascism and communism led to most of the major wars in the last 100 years, but nationalism, religion, sheer greed, the drug trade, and simple political games have all had their large shares in creating violence. The United States was at war virtually the entire twentieth century, and the twenty-first until 2021. The American role in World War II was surely a just war, but American values declined until the slimmest of excuses were adequate for war by 2000. Most other countries worldwide, democratic or autocratic, have had their periods of unedifying violence.

Fascism continues to grow and flourish worldwide (Traverso 2019). The connection of Hitler with giant German firms, and later of Mussolini, Franco, and other fascist rulers with giant economic interests, is well known. Current

‎‎

totalitarian and far-right regimes are similarly linked with reactionary economic interests. Often (as in, for example, Orbán's Hungary) the links are unclear. Where they are visible, they tend to be with fossil fuels above all (Auzanneau 2018): Oil and gas in Iran, Russia, Saudi Arabia, Venezuela, and several other countries; coal in China and India. In Brazil, Bolsonaro's moneyed support has drawn heavily not only on the energy sector but also on cattle ranchers and others whose interests lie in destroying the Amazon forest (Artax 2019; Hyde 2019. Russia's oil and gas wealth financed its Ukraine war, and European dependence on Russian oil makes it impossible for Europe to stop that war. Russia's military depends on fossil fuel money, as do its oligarchs. Defunding this treasure trove is critical to stopping war in future (Romanko and McKibben 2022).

In all cases, fascism and totalitarianism require enormous inputs of money to keep them viable. They must win votes where any pretense of democracy remains, they need resources to suppress dissent, and they need powerful allies in the productive sectors of the economy. Classically, large landlords and other resource-lords financed war and repression, as during World War II and most wars in history. Over the last seventy years, fossil fuels, munitions and armaments, and giant agribusiness interests have been the major funders and supporters of war and repression worldwide.

Many countries are now either run outright or strongly influenced by a worldwide oil-coal-mining-agribusiness-armaments linkage. These interests frequently play zero-sum or negative-sum games with their own people, hurting their own self-interest if they can hurt others more. The worst problem recently has been that interests formerly considered "good" have turned out to be bad: tobacco, oil, coal, chemical farming, monocropping, plastics, beef, palm oil, and other commodities. The history of these commodities is that they are first adored, subsidized, supported. Then they overreach themselves, polluting or otherwise destroying the environment. Then they make desperate moves to question, then deny, then lie about own product. Finally, they make even more desperate moves to get support by going with any and all reactionary hate, bigotry, and evil. This leads, increasingly, to backing fascist takeover and repression.

Subsidies are often a gateway drug. The term includes government "cash grants, tax breaks, loans at below-market interest rates, loan guarantees, capital injections, guaranteed excessive rates of profit, below-cost or free inputs including land and power, and purchasing goods from firs at inflated prices" (Rickard 2018:66). Also included are provision of infrastructure; governments routinely build roads and dams for the benefit of specific industries. Also involved are conspicuous failures to enforce the law against miscreants such as polluters, and even special laws that exempt some industries from paying for spills, pollution control, damage to health, and the like. At worst, governments will even foot the bill for cleanup, when an ordinary individual would be jailed for equivalent (but far smaller) damage. These "posttax" subsidies are far greater than the "pretax" ones, the outright donations of funds by government. They are also insidious and hard to stop.

The great worldwide spinner of reaction is big oil. Matthieu Auzanneau (2018) documents this at enormous length. (See also Clarke 2009 for Africa; Heinberg 2017 for the connection of oil and authoritarianism; Juhasz 2008 for the Western world; Ross 2012 for the effects of big oil on poorer nations.) Worldwide subsidies to fossil fuel companies ran to $4.9 trillion in 2013 (Coady et al. 2015, 2017; Edenhofer 2015; figures from International Monetary Fund, counting both direct and indirect subsidies; Overland 2010). By 2020, an IMF report by Ian Parry and coworkers finds that subsidies had climbed to $5.9 trillion, 6.8 percent of the world's economic product and $11,000,000 a minute (Parry et al. 2021). Eight percent of this total is direct subsidy; the other 92 percent represents environmental and human costs that are absorbed by governments and taxpayers rather than being specified on the fuel corporations. Alex Kirby (2017) has pointed out that the taxpayers not only subsidize big oil directly, they then absorb literally trillions of dollars in medical costs caused by pollution from fossil fuels.

Pricing to IMF standards would reduce fossil fuel consumption by 36 percent, allowing the world to meet goals for greenhouse gas release. It would also spare 900,000 people who will otherwise die of pollution—unfortunately a foregone hope for the next few years (Parry et al. 2021:1). The Parry report gives full details on government pledging for slowing climate change, and notes how far out of line the fossil fuel subsidies are with the stated goals. They find that the United States is actually a lesser offender, in terms of percentage of government money spent, though not in absolute dollars. Russia, Turkey, and other autocratic countries do worse. The Commonwealth of Independent States (Russia and allies, basically what is left of the USSR) is a major offender in terms of percentage of public funds so used, especially in direct subsidies.

In 2013, China spent most at 1.8 trillion, the United States was next at $600 billion, then came Russia, the European Union, and India, each with some $300 billion. "Eliminating subsidies would have reduced global carbon emissions by 21%," raised GDP by that 6.5%, and otherwise benefited us all (Coady et al. 2017). By 2020, these figures had climbed to 2.203 trillion for China in spite of some reforms, the United States to $662 billion, Russia to $523 billion, India to $247 billion, and the rest far behind (Parry et al. 2020:38). This is all government and taxpayers' money, gone to keep feeding the fossil fuel industry that is literally killing the planet. This information is from the International Monetary Fund and the World Bank, those bastions of capitalism—not from some "wild-eyed" leftist source.

These figures include the indirect subsidies: infrastructure; legal protection from lawsuits over pollution, oil spills, and the like; cleanup for that same pollution and spillage (the corporations pay little or nothing of those costs); legal favors, military procurement, government business to chosen firms, bailouts, sweetheart deals, and dozens of other special favors that small businesses cannot get. It is virtually certain that without these subsidies the fossil fuel corporations could not compete with wind, solar, and other clean energy, and would have died long ago.

As Stephanie Rickard points out in *Spending to Win* (2018), subsidies cost the taxpayers a great deal to benefit special interests by a smaller amount. Possibly worst of all is the fact that subsidies pay firms not to modernize. The government eliminates the need to be competitive or efficient or compliant. Firms recycle the subsidy money in lobbying and political donations, to make the cycle go on endlessly (Rickard 2018). In 2018, giant oil firms spent millions on lobbying to block climate change legislation: BP $53 million, Shell $49 million, ExxonMobil $41 million, Chevron $29 million, total for all firms $201 million (McCarthy 2019). This is only documented totals; the reality is far more. The true sums are hidden, thanks to "dark money" rules.

Ana Revenga writes in a World Bank report that energy subsidies are "one of the most expensive and most regressive fiscal policies in low- to middle-income countries. In fact, public expenditure on subsidies often exceeds the entirety of these countries' social safety net expenditures many times over, making this a critical area of reform. . . . In some cases, the energy subsidy bill is enormous" but they are very difficult to reverse, getting general support, powerful lobbying, and cooperative legislators (Revenga 2017:ix). The report continues to document the massive failure of subsidies to help the poor (in most cases worldwide), the enormous wealth transfer to a few rich, and the extreme difficulties encountered in reforming the situation (Inchauste and Victor 2017). It also stresses, over and over again in the many national examples, the extreme difficulty of cutting these subsidies, because cutting them makes the price of gas and fuel go up, leading to riots and the fall of the government responsible. The sometimes desperate needs of people in the short term lead to the perpetuation of the situation. The earth is poised to shift to a Venus-like situation of extreme heat if ice caps disappear and oceans get seriously heated (Turbet et al. 2021). Burning all extractable fossil fuel would almost certainly accomplish this.

Coal is the biggest beneficiary of world subsidies to fossil fuels, getting 60 percent of the subsidies (Edenhofer 2015; Parry et al 2020); China and India were the biggest friends of coal. The United States spends almost as much on subsidies as on the defense budget, and more than ten times the total amount spent on education in the country (Ellsmoor 2019). In addition to these national subsidies, there are enormous local ones, adding up to tens of billions (Jensen 2018), a large percentage of them for fossil fuels. In the United States, state governments have been especially friendly, particularly to interests within said states.

Obviously, the best way to combat global warming is to eliminate these subsidies (Overland 2010). Much progress has been made in some countries. The secrets of success begin with transparency about the whole process of reducing subsidies. Reduction is most easily done by a stable, popular government with good credibility; a weak one crumbles in the face of opposition from those hurt. Relief for those severely impacted is necessary, such as providing help to nonaffluent individuals who live by driving long distances (delivery personnel, small truckers) or live in very cold regions. Many stories of success and less-than-success are told in an excellent collection by Benedict Clements and colleagues, *Energy Subsidy Reform* (2013). This book also reveals that subsidies to fossil fuel are vastly higher in producing nations than in importing nations (oil in the Near East is an extreme case), and this is especially true for the insidious posttax subsidies.

Big Oil and far-right politics are in mutual dependence in many countries, including Azerbaijan, Iran, Kazakhstan, Russia, Saudi Arabia, Sudan, Uzbekistan, and Venezuela (which claims to be "socialist" but is de facto fascist). Big Coal has played a similar, though less direct and important, role in the transition of China from communist to fascist (by the definitions above). Worldwide, right-wing politics is dominated by the most direct types of extraction: logging, mining, and the like—anything that can be owned by great landlords and worked by starving laborers without rights. Oil drilling is a partial exception, since it requires skilled workers, but it is so far into the category of bulk extraction that it still feeds right-wing politics.

Class, ethnicity, nationhood, economic organization, and other variables are far less important in determining on-the-ground politics, as a quick global tour will show. Everywhere, countries dominated by giant extractive interests tend to be authoritarian and poor (for the dynamics of this, see Bunker and Ciccantell 2005). If a free country with numbers of roughly equal smallholders gets taken over by such interests, it rapidly splits into a tiny, rich minority and a vast majority becoming ever more impoverished, as we see today in Venezuela, Brazil, India, and elsewhere. Communism briefly provided an alternative, but, in many cases (Mao's China stands out), democracy leveled up, communism leveled down, creating a worse hierarchy than capitalist firms. Bureaucrats instead of workers took over.

In 2021, six hundred journalists from 150 media outlets all over the world went into worldwide bank data and found hundreds of billions, if not trillions, hidden in numbered bank accounts, invested in real estate, and otherwise squirreled away safe from taxes and removed from the economy. Much of this was illegal. A great deal of the money came from the illegitimate drug business. King Abdullah II of Jordan is a major money-hider, as well as a large percentage of the American rich. The British charity Oxfam noted in a press release: "This is where our missing hospitals are. This is where the pay packets sit of all the extra teachers and firefighters and public servants we need. Whenever a politician or business leader claims there is 'no money' to pay for climate damage and innovation, for more and better jobs, for a fair post-COVID-19 recovery, for more overseas aid, they know where to look" (Liedtke and Mattise 2021). Nothing was done. Campaign promises to tax the rich and reduce inequality are invariably blocked by politicians supported by the interests in question.

The rise of fascism in modern times is thus largely traceable to the giant multinational firms, especially the oil industry—the wealth-maker for extremists from the Koch family to Saudi Arabia's Wahhabist government. They invoke fascism to crush regulation, install friendly governments, eliminate dissent with them, and above all to keep the subsidies flowing. Fascism could easily take over as resources really tighten in the years leading up to 2050. In other words, the world's taxpayers are paying the giant polluting firms not only to keep heating the planet, but also to empower authoritarian regimes that stifle dissent, including honest science.

SOCIAL CONFLICT: THE UNITED
STATES AS EXEMPLAR

The United States was founded on principles of equality and justice, but many of the founding fathers were slave owners. Many of them realized the contradiction. Since then, the country has had a consistent divide: antislavery vs. slavery, Reconstruction vs. the Ku Klux Klan, genocide of Native Americans vs. defending them and giving them citizenship. The majority has generally been with the more egalitarian and just cause when the chips were down, as in the Civil War and the 1930s. On the other hand, the minority has been vocal, well-funded, and powerful. The country remains as divided as ever today. A large segment of the left counters "American exceptionalism" with narratives of an America almost unique in the world for its violent racism, but surveys of genocide show that slavery, settler massacres, racism, and outright genocide are widespread in the world, not limited to left or right, Western or Eastern, rich or poor, capitalist or socialist.

The correlation of slave-owning and reactionary politics in the United States is well known (MacLean 2020). The slave owners of the pre–Civil War era, above all John Calhoun, created American right-wing politics. In particular, they perfected the pattern of setting the poor whites and the African Americans against each other, deflecting poor-white and middle-class white opposition to elites by setting them against Black people instead. Slavery was maintained by ruthless government suppression of enslaved and free Black persons, and by structures of international trade.

This led to a society that persists today, in which the most reactionary sectors of the elite fight down labor unions and maintain dismally low wages and working conditions by setting Black people and white people against each other. The playbook has not changed. In spite of the enormous contributions to American economy and culture, Black people were demonized; racism created a whole "frame," a narrative and structure going beyond simple racist beliefs (Feagin 2015, 2020). Other ethnic groups had their own frames, with Native Americans subjected to genocide based on framing narratives (Madley 2016). It also reinforced the tendency to see bosses vs. workers as a limited-good game, where workers had to lose for bosses to flourish. The idea of mutual support for mutual benefit shrank into near-oblivion.

When slavery was abolished, de facto slavery was maintained by debt and by brutal terror, leading to giant plantations in Mississippi in the 1950s that differed little from those of the 1850s. Senator James Eastland (D-MS), in the mid-twentieth century, owned the Sunflower Plantation, a huge estate that held some of the richest lands in the Yazoo Delta, and was worked by landless African Americans under conditions of starvation and early death. With his colleague John Stennis (D-MS), another Mississippi landowner, he dominated American politics through the 1950s.

People tend to vote their self-interest or their hate. As one might expect, the breakdown is about 50/50. Racist, minority-crushing presidents from Andrew Jackson to Calvin Coolidge are as common as presidents who advanced the general good. In the United States, voting one's self-interest peaked from 1930 to 1970, after which voting one's hate grew steadily. It now dominates the right and a growing segment of the left.

In the period from 1900 to 1970 self-improvement, education, science, artistic quality, liberal values, civil rights, environmental concerns, and other public goods flourished. Above all, learning from other cultures was diligently pursued. In general, people believed we could all progress by helping each other up. The old left goals were, first, equality before the law, equal access to basic services, equality of educational and economic opportunities, and smooth functioning of society. Equality may not be equity, but equity cannot happen without equality. On the other hand, ominously, folk society came to an end, replaced by mass media. People oriented to television and other top-down mass media that allowed no participation. Making music together declined. The corruption of religion by right-wing megachurches and of government by giant firms was inevitable.

The forward agenda began to unravel in the 1968 election of Richard Nixon, and has continued to unravel, erratically, ever since. Most of the reason was decline of power and prestige of ordinary people relative to the giant firms, but also the superficiality and quickness of our contacts (Putnam 2000). If one sees a person only briefly at work, rather than being in family and community together, one naturally goes for the episodic, brief, shallow, rudimentary, and superficial. Also, of course, the extreme stress of modern life (long work hours, computers, commutes) means that few have the time, energy or clear space to deal with community welfare. All this perfectly explains the decline of good (including self-improvement) and rise of evil. We are now in a bizarre situation: science progresses, environmentalism grows, and the scientists can solve all the problems, but the environment gets worse at an ever-increasing rate, while governments get less and less sympathetic to human or environmental concerns. Finally, we reach a stage when voter suppression is eliminating democracy (C. Anderson 2019). Giant corporations came to resemble more and more the slave plantations of old, as they successfully crushed unions, cut wages (in real terms), used racism to divide the working classes, and relied more and more on government subsidies and protection (much of the history is covered by MacLean 2020 and Schiff 2021).

Nancy MacLean's book *Democracy in Chains* (2020) reveals the Calhoun legacy of the great architects of fascist America: James Buchanan from a Tennessee farm, the Koch brothers from border-south Kansas (Leonard 2019; Mayer 2016). One can add Mitch McConnell from Alabama, Ted Cruz from anti-Castro Cuban background in Texas, and many other southern right-wing extremists who are re-creating in America the society of a southern plantation in 1850. Slavery still shapes southern politics (Acharya et al. 2018). Oil states like Louisiana remain right-wing, with even the poorest sympathizing with the giant corporations; a sensitive, insightful inquiry into their hard lives and choices by Arlie Hochschild (2016) creates empathy, but also the recognition that they are trapped in a pre–Civil War ideology.

The transition of the Republicans from the party of the affluent to the party of white supremacy and other culture wars was a product of the "Southern strategy" in Republican politics, which began when Senator Strom Thurmond switched from Democrat to Republican in the 1940s (MacLean 2020). It continued to grow and develop in Nixon's presidency (with Karl Rove, Lee Atwater, and Roy Cohn as gurus), consolidated under Reagan, and finally triumphed under Trump, when almost all other elements in the Republican Party were relatively sidelined (Schiff 2021). With the Southern Strategy, the Republicans put together a coalition of the right-wing superrich, the old-fashioned local conservatives, and the outright bigots (see Dean and Altemeyer 2020; Frank 2004; Johnson 2018, 2021). The Republicans have become identified with hatred, but the Democrats too have developed more and more antagonism, identity politics, fiery and overdone rhetoric, and self-destructive hate-voting.

As of 1968, the main right-wing power bloc was the military-industrial bureaucracy. Against it were, above all, the labor unions, with up to 37 percent of workers unionized. The knowledge industry, a large slice of religious people, and ordinary working people were voting for furthering democracy. Now labor unions include only 10.8 percent of the workforce, and a considerably lower percentage of the nongovernmental workforce. Religion is usually a force for hate, as is sadly true worldwide; it tends to appeal to people who feel they are both absolutely and relatively downward-bound, like less-educated white workers facing falling wages and increasing competition from minorities. This creates a mindset of despair and reaction, and religion appeals under such circumstances (Kay et al. 2010). The most dangerous thing, abundantly visible worldwide today, is that groups who fear they are losing due to progress and modernization will take over and reverse that process. The fact that health care and education are deteriorating in the United States is abundantly proved by declining life expectancy, rising maternal mortality, and declining academic test scores across the board. The reason is the increasing success of the resentful voters at reversing progress on these fronts. Similar trends are visible from India to Venezuela.

Another problem has followed the rise of urban educated workers, who may not make more money but who look down more and more openly on the "rednecks" and "trailer trash." The white working classes, used to being respected if not well paid, are increasingly hostile toward those who presume superiority. When the urban workers are nonwhite, the racism of the white workers is mobilized.

The leader in all this was suppression of the labor union movement. That devastated the liberal and centrist side of politics, gave the right tremendous power, and set the working population against themselves. Many felt threatened by poorer, immigrant, or "racially" different workers. Racism replaced the competition of workers and bosses as the defining opposition in the United States, and to some extent in other countries. The general welfare took an increasingly minor role. The result has been a rise of more extreme right-wing forces, and decline of the left and center. It appears that the defensiveness that makes the right violent and hateful makes the left give in. The stress that makes the right increasingly deadly makes the left increasingly meek.

Some individuals and corporations get unlimited subsidies, direct and indirect, from Republicans, but will face challenges if Democrats restore a rule of law in the United States. This includes at least some of the corporate lobbyists and high administrators of fossil fuel corporations, among others. Decades of deliberate poisoning of thousands of people and breaking countless political-advocacy laws is only the tip of a huge iceberg. Subsidies once started are hard to stop, and the huge subsidies and tax breaks given by Republicans (in spite of their claimed commitment to the free market and small government) never get repealed by Democrats (see Rickard 2018:54).

Farm subsidies are problematic also. In the United States, they run to over $20 billion a year. About 40 percent of farm income in the United States is now from subsidies (Held 2020). Some 39 percent of farms get some subsidies, though most go to the giant agribusiness firms. The vast majority of subsidy spending goes to the "commodities," staples including maize, soybeans, wheat, rice, and cotton (Hojjat 2021:29). This leads to worse nutrition, since the processed starches and sugars from subsidized foods are artificially (thanks to subsidies) much cheaper than nutritious foods (Hojjat 2021:29).

An extreme case is provided by sugar growers: "Subsidies to the US sugar industry . . . sustain a domestic sugar price two to three times higher than the world's market price. As a result, approximately 20,000 US sugar cane farmers receive an extra $369 million dollars a year. . . . These benefits come at a cost to American taxpayers and consumers who pay an additional $2.3 billion dollars a year for sugar. . . . Nearly 60 percent of this money goes to just 17 growers" (Rickard 2018:17–18, 39). These same seventeen growers have almost destroyed the Everglades, including Everglades National Park. The diversion and pollution of water has led to well over a 90 percent decline in wildlife, especially birds, in that once-marvelous region. The total failure of Florida, and near-total failure of the United States, to enforce pollution controls is yet another subsidy to sugarcane growers, probably bigger than the $369 million noted by Rickard. Failure to enforce on the rich the laws that are condignly enforced on the rest of us is possibly the biggest of all subsidies worldwide.

In the United States, the tie is direct (e. g. Cahill 2017; Loki 2019). Big oil, big coal, and in Florida big sugar, donate heavily to extreme right-wing legislators (Goldberg et al. 2020; Good Jobs First website). The oil industry began in Pennsylvania, but soon became dominated by Texas and Oklahoma, where social institutions carried directly over from the antebellum south. Oil billionaires tend to be far-right-wing southerners, with all the beliefs and attitudes of their lineage, back to John Calhoun. The above-cited sources show that they and their allies in big mining, big logging, big agribusiness, and other basic extractive industries are major sources of funding for the right in the United States. They were preadapted by sharing right-wing views in the first place, but their enormous success at dividing the working classes—setting Americans against each other to distract them from opposing the corrupt industries—led to more and more imitation of this technique. Often, these interests would whip up anger against science and environmental protection.

They eventually came to create "Astroturf" (phony grassroots) organizations, such as the Tea Party, to mobilize right-wing citizens.

Recall that the full subsidy amount to fossil fuels in the United States is well over $600 billion dollars—about $2,000 for every man, woman and child. This includes not just direct subsidies, from the oil depletion allowance and the enormous tax breaks for production on down to sweetheart deals for military fuel. Far greater are the subsidies involved in providing infrastructure such as roads and port facilities. Beyond that are the taxpayer-funded efforts to clean up spills and water pollution, fight air pollution by smog, detoxifying soil, and, above all, dealing with the national health crisis caused by this pollution and by the toxins in fossil fuel products from plastics to industrial chemicals. The full cost of this cleanup and of damage to the environment and to individuals' health is still not covered by the $600 billion figure. Still beyond that, the loss of wildlife and wild landscapes is unpriced and beyond valuation. Those who complain about the price of gas might recall that they are paying an additional $6 a day in subsidies.

Koch Industries (oil and forestry, plus minor other items), for instance, gets a mere $9 million in direct federal monetary subsidies, but about $530 million from the states, and billions in exemptions from pollution laws, taxes, and other legal obligations. ExxonMobil, Koch's rival in leading the global climate change denial industry, gets nothing directly from the federal trough (though enormous indirect subsidies), but over a billion from state and local governments (Good Jobs First, "Koch Industries: Subsidy Tracker" and "Exxon Mobil: Subsidy Tracker," accessed Oct. 22, 2021).[2] Other environmentally destructive corporations do as well. The oil industry and its allies—especially the Kochs—were the key funders of far-right politics. The tradition of fascism goes directly back to Hitler. The father of the Koch brothers, Fred Koch, worked for him (Mayer 2016; see also Schulman 2014). Fred Koch, one of the founders of the John Birch Society, raised his sons to be fascist. The Coors family and many other right-wing dynasties in the United States were also pro-Hitler, and continued Hitler's policies and politics quite directly (Bellant 1990).

The full story of the Kochs and their supported theorist, the Nobel-Prize-winning economist James Buchanan, has been told by Quinn Slobodian in *Globalists* (2018; see also MacLean 2020), and it is a terrifying story. The "neoliberal" Buchanan-type economics is most appealing to dinosaurs—giant firms that lose from free competition—and to those who have inherited wealth but are too incompetent to keep it in a free market, like Trump and many another rich heir. This neoliberal and libertarian rhetoric also plays well to shady interests, and to any giant firm with vested interests and investments that does not like competition. It is least attractive to real Adam Smith capitalists: small businesses that rely on consumers with money who can choose and thus be lured by good service. Obviously, nobody with any concern for rational economic self-interest is going to buy into neoliberalism. Adam Smith championed small businesses in opposition to the giant government-sponsored firms of his day. He saw good competition among the former—they competed to serve the public—while the latter simply colluded with corrupt rulers to fleece said public. Conditions today are not notably different.

MacLean makes one major error: she thinks the libertarian protestations of the Kochs and their fellows were sincere. In fact, the Kochs were oil men, later expanding into timber—two of the industries most heavily subsidized by the US government. The Kochs lived off the taxpayers as surely as any stereotypic "welfare bum," and more surely than most who actually receive government help. By contrast, the Social Security, attacked by the GOP as a "dole," is actually paid for by special taxes on workers; it pays for itself, when the government does not raid its funds. Rich right-wingers' attacks on other government spending are best seen as ways to get more government money for themselves. Charles Koch has actually admitted many of his sins, and apparently repented, in a new book (Koch 2020) that is surprisingly good both intellectually and morally. Among many indications of a change of view, he says: "At this point, you may be thinking, 'Oh no. Here comes the anti-government rant.' Prepare to be disappointed" (Koch 2020:13). "America is sprinting toward a two-tiered society" and he sharply disapproves of this (Koch 2020:88–89). He has read Case and Deaton on deaths of despair, and is both sad and highly insightful about the issue, saying we need to hear from the despairing: "As a general rule, the people best suited to end an injustice are those closest to it" (Koch 2020:95). More dramatically, on entering politics in general and Republican politics in particular, he comments: ""Boy, did we screw up. What a mess!" (Koch 2020:219). One hopes he is sincere. It presents a striking insight into the mind of a repentant far-rightist.

A further insight into the morality of the (hopefully former) Koch universe is that the American Legislative Exchange Council (ALEC), a Koch creation, led the fight to "reopen the economy" by forbidding masks, shutdowns, and required vaccinations during the COVID-19 pandemic (Kotch 2020). It has long served to write laws protecting the giant firms and restricting civil liberties; cooperating legislators, generally beneficiaries of Koch campaign donations, get these passed in Republican states. First the military, then tobacco and pesticides, then oil, coal, and chemicals, then everybody else that damages the public interest through pollution and other environmental and medical harms, developed a technique of spreading doubts or outright lies about science, to protect themselves from lawsuits and regulation. ALEC has also consistently backed laws aimed at limiting the vote, and limiting the ability of nonwhites to compete socially and economically.

Another of the Koch brothers' political creations, the Tea Party, has led to a massive right-wing swing of the Republican Party (Nesbit 2016). It has succeeded in taking over many states for Tea Party slates of legislators. The Tea Party early fell into the hands of white supremacists and religious bigots (categories that overlap broadly), and the result has been an extreme swing toward racism and religious oppression in Republican states. Other beneficiaries of Koch money range from the Heritage Foundation (a spreader of right-wing views) to far-right-wing candidates. Particularly revealing is support from the Kochs and Robert Mercer for the extreme white nationalist hate group VDARE (Kotch and Hayden 2021). American consumer and taxpayer dollars, recycled by the giant fossil fuel firms and their allies, have financed the political extremism of the last twenty years.

Big oil has been the main supporter of the disinformation and outright lies denying global warming. ExxonMobil has not only donated millions to this cause over more than thirty years; they also fight critics and lawsuits by every means possible, including harassment, personal attacks, and forcing those who sue to document everything with full sources, even in group suits. One tactic involves appeal to a Texas law (ExxonMobil, like much of big oil, is based in Texas) that protects corporate lying as "free speech" in spite of national and worldwide limits on fraud and deceptive advertising. The law applies only in Texas, but is used to silence Californians and others (Hiltzik 2021). Chevron has also engaged in massive public relations masquerading as news, to the extent of starting a local newspaper to defend their Richmond, California, refinery (Hiltzik 2022b).

This process has been meticulously documented, for instance by Lindsay Abrams (2015), Neela Banerjee (2017), David Michaels (2008, 2020), Sara and Jack Gorman (2016), David Helvarg (1997), Michael Mann (2021), Chris Mooney (2006), Naomi Oreskes and Erik Conway (2010), and recently Gale Sinatra and Barbara Hofer (2021) and James Gustave Speth (2021). Matt Hope reveals the major organizations that spun anti-science lies in the Trump era; most, including the powerful and important American Enterprise Institute and ALEC, were funded by giant oil corporations (Hope 2019a) and especially Koch money (Hope 2019b). Several states have sued. European countries have had their own issues with comparable abuses of public trust.

The US Congress may yet get seriously involved (Lynn and Supran 2021). The extremism of Koch, ExxonMobil, the American Petroleum Institute, and other far-right oil interests has even alienated other oil companies (Banerjee 2017). The US government, highly responsive to fossil-fuel firms at the expense of the public, kept on with extreme pro-fossil-fuel policies for decades, in spite of near-universal advice from scientists and even its own environmental administrators (Speth 2021). As long ago as 2013, an American family making $72,000 a year and paying the standard tax rate is giving away $6,000 to big firms in this way, and $4,400 of that is for the fossil fuel corporations (Buchheit 2013). The figures are now much higher.

Fossil fuel corporations are far from the only subsidized entities that produce pollution and destroy value. Big agribusiness does as much, notably the cattle-producing sector. The logging industry is subsidized, as is much of mining. Larger than the dollar payouts are unenforceable subsidies: pollution laws are not enforced against such entities. Frequently, at the state level, the laws controlling these firms were actually written by their lawyers, often via ALEC. Biggest of all, and most dependent on government money, is the armaments industry, from gunmakers to aerospace contractors. After oil, the heaviest subsidies go to such firms as Boeing and Lockheed, and this over and above government procurement for "defense."

A great deal of this subsidy money is recycled in lobbying fees and political "donations" (in other countries these would be legally defined as corruption), for the purpose of getting yet more subsidies. The facts about that are hard to tease out, because of the "dark money" laws in the United States. Identities of givers to leading political action committees (PACs) and the like are protected. The biggest donor to politics in the United States in 2020 was the Senate Leadership Fund, which donates only to Republicans and provided about $167 million; its own donors are obscure. Tom Cahill (2017) found that ExxonMobil donated from $184,250 to $3031,956 to pro-oil senators to shore up their opposition to action on climate change.

Koch Industries is known to have donated $13.75 million in 2020 to far-right-wing groups, and Charles Koch's various creations and affiliated groups gave tens of millions more. Other fossil fuel interests including Chevron, Conoco-Phillips, Exxon, and Phillips 66 gave $8.8 million to candidates who supported the January 6 insurrection. Other major donors to the far right included the late Sheldon Adelson and his surviving wife Miriam Adelson (unusual in that they are open about their $100 million a year in donations to Republicans); the Mellon, Prince-DeVos, Mercer, and Coors families and their affiliates; and a number of long-term Republican donors (Kotch 2021; see also D'Souza 2020).

Other large donors to the Republicans, notably big banks and financial firms, often donate more or less equally to both parties, to maintain their access; Goldman Sachs, one of the very biggest donors (over $5 million in contributions and over $3 million in lobbying in 2020) splits almost exactly 50/50 (OpenSecrets, Goldman Sachs Profile: Summary, retrieved Oct. 22, 2021), explaining why so many secretaries of the treasury and other high officials of both parties have come from that corporation.[3]

Funding for the far right extends its effects much more widely. Corporations donate to Republicans that support subsidies and special breaks even if those Republicans also support depriving voters of their rights and otherwise attacking democracy quite directly. An investigation by the *Los Angeles Times* (reporting further on other investigations) revealed that not only the expected Chevron, ExxonMobil (cf. Coll 2012), Altria (tobacco), Lockheed, and Boeing (the latter two being aerospace companies and thus connected with military spending) but also Wells Fargo, AT&T, Toyota, Comcast, and even Google had donated to far-right candidates supporting voter suppression as well as other extremist causes. Even the Republican legislators who supported and even took part in the January 6, 2021, attack on the US Capital continue to get corporate donations and support. Toyota stated: "Toyota supports candidates based on their position on issues that are important to the auto industry and the company," which caused *Los Angeles Times* writer Michael Hiltzik to say "In a rational world, this would be taken as a concise description of graft" (Hiltzig 2022a:A2).

It is also well known that congresspersons invest in firms they legally regulate (Kotch 2019, 2020), and that key regulators come from firms the government is supposed to regulate. This is described as "the revolving door" and "regulatory capture." Trump drew on the fossil fuels world for most of his environmental appointees (see, e.g., Friedman and O'Neill 2020). Two of his nominations for the Supreme Court had oil backgrounds: Neil Gorsuch with family ties to the Coors family (which long ago abandoned beer for energy resources); Amy Barrett's father was a lawyer for Shell. It is not too much to say that big oil and coal ran environmental management under Trump. The recycling of corporate officers and lobbyists as government regulators, and their frequent return to their home industries, has long been known, especially for the military-industrial complex, but now is more common for giant polluting firms. Ordinary criminals cannot manage this—they never get the support and power in the first place, they never think they are in the right, they never can successfully lie about their game. Even if they take over a country, they cannot do much to legitimate themselves.

The giant corporations are donating to racist politicians and racist causes, not only because they need subsidies and find support this way, but because the leading figures in the relevant political actions are personally motivated by far-right ideologies. Sometimes the racism is open and outright, as with many Koch family donations to racist educational and public information causes (Howie 2018; Kotch 2018) and political groups (Ahmed 2019). More often the link comes from funding openly racist or "dog whistle" racist (Lopez 2017) candidates, from Trump on down (cf. Acharya et al. 2018). This is typical of Europe as well as the United States, and in fact racist politics is linked (Ahmed 2019; Fekete 2019). In general, big business funds hatred and the Big Lie, as stated bluntly in the *New York Times* by Paul Krugman (2018).

Allied to the fossil fuels industry in politics and donations are the giant military-industrial and gunmaking firms. These have always engaged in a rhetoric of security and strength through availability of deadly force. In recent years, the rhetoric has become more strident. Gun dealers (largely through their public face, the NRA) allege increasing threats from crime and violence. "Dog whistles" about minority criminality have become less and less hidden. Sympathetic public groups are often openly racist. The more extreme "Second Amendment defenders" have more and more openly championed public violence, and defended police shootings of minority individuals. An interesting success of the right-wing corporations is getting antiestablishment sentiments directed against the government, and specifically against its rules about individual behavior, and promoting the giant government-subsidized firms as the antiestablishment that all good American individualists should support.

The giant agricultural interests—today's equivalent of the plantation owners and great landlords of the past—have similarly engaged in more and more extreme rhetoric against government regulation, especially environmental protection. An open insurrection by cattle interests, led by the Bundy family, briefly took over and vandalized the Malheur National Wildlife Refuge headquarters in 2016, and were released by a jury of their peers in local court, sympathetic with destruction of federal property and threats to government personnel. This was merely the most visible part of a large movement, spearheaded in the past by Coors associates James Watt and Anne Gorsuch (who served in the Reagan administration), and other public officials with western rural backgrounds and support. Unsurprisingly, Koch money supported the Bundy agenda (Rowland and Lee-Ashley 2016). The rural areas of the United State strongly support Trump (see, e.g., the excellent discussion of the situation in Wisconsin in Cramer 2016).

Rhetorical excess is thus not only coming up from below, but more stridently and visibly from above—the great interests threatened by progress and modernization. They continue to divide the public by racism and other traditional bigotries, but they have gone on to raise radical opposition to all government protection of the environment. As so often happens, the resulting movement has gotten away from them and become a real threat to national survival, causing more than a few of them to regret their more extreme actions (Koch 2020). Following the money means following both the financial interests of the supporters and following their personal ideological and emotional commitments. Trump let these large funders tell him what to do (Abramson 2020). The Trump administration fought legitimate science tooth and nail on every front, even banned a range of words from use by any government agency relating to global climate change and liberal politics (Friedman 2017; Sun and Eilperin 2017). (See Figure 5.2)

Trump promised much, but gave his followers nothing but the satisfaction of their dislikes. He cracked down on migrants, up to and including shutting down even amnesty and refugee programs. He ramped up racism and fought civil rights. He supported white nationalism (Guerrero 2020). He supported openly fascist groups and demonstrations. However, he did nothing positive for his base. His positive measures—tax cuts, subsidies, government programs—were all for the rich, and most of them were for the fossil-fuel firms, the right-wing financial interests, and a few other narrowly targeted interests. A detailed insight into the Trump presidency is the memoir *Midnight in Washington* (2021) by Adam Schiff (D-CA), who was in charge of several investigations into presidential misdoings. It is a disturbing story of political manipulations (see also Browning 2018). Studies show that, to quote one title, "the authentic appeal of the lying demagogue" is a general phenomenon well worked by strongmen everywhere, and certainly by Trump (Hahl et al. 2018).

Henry Giroux, one of the sharpest writers on the left, was unhesitatingly calling Trump neo-Nazi by 2017 (Giroux 2017b), and listing the already-emerging fascist traits of the Trump administration: fiery language encouraging irresponsibility and violence; "survival-of-the-fittest discourse provides a breeding ground for . . . hypermasculine behaviors and hyper competitiveness"; alternative realities; labeling whole groups as dispensable and criminal and bad; ignorance, anti-intellectualism, anti-fact; regarding the weak as worthless losers; "language of borders and walls"; violence as the solution; criminalization of homelessness, Blackness, and many other issues; hate of democracy (note that Trump banned the use of the word by the State Department); opposition to public education and to "think[ing] critically and act[ing] responsibly"; fears of others who demonstrate responsibility; ending of welfare state and safety nets; increasing inequality; ultranationalism and militarism; oppression of mainstream media and control of them when possible (Giroux 2017a).

More recently Alexander Hinton, leading anthropological expert on genocide, has added his voice, in a book significantly titled *It Can Happen Here* (2021). He reviews in detail the rapid rise of white supremacy into visibility and even mainstream politics under Trump. It is not the only riff on Sinclair Lewis's title; Jonathan Greenblatt's *It Could Happen Here* (2022) covers some similar ground, but is less balanced and temperate, attacking the tiny power abuses of the far left as if they were equivalent to the enormous fascist movement.

This attack on science bore dreadful fruit in the COVID-19 pandemic that began to affect the United States in 2020. Many interest groups, including the familiar fossil-fuels firms, launched attacks on public health regulation. These were mobilized and exaggerated by the Trump administration and their right-wing allies at all levels, leading to widespread and often violent resistance to even the most minimal public health regulations. The result was hundreds of thousands of deaths, almost all preventable, all the result of deliberate policy choices conditioned by the decades of war on science.

The right-wing politicians joined the system, getting more and more close to the world of conspiracies. Even the fast-food companies are strong Republican donors, though their less-than-affluent clientele is hurt by Republican policies, from opposition to minimum wage to opposition to public health care. At this point we recall the "limited good" idea; the fast-food companies would greatly increase their profits by allowing their working-class customers to have more money. Maintaining position, and keeping down labor costs and health regulation enforcement, mean more to them than actually maximizing profits. And sheer size of an enterprise, especially relative to everyone else, has tremendous negative social effects, as shown by Thomas Piketty (2017, 2020) among others.

The increase in right-wing corporate gigantism since 1900 is enough to explain all the ills of the United States since. There have been many other problems—anti-environmentalism, fascism, racism, and the rest—but bigness, specifically bigness of right-wing firms (notably fossil fuels and agribusiness), would have been quite adequate even without them to drive the economic problems and political declines of the last few decades. A clear indication is the virtual elimination of taxes on the rich. Marginal rates have gone from 91 percent in the 1950s to literally zero for the more successful tax evaders among giant firms.

Not only does bigness explain the political changes—they trace back to overwhelming amounts of money coming from these firms—but it also explains the decline in attention to serious art, music, literature, and other cultural matters, including the tragic destruction of small-scale cultures and traditions. With them go all our alternatives to current politics, arts, and environmental policies. Ordinary people become more and more passive. From having less and less free choice between firms to having worse and worse fare on TV, ordinary people have been led into something between surrender and despair. A rising number of American right-wingers are involved in local militias, increasingly involving themselves in extremist actions ranging from racist intimidation similar to the Ku Klux Klan to disrupting liberal demonstrations (Klaas 2017). Militia activity and politicization increased greatly under Donald Trump.

There has also been a shift to defiant anti-government and anti-science positions. Many states that used to have strong traditions of social responsibility have shifted to this attitude. The Dakotas, formerly very high in mutual support (partly thanks to Scandinavian settlement), were a center of opposition to masking and social distancing during the COVID-19 pandemic. The

United States has also seen a considerable loss of mutual-aid voting among the working class; white workers whose fathers voted with the labor unions now tend to vote against minorities and the poor, even if it means devastating harm to their own interests. Unions have declined accordingly. (On the general case of such self-destructive voting, see Arzheimer 2017; Frank 2004.)

The old-time split between Republicans as the party of bosses and the Democrats as the party of workers is increasingly replaced by the Republicans as the party of older, defensive whites and the Democrats as the party of minorities and the young. Appalachia has shifted from being Republican in the nineteenth century to Democrat in the twentieth and then back to Republican. Appalachian people suffer about the same level of poverty, sickness, and high mortality as Black communities, but display opposite political reactions—though only since the "southern strategy" took off. Some 12 percent of Americans—24 million people—are supporters of the "alt-right," i.e., outright fascism (Beauchamp 2018). They have the expected constellation of bigotries, and largely supported Trump in 2016. Their hard core produced about 10 percent of his vote (Forscher and Kteily 2020). Extremism was fed by Trump's deployment of scare rhetoric, to the point that Republicans in one survey believed that 18 percent of the population of the United States was illegal immigrants (Gelfand and Denison 2019; the real figure is less than 3 percent).

This has led to Republicans dropping to 29 percent of registered voters, with Democrats and Independents splitting the rest. However, Republicans get large turnouts of voters, suppress voting in Republican-governed states, and continue to get about 50 percent of the total vote. Even the 29 percent hard-core is not all racist; many old-fashioned business conservatives and others remain in the party, uncomfortable to varying degrees with Trump and his movement. However, the Republican Party has abandoned its long defense of small government and fiscal conservatism. As veteran conservative Jonah Goldberg says, "What unites [today's Republicans] is rejection, in whole or in part, of the American right's traditional laissez faire dogma about not using the state for picking winners and losers" (J. Goldberg 2022). Republicans now support enormous military expenses, enormous subsidies, and heavy policing and surveillance. Fiscal responsibility was abandoned in favor of vast tax cuts to the rich, without proposals for cutting spending besides cutting the much smaller amount spent on "welfare" and related public goods. Military spending and subsidies are many times greater than the total spent on "welfare," the environment, education, and other social services.

There remain several classic conservative factors that make non-racist, non-fascist people vote Republican. One is the defining principle of conservatism: hierarchy. People vote to maintain and strengthen social hierarchies, as matters of security. Second is personal freedom to act against community welfare. Many people feel they are "entitled" to sacrifice general welfare for their own personal comfort. This came out strongly in the battles over vaccinations, masking, and public distancing during the COVID-19 pandemic. Those measures were actually called "communist" by large sections of the right. Other social-welfare measures, especially for public health, have consistently run into the same opposition. Anti-litter laws, seat belts in cars, helmets for motorcyclists, and other such regulations all had the same history.

Another reason for non-racists to vote Republican is self-reliance. This is a classic American value. It is commendable enough in itself, but it can lead to opposition to all spending on the poor or the less fortunate. They are expected to be "self-reliant," while the rich get their subsidies. Religion is also involved. Many deeply religious people are captured by the rhetoric of the right-wing evangelical preachers, such as Franklin Graham and Kevin Swanson.

Alexander Hinton (2021) and others who concentrate on the white supremacist movement miss the far greater danger of misled conservatism coupled with billions of dollars from the right-wing establishment. These various principles, often deeply held, allow conservatives to feel they are defending freedom rather than attacking minorities. (For deeper and more dispassionate study of these issues, see George Lakoff 2006, 2016). Democrats want very modest background checks and controls on further sales of automatic weapons; Republicans say Democrats are taking everyone's guns. Democrats want face masks to protect people; Republicans call this an intolerable crackdown on personal liberty. Democrats want to maintain government social services; Republicans call this communism. Conservatives either ignore racist hatred and fascist ideation, or see them as less bad than the egalitarianism and social welfare of the liberals. Politics becomes more polarized and uncivil. Shouting, intimidation, and threats are driving people out of government service, from public health to school boards. Often only opportunists will take such jobs now (Klaas 2021). Demographics and political ideology are described in Figure 5.3.

Brynn Tannahill in *American Fascism* (2021) has shown in detail that Trump was a straightforward Hitler fascist, and recorded the progress of tactics copied from Hitler's Germany in the Trump administration. Reading Jason Stanley and Timothy Snyder verifies that all their markers of fascism were present in the Trump years. Pippa Norris and Ronald Inglehart (2019) have followed the rise of "authoritarian populism" in England as well as the United States. The failure of unwritten rules and norms of civility, decency, and due process are also deadly (Levitsky and Ziblatt 2018). If Trump wins in 2024, the future is predictable.

Today, suicide, drug overdoses, and death from sheer self-neglect are common and increasing, as documented by Anne Case and Angus Deaton in *Deaths of Despair and the Future of Capitalism* (2020; see also Case and Deaton 2015). These deaths are the tip of an iceberg. The parts below the water line are denial, defiance, bad-boy acting out, failure of self-care, passivation, giving up, and decline of personal responsibility. Vulnerable and lacking hope, many abandon self-improvement, which seems a threat and makes an "improved" person seem a fold breaker.

Suicidal anomie hit British Columbia First Nations in the 1960s and 1970s, and in fact suicide and substance abuse have been a problem for all Native American groups particularly hard hit by racism and economic discrimination. Deaths of despair peaked among Black people in the United States in the 1980s. The cause has been the decline of traditional culture followed by vicious racism that forced people out of new economic adjustments. With traditional religion and ideology dead, new spiritualisms and ideologies flourish, but do not substitute for strong tradition. Without community or tradition, people succumb to pernicious conformity (faddism, toxic masculinity), disempowerment, hopelessness, (consequent) cynicism, low self-efficacy, alienation, anomie, loss of meaning, random violence, and extremist politics. Abject sociability—subjecting oneself to social conformity at the lowest level—leads to sublimating resentments and greed into group hate.

Today, deaths of despair remain common among Native Americans, but have exploded among whites. They are especially common in downward-bound working-class communities, and—significantly—are particularly common and fast-increasing in areas that voted for Obama but then for Trump (Case and Deaton 2020). Overall, thanks in part to these factors, life expectancy in the United States has entered a sharp decline (Case and Deaton 2021). COVID-19 is the most obvious direct cause, but the rapid rise in suicide, opioid overdose, murder, and attendant deaths of despair and social breakdown are part of the picture. Above all these ride social irresponsibility and defiance of science and medical advice, as seen in drug abuse, rising alcohol consumption, declining exercise (with COVID-19 shutdowns), higher obesity, and other such issues. Meanwhile, COVID-19 has seen a decline of 25 percent in the US health-care workforce. The proximal cause is COVID-19, but the ultimate cause is chronic underspending on educating doctors and nurses, funding hospitals and health-care plans, and preventive actions. Trump has been a master of controlling the discourse about despair—getting the public media to focus on his view of the world, ignoring or downplaying counterviews. His strong statements get the media attention, drawing it away from inevitably late and inadequate rejoinders.

Trump and other modern fascists follow Hitler in directing hate against every traditionally devalued group (and some new ones), and against every group considered by the dominant majority to be upwardly mobile and thus a challenge. Trump's Republicans galvanized hatred of LGBTQ persons, feminists, minorities, Muslims and indeed any non-evangelical-Christian believers, liberals, and many other groups. This level of indiscriminate hatred is typical of Hitler fascism, but of no other belief system (see, again, Snyder 2015, 2017, 2018, 2021).

Trump is a master at testing any and all lies and hates until he finds ones that catch on. He has taken advantage of every crisis to promote lies to inflame hatred. He moved from attacking immigrants (especially, but not only, undocumented ones) to attacking Islam to attacking liberals, and then various other groups, and then to Black Lives Matter and other African American causes. He is smart enough to be fully confident that extremists on the left will match him—though on a far smaller scale—in being rhetorically or literally violent or extreme, thus justifying massive reaction by conservatives.

Trump's followers' America was a dream of the 1950s: white supremacy unquestioned, peace unbroken, women happily staying home. Trump's actual followers were anti-intellectual, anti-aesthetic, anti-nature, and anti-deviant. (The identification of the American right wing with fear and hate of the natural environment, and felt need to control or eliminate it, goes back to early settlement; see E. Anderson 2014; Louv 2005.) Their "patriotism" was shaky; they supported Trump's Russian dealings and they flew Nazi and Confederate flags. They go back to an American tradition of honor culture: violence is idealized in defense of "honor" and "law'n'order." One recalls the emphasis by writers such as Snyder (2018, 2021) and Stanley (2020) on the nostalgia of fascism for an idealized past.

Trump and other authoritarian strongmen are masters of encouraging motivated belief. Followers believe what they want; the leaders promise them anything. Fox News and the right-wing think tanks have figured out what people want to believe. The masters of this art are the right-wing preachers, of "pie in the sky" fame (it could be argued that religion was original inventor of the technique). These preachers know exactly how to talk to conservative Christians, just as Fox News knows about communicating with the right-wing side of the working class. Left-wing attacks on all whites, and above all on "rednecks" and "poor whites," merely repeat his behavior.

All these things encourage infantilization of the public, leading to the mindless conformity and obedience, as described and prophesied by George Orwell in *1984* (1950) and Margaret Atwood in *The Handmaid's Tale* (1998). These books are particularly chilling, and particularly accurate, because they predicted a world of blind obedience to emotional, irrational leadership policies, with secrecy and surveillance—and ultimately terror—as the ways the rule is maintained. This is what has happened in North Korea, China, Afghanistan, and several other places. Utopias based on technology or rational self-interest have not been even remotely approximated. Dystopias based on fears of brute force met with serious opposition have reflected the reality of Latin America and some other areas.

In recent years, many progressives have turned against some of the best ideas of the past, such as learning from other cultures. Radical thought is sparse, almost nonexistent. The ideas of the "progressives" are largely New Deal ones. The biggest problem faced by the left is a lack of any ongoing idealistic organizations. The labor union movement is on the ropes. Religion has been largely hijacked by the extreme right. The Democratic Party is disorganized and meek. A movement is awaited. "Democrats should try campaigning on the truth: the Republican Party is controlled by intelligent, college-educated, affluent elites who concoct dangerous nonsense to paper over a bigoted, plutocratic agenda and to justify attacks on the democratic process" (Nwanevu 2021). As Ian Bassin and Justin Florence wrote in 2020: "We came far too close to a full authoritarian taekover. . . . Disinformation," corrupting agencies, "delegitimizing vulnerable populations . . . quashing dissent . . . corrupting elections. . . . Immediate reform legislation should be passed to impose stronger guardrails against executive abuses. . . . Barriers to voting should be removed while better protecting our elections form foreign interference." We need "a diverse set of experts and citizens" to deal with electoral college and all downstream; "we must reclaim our national identity as a country that derives its strength from its diversity" (Bassin and Florence 2020).

The current goals of the right wing, from Trump's America to Taliban Afghanistan, include strict hierarchical systems with individuals and groups "knowing their place," maintained by military and police; repression of freedoms; economic growth but only for the powerful. Much of this is being integrated on a worldwide level. The far-right politicians and secret police are meeting globally. Recently, Michael Pence and Ted Cruz attended a meeting in Europe with Viktor Orbán, the Spanish Vox group, and other fascists of that continent. Cas Netherlands Institute for Neuroscience (2020) identifies components to this international right-wing movement: the Christian right, "national conservatism" (an openly fascist movement started by an Israeli politician), and standard far-right-wing politics as known since Hitler.

We need to go beyond that to reaffirm American ideals of tolerance, justice, equality, and the rule of law. We need to call out churches and "charities" that are strictly run for profit, and defend themselves by continuing the circulation of lies. Corruption and the status of the superrich as above the law must end.

NOTES

1. The website can be found here: www.genocidewatch.com.

2. The Koch Industries subsidy tracker can be found here: https://subsidytracker .goodjobsfirst.org/parent/koch-industries, and the Exxon Mobil subsidy tracker can be found here: https://subsidytracker.goodjobsfirst.org/parent/exxon-mobil.

3. The full report can be found here: https://www.opensecrets.org/orgs/goldman -sachs/summary?id=D000000085.

Chapter 6

Moralities

SOLUTIONS ARE DIFFICULT

Appealing to people's better instincts is not enough. Locke, and later the founding fathers, realized that one must marshal public opinion, and then mobilize it to create institutions that can enforce it. The United States has been somewhat successful until now, but today the laws are inadequate to protect democracy. It is necessary to appeal to better instincts and to common sense, but then to follow through with a sober, strictly defined plan to fight evil by legislation. The problem is not that better instincts and common sense do not work; the problems are that not everybody has them, and that nobody follows them when strong emotions intervene (recall David Hume's cynical but accurate remark). Ataraxia (the stoical attempt to avoid emotion) and meditation are not successful at conquering hatred. They can wipe out all the emotions except fear and anger—those, being concerned with immediate survival, are too strong to kill without extreme effort. Meditation to the point of ataraxia leaves people open and defenseless in the face of evil politics.

The opposite of concentrated hierarchic power should not be total anarchy. Even Adam Smith's free enterprise is hopeless in a world where giant multinational corporations have replaced small shops. Power now flows upward, partly because voters tend to opt out and let the power-mad take over. As it concentrates, corruption supervenes, and collapse ensues. Humans do have some advantages. They are much more prosocial than Hobbes or Freud or the neoliberals make them out to be. They also were usually taught by their parents to follow at least minimal rules, on a "what if everybody did that?" theory. (Do any parents *not* say that? And it works; see Levine et al. 2020.)

Yet overoptimism about people fails. People are a mix of good and evil, and the evil can usually be mobilized without too much effort. People do not often want to self-improve, because it would be admitting they are not

"good enough," and because they and their society generally want conformity instead of improvement. (These two points derailed the "humanistic
psychology" of the 1950s and 1960s, with its assumption that people wanted
to "grow.") If they do self-improve, it is because some very prestigious figure
is the target to imitate, thus neutralizing the admission of inferiority. Thus,
people like Jesus and Martin Luther King Jr. are even more important than
usually thought: even if mythologized, they give the rest a mark to shoot
for—someone so good we can never equal them, but do not feel particularly
bad about admitting that, and thus feel good about any attempt to follow in
their directions.

The good does not always sell well. The appeal of great music, art, and
literature, the appeal of building a better society, even the appeal of doing
better in life, are all strongly limited because of lowest-common-denominator
conforming to get along and to be able to talk to everyone. This in turn leads
to militant defense of trash because everybody else also pretends to like it.
(Orwell foresaw this in *1984*.)

Thus, predictably but unfortunately, liberals are often both too gentle and
too prone to appeal to narrow and crass pocketbook issues, instead of high
ideals. As Ruth Ben-Ghiat says, "Liberal values don't have to seem 'tepid
and boring,' the philosopher Martha Nussbaum argues, if compassion and
love are recognized as fundamental to the democratic model of politics. Too
often, we have left the work of shaping emotions—including patriotism, our
love for our country—to democracy's enemies" (Ben-Ghiat 2020a:254). A
movement should inspire everyone, but concentrate on reasonable appeals to
pocketbook issues and on outlawing and destroying evil, especially the hateful lies that sell evilness beyond the 10 percent or so who willingly embrace
it. This requires that people face their real fears and insecurities and recognize
the grounding of those in social threats and hates. Liberals often underestimate the sheer meanness out there, in every society and culture.

Almost always, good must be united with some desire for power or prestige. It helps to be "doing well by doing good." Successful change in a good
direction also requires some real antagonism, even hate, against the bad elements. This is obviously a delicate balance; hate can easily take over. The bad
wolf wins unless there is a strong structure of morals and also self-interest
in doing good. A chainsaw can take out a two-hundred-year-old tree in a few
minutes, and then replacing that tree takes another two centuries. The same
applies to most social evils; a bad man in power can undo decades of good
work in a year or two, and then regrowing it can take decades again. (Partly
through sheer gentleness and desire to seem inclusive, the Biden administration could stop but not reverse the damage done by the Trump years.) Good
is limited by the gentleness and local activity of most saints, by sheer inertia,
by conformity to often-hateful social traditions, and by despondency.

Deeply entrenched are human thought patterns, the "heuristics" of the psychologists (Kahneman 2011). People excessively discount the future, and routinely sacrifice an enormous future benefit for slight immediate returns. The extreme example today is ignoring global warming: even without the denial machine funded by fossil fuel corporations, people value cheap gasoline now, and ignore the destruction of civilization and possibly of all life on earth if nothing is done. The same discounting extends to wide-flung concerns as opposed to narrow ones. Modern nation-states, and the checks and balances endemic to most political regimes, allow the worst, stupidest, and most irresponsible to block almost any forward action. They have blocked attention to global warming for decades (Oreskes and Conway 2010; Speth 2021).

Related to this is a very long-standing and widespread tradition of seeing government as largely about military protection. An old principle holds that the most basic and vital purpose of government is to protect its people. Throughout much of history, that meant maintaining a huge army, typically funded and led by the elite landowners—the dukes, barons, knights, and so forth, raised to fight to defend their landholdings. Thus, governments today spend much of their money on the military and on subsidizing the rich resource-owners. The United States spends the vast majority of tax dollars on these two things. Yet, in the modern world, ill health and environmental damage are far more dangerous than military invasion. A government attending to protection would spend far more effort, attention, and money on them than on military matters, let alone subsidizing the rich.

Fortunately for humanity, morality and common sense exist in all functioning societies. Without them, breakdown and chaos would occur. In fact, even in breakdown, as Hobbes predicted, people "desire peace" and quickly develop some sort of peaceful government. Entitlement, made worse by insecurity and still worse by brooding on those who are believed to threaten entitlement, is particularly hard to fight. Uniting people for a common cause is the only cure, and this fact is too often exploited by aggrieved high-entitlement figures like Hitler, who use unity for their own evil ends. Substituting general welfare as a goal is difficult, but necessary. If there is no hope in unity except through opposition, the only valid group to oppose in the modern United States is the extremist right. The need is to unify everyone else, from left to moderate-right, against that.

Visionary plans to advance the good often convince the best 10 percent or 20 percent of people, and often get them to come on board and help. But then such plans run into a wall: the other 80 percent find them too good for this world. They want more immediate and practical goals. Intentional utopian communities usually fail. They succumb to personal conflicts, or the energy runs out, or at best they merge back into being just ordinary towns. The religious ones collapse into frozen dogma and patriarchy. The political ones succumb to conflicts. By contrast, newly settled small towns that simply reproduce their origin culture do fine, if they keep supply links up. Having conflict resolution mechanisms in place is a key. The western small towns of the nineteenth century brought with them a set of political institutions. The many intentional communities that were founded at the same time (Hine 1966; Nordhoff 1875) rarely did, unless they were highly structured religious settlements.

Pocketbook issues like wages, economic growth, and medical care remain essential to politics, and for good reasons. On the other hand, without inspirational and visionary politics, states tend to stagnate. The Democrats have learned the hard way since 2016 that opposing pocketbook issues to hatred guarantees a win by hate. Democrats need to start and end with ideals—stressing pocketbook issues, but only within that framework. Individuals range from psychopaths to saints. Society needs the latter. It is ideals that motivate saints.

Yet, any social movement must also push practical reason as hard as possible. It is, after all, the source of all progress: science, economic growth, environmental protection, medical care, all the ways to improve. Love and care have been promoted since time immemorial, and must be promoted again and again, but have a thin track record of actually improving any major group's lot. More important are fairness and a sense that "we are all in this together."

Altruism tends to be based on extending fictive or imagined kin links: "all people are siblings," "brotherly love." Some people do indeed manage to think of all humanity as family and help all the world. At worst, such language makes people think. Ordinary reciprocity encourages altruism (Barragan and Dweck 2014). It depends on empathy. Pure altruism—doing something for the sheer "eudaimonic" pleasure of helping—is fairly rare (Batson 2011); most people do it occasionally, but not much of the time. Fortunately, similar effects from reciprocity, consequentialist ethics, childhood teaching, and other causes are common.

To summarize what has gone before, we need a whole range of solutions. To fight malevolence and spite, society must deploy caring and compassion. To rivalry, greed, and fights over control, the need is to support cooperation and work for the common good. To oppose conflict, the Maya concept of *tranquilo* should be deployed, and conflict resolution made systematic and universally available. Most serious and important of all, hatred and callousness must be opposed by tolerance and valuing others' lives and attainments.

SOME SUCCESSES

The authors of this book have lived and done research in a few communities that had solved the problems of minimizing conflict, hatred, and abuse to a remarkable degree. The most astonishing were the Maya towns of central Quintana Roo, Mexico, studied by ENA over many years (1989–2012), with periods of residence (living with Maya families) totaling a year and a half (Anderson 2005). In that time ENA saw one fight, between two drunken young men, and it was broken up by onlookers before three punches were landed. Children were treated gently, rivalry was handled with good humor, and serious community tensions were mended by moving out. Groups sometimes budded off from a village to start their own communities. Domestic violence was not unknown, but was usually damped down by relatives and neighbors before it became serious. Several religious sects existed in the larger villages, but got along perfectly peaceably. Community leadership is by election, or informal choice in small communities, and can (rarely) occasion considerable noise and argument, but it stops short of violence or serious long-term disruption.

All this was even more striking because of its contrast with behavior in some Maya towns in old plantation agricultural areas to the west, and with many other villages in Mexico, where violence is endemic and "honor culture" and machismo are rife, and religious differences can lead to serious trouble. The Quintana Roo Maya are the heirs of revolution; they successfully rebelled against Mexico in 1846–1848 and ran a de facto independent country until conquest beginning in 1901 (Villa Rojas 1945). Their peacefulness today is often explained by them as due to their ability to band together and fight down oppression. This is confirmed by outside observers (Anderson 2005; Sullivan 1989; Villa Rojas 1945; all with reviews of further sources).

The Quintana Roo Maya put a very high value on being *tranquilo*. This means tranquility, but is extended to include proactive stopping of conflict when it occurs. Individuals mind their own business, and avoid any conflictual situation. Individuals and groups talk out their problems with as much good ill as possible. Child-raising is nonviolent, and parental and older-sibling directions to be *tranquilo* are constant.

Closer to home was a community studied by ENA in northern California, made up of Appalachian, southern, and Midwestern Anglo-Americans so close in origin and culture that the area was actually named after a probable relative. (Anthropologists do not confine their research to "exotic" people.) Despite the famed "honor culture" of this population (Nisbett and Cohen 1996), there was little conflict or crime, in spite of enforcement that—in the words of one resident—consisted of a sheriff's deputy coming once a week and asking "any trouble here?" and getting the inevitable answer "No, Sheriff, nothing happening." As in Quintana Roo, leadership was informal, people minded their own business and lived in widely separated farms, and maintained a strong value on "quiet" and "getting along." Honor was certainly a matter of explicit concern, but it included *avoiding* fights and being a peaceful citizen.

Both authors of the present book have lived in very different communities, where violence was endemic and fights were not easy to miss. In general, folk values on peace and on conflict resolution always operated to keep violence down, but counter-values on maintaining status and power by violent means kept tranquility limited. The success of conflict resolution in a Chinese community reaching successful peace after long periods of trouble has been analyzed by one of us (Anderson 2007), and the failure of another very similar community to maintain peace or even to survive has also been our concern (Anderson 1978). Suffice it to say that very similar communities can differ astonishingly in their success at avoiding conflict, hatred, and evil, and that detailed analysis of values and actions is necessary to explain this. Two things stand out: first, conflict, violence, and hatred are three different things that have to be addressed separately; second, rivalry was the most usual source of conflict in the communities we studied (and probably in most cases worldwide), and can produce all three of those ills, thus needing special attention.

A canonical ordering is either negotiate, compromise, cooperate or defend, aggress, fight. The real need is intervening at every stage. Basic is how one gets one's needs met: competition, cooperation, or individual work.

ENABLING CONFLICT RESOLUTION

For reliable success, the good (including avoidance of evil) must be taught constantly through life, formally and informally, and made into social rules. Then laws must be passed, because the most difficult 10 percent or so of people cannot be reached by social rules. The laws must appeal to well over 50 percent, or people ignore them. This fact is a problem for lawmakers. Moreover, laws must be enforced strictly and incorruptibly. When the rich are above the law—as they are in much of the world today—society suffers. Inequality needs to be kept low. Meanwhile, counter-messages against the endless lies and seductive messages must be kept up. Self-reliance and self-confidence are needed, so that the natural gentleness of good does not lead to failure from sheer inanition. Irrational hate is the basis and foundation of evil, and politicians at the extremist ends of the spectrum are often successful at preventing rational thought from interfering with their hate campaigns.

Conflict resolution, ideally by respected people, is effective. So is legally cracking down on incitement to violence and on fraud and corruption. It is vitally important to forbid evil behavior by every possible legal and social mechanism. Trying to harness power for the sake of practical reason is self-limiting, since it becomes nonfunctional at a certain level. Trying to harness totalitarian power in the name of the good has given the world the Inquisition, Wahhabism, Stalinism, Maoism, and many more such cases.

Some problems are particularly intractable. Global climate change is probably the worst mess humans have ever faced, because it requires everybody on the planet to give up something—often a great deal—for a large but distant and uncertain future benefit. It requires unity, and trust in leaders—two things hard to find under the best of circumstances. So far, the immediate needs of ordinary people for fuel, food, transportation, and other things have run against sacrificing for the long term. Many people worldwide now depend on fossil fuels not only for heating and the like but for work: they are truck drivers, delivery workers, gas station employees, or any of thousands of other job categories dependent on gas, oil, or coal. They will not be able to give up fossil fuel use until electric vehicles and other alternatives are easily and cheaply available.

THE VALUE OF MORAL PHILOSOPHY

Today, in English the word "ethics" tends to mean abstract high-level systems, "morals" tends to be used to refer to everyday working morality. Sometimes ethics are considered secular or philosophical; morals are religious. Ethics and morals were originally the same thing—just the Greek and Latin roots, respectively, for the same concept. They meant something slightly different from our ordinary meaning. For the ancients, and for many since, they referred to the regulation of individual behavior. Aristotle, who had much to do with making ethics a separate and important topic of enquiry, used it that way. He contrasted ethics with politics; politics was about governing the realm; ethics was about governing oneself. Thus, a great deal of his writing focused on what we would now call "self-care" rather than ethics. His "ethical man" (Aristotle was writing for upper-class males) was accurate in self-assessment, had a positive yet reasonable self-image, and knew when to stop eating and drinking (Aristotle 1955). These we would still value, perhaps, but we would not necessarily call them central to ethics. We lost an ethical valuation of positive self-image partly because centuries intervened in which Western ethical philosophy was dominated by Christian ideas of meekness and humility. Conversely, the social side of virtue was "politics," not ethics, to him. Again, Christianity, with its social message, changed this.

Aristotle gave us one unfortunate bias in ethical examination: he made ethics an individual matter. Philosophers still write as if ethical standards were worked out by individuals meditating alone. This stands in very striking contrast to East Asia, where moral codes have always been seen as thoroughly social. Confucius and his followers in China were particularly clear on this issue, but to varying degrees it is generally held. Daoist, Buddhist and Hindu hermits are a partial exception, but they have self-consciously severed ties with society; they are not prescribing for a society of isolated individuals.

The Chinese equivalents are *ren* and *li*, "humaneness" and "principle." *Ren* was originally simply the word for "person." To make it an ethical term, the number 2 was added, so the character is now an abstract picture of a person next to the two parallel bars that mean "two" in Chinese. It thus means how two people should act toward each other. By extension, it shows how we all should act toward each other. The word *li* originally meant "sacrificial order," with a small picture of a sacrificial vessel as the character. It rapidly evolved from conforming to social rituals to mean loyalty to abstract principles and integrity in life—"principle" and "principled behavior." The fact that the Chinese words are based in social usage, the Western ones in individuality, is obviously significant.

Every society has its ethical and moral codes, and in all societies they are social constructs, worked out through interactive practice. These codes hold society together and keep individuals from getting out of line. People exhort others to help them or to work together to fix a problem, or they blame others for hurting them or for failing to work together. They censure the unsocial and praise the sociable.

In everyday life, there are various levels of justification. One explains moral rules to a child by recourse to very simple, low-level constructs. The subtle thought of Rawls or Habermas (1984) is far different. Yet, the child may still receive fairly high-level philosophic generalizations. If told that people will be hurt if she acts in such-and-such a way, or that such-and-such an act is unfair, the child is getting the condensed wisdom of the ages. On the other hand, children often hear that such-and-such an act is done "just because everybody does it" or "just because I say so." This does not pass muster as ideology, though it often gets the right behavior established.

It thus follows that there is often more consistency in the low-level behavioral rules than in the ideology. The more remote and sophisticated the interpretation, the less it is apt to be shared (other things being equal). Thus, cultural behavior is most clearly shown in practical daily acts, not in high-level philosophy.

People often agree on broad principles, especially ones that arise easily from experience, such as "fairness" and "not hurting others." A moral code is structured, usually around such elementary insights as these. People deduce logically, from the code, what is right in a new situation. This provides grounds for debate. How dangerous is a new chemical? Is it "fair" to restrict its sale until it is known to be safe? Can society assess the risks?

Practice and structure constantly influence each other. People deduce, logically (but on the basis of prior experiences), what to do in a new situation. They then try out the logical deduction, and revise or refine their plans accordingly. Usually, logic is imperfect, and plans are revised. New rules or generalizations, with more or less extent and power, are the result. An individual does this on the basis of internal "dialogue." Social groups do it by talking everything out as they go along. Morals are thus means to an end: successful social systems that allow tolerable life for the members of the society. Morals are practical rules. They are not, in everyday practice, the elaborate comprehensive systems that philosophers love.

Modern ethicists pride themselves on transcending the old group morality and developing a morality for the Individual. Ancient Chinese and Indian philosophy was filled with speculation on the individual's role in society, and there were those, like Zhuangzi, who espoused an individualism as radical as anything in the West. Even the small, kin-based societies have their individual moralities, as Paul Radin showed in *Primitive Man as Philosopher* (1927). Even so, the radical individualism of ancient Greece really was different, and it survives in the modern West, for good and ill.

Aristotle had to work out a whole new language, inventing words or giving them new meaning (see, e.g., Aristotle 1955:126–27). Confucius and Mencius did similar things in China, at about the same time. This is anthropologically interesting, because it shows how cultural concepts form. It shows that a thinker in a highly traditional society was not bound by the conventions of language and culture. Thinkers could examine and change them at will. Similar conscious changing of moral concepts is well documented from many societies, giving us hope for the future.

In every society, people expend a great deal of effort "pushing the envelope." Thus, societies change, and can change very fast. Consider the sexual mores of the United States over the last seventy years, and the constant debate that has gone on about sexuality. As people interact, their experiences lead them to have particular ethical and moral views. James Scott has used the concept of the moral economy, the grassroots rules developed by individuals (farmers in Scott's cases) working with each other every day. They developed an economy in which trust, cooperation, rough equality, and expectations of mutual aid are a pragmatic necessity. Naturally (remember "natural man" here), their morals reflect this (Scott 1976, 1985). Scott has been criticized for being too optimistic or starry-eyed about peasants (Popkin 1979), but that is not the point: the point is that peasants do have to take account of needs for cooperation and mutual aid in their moral codes. Whether they live by their moral codes is another matter.

Moral codes are *intended* to be too perfect for this world of ours. Since humans never quite live up to codes, the only way to get people to be even sort of good is to have perfectionist codes. The alternative, common in politics, is what Caribbean islanders call "crab antics." If you put crabs in a bucket, you need not cover the bucket, because whenever a crab begins to climb up and out, the others promptly pull him down.

Recognizing the social nature of morality leads us to realize that ethical philosophy since Aristotle has had rather a split personality. The expansion of "ethics" to include general morality never quite shook Aristotelian individualism. It was reinforced by mainstream Protestant and liberal Jewish thought, which privilege individual conscience. Several Catholic and Fundamentalist writers dissent sharply and provide more communitarian views, but are apt to be more interested in providing arguments for specific tenets of conservative Christianity than for a generalized social ethic. Consider, for instance, their positions on the family and on gender roles within it. Alasdair MacIntyre (1984) is the most sophisticated of these, but argues for little more than acceding to power, divine and human.

THE VALUE OF MORAL ACTION

People being social animals, the irrationally social individuals tend to win out in society. A world of rational individual choosers in the classic Hobbesian sense would be defeated, one by one, by even a pair of "irrationally" social humans that could cooperate to take them on one at a time—let alone by Hobbes's group forming a social contract. (Much of what follows is extracted from the posting "Ethics" on ENA's website; the full post at www. krazykioti. com has further backup data.)

Providing an ideal ethic for a highly moral and rational individual is, no doubt, a praiseworthy and desirable thing in itself. However, it does not provide a social charter or a social code. It attempts too much—no society will ever be composed entirely of highly moral and utterly rational people. Every society has its cheaters, and there must be at least a few self-sacrificing individuals who balance them out. Society runs on tit-for-tat games; people exchange cooperation. Society requires simple, clear, memorable codes; the tax codes and civil codes would be hopeless as general moral guides (Gigerenzer 2007). Moses held it down to ten commandments, not because those ten covered everything but because the human animal has enough trouble remembering seven items at a time, let alone ten. Every society has its unfortunates—at least, the mentally handicapped and mentally ill persons; at most, the millions of unfortunates that follow a war or depression. There must be people self-sacrificing enough to care for them; otherwise, the society falls victim to a downward ratchet in which more and more people fall into the needy category and fewer and fewer can help them.

Social gift-giving is notoriously prone to sabotage by "rational" freeloaders. Only the most powerful social sanctions, coupled with very strong social needs on the part of individuals, can keep people writing letters, giving Christmas gifts, throwing dinner parties, and celebrating festivals. Yet, in every community on earth, things of this sort go on all the time. Cooperation after assurance contracts provides one notably successful method that people use to effect such results (Anderson and Anderson 2020; Schmidtz 1991; see Brown 1991 for other mechanisms). By themselves, they fail for the usual reason: irrational individuals will violate the most reasonable of contracts. Thus, there is need for stronger moral suasion, and it usually is forthcoming.

Conversely, from the social and interpersonal point of view, self-destructive behavior by an individual is to be condemned only if it threatens others. Most moral codes have relatively little to say about drunkenness, profligacy, and individual stupidity. Significantly, the Protestant codes of Northern Europe are the main exceptions. These codes, based on individual guilt and on liberty of conscience, were developed to sustain persons in their faith during times of conflict and persecution. They also have a strong individualism derived not only from Greece but also from the highly individualistic Celtic and Germanic cultures of the area (E. N. Anderson 2014) and greatly augmented by the rapid rise of commerce and trade after 1600 (Lerro 2000). Moreover, as befits the codes of nascent capitalist societies, but unlike almost every other moral code in the world, they value thrift over generosity (Weber 1958). Many Protestant codes born in different social circumstances are more concerned with social matters; the Hutterite, Mennonite, and Amish ethical systems come to mind. Even the most individualistic Protestant codes, however, place a value on self-sacrifice and are rather tolerant of personal foolishness. Still, it has been argued that Americans have gotten too individualist for our good (Putnam 2000).

One basic moral code is that of Dumas's Three Musketeers: "All for one and one for all." Individuals can be expected to take care of themselves without the urgings of a moral code. The moral code is needed to make us see that "an injury to one is an injury to all." Thus it occurs that all societies place a strong moral value on self-sacrifice and generosity and a lower value than "rational self-interest" would predict on individual self-protection and welfare.

In practice, there is a firm rule that can be extracted from all accounts of human action: No long-term interest wins without moral and ethical institutions supporting it. Robert Frank (1988) demonstrates this point at length.

Short-term considerations will tend to govern or undermine rational choice. In a society, even if most people look to the long-term and wide-flung interests, those who go for maximization in the short term will flourish quickly at the others' expense, and destroy the society in a short time. The behavior of the oil corporations in today's world is a monstrous example.

Long-term reckoning leads to development, within individuals, of concepts we sum up in the words "responsibility" and "commitment." People are expected to be responsible for their behavior—to regulate themselves, to follow the social codes even when not being watched. They are also expected to commit themselves to those that depend on them, and to the social group and its needs. A moral individual owes certain duties to all living things, or at least all humans; but he or she owes more to *some* beings. Commitment to family, friends, livestock, fields, and even a favorite wilderness is a real moral choice. It entails many obligations. Many or most people would sacrifice their lives for their families, and would defend them by killing enemies who could not be stopped any other way. Confucius emphasized this aspect of morality, and gets blamed for it by Western moralists who believe in equal morality for all, but it can be confidently assumed that they too take care of their families first.

A major worldwide study by P. J. Henry (2009), backed up by experiments and interviews, led to the conclusion that violence is particularly valued in bottom-dog cases: poor and marginal groups that still have enough autonomy to get away with it on a social level and are not scared into pacified tranquility. Henry was testing a theory that herding societies were especially violent; he found it to be wrong. ("Explanations exist; they have existed for all time; there is always a well-known solution to every human problem—neat, plausible and wrong"—H. L. Mencken 1920:158.) Herders are violent when they are marginal players in wider social worlds, and have on the one hand very little vested interest in peace, on the other a good deal to gain by maintaining "honor" and by taking land. Thus, indeed, many herding societies are violent—one thinks of the Mongol hordes and the ancient Israelites. But so are farming societies in the same situation, as in highland New Guinea, the Caucasus Mountains, and Afghanistan. Conversely, herders in tranquil settings are peaceful enough. The tranquil shepherds of Arcadia are proverbial. Herders sometimes get a bum rap; America's Wild West gunslingers are popularly thought of as "cowboys," but the violence actually centered in mining communities, and even then was usually carried out by bandits, gamblers, and other shady elements (see Mark Twain's memoir *Roughing It*, 1913).

Moral codes are also internalized and continually individualized and reconstructed as individuals grow up (Tomasello 2016). The biological substrate of morality, such as it is, becomes supplemented almost immediately by parental teachings. Long before they can consciously think about or choose their morals, children develop a "habitus" (Bourdieu 1978), an internal representation of the social codes of family and peers. This habitus is accepted unthinkingly, and rarely changed. It is what gives us the picture (so often remarked by grave authors) of the modern ethical philosopher constructing arguments that clearly are intended to prove a preexisting belief, not to construct a new vision. (This point is, for instance, often argued against John Rawls; see below, and also Schmidtz 1991:161–63.) Some attributes considered moral almost everywhere are usually directly beneficial to the person who has them, such as courage, patience, wisdom, useful knowledge, industry. Others are pure cost, in rational-individual terms: generosity, self-sacrifice, tolerance, accommodation. Naturally, moralists have to work harder to sell these latter morals, and thus these morals often become privileged and specially honored.

This constant negotiation gives moral codes the necessary flexibility to allow them to function in this rapidly changing world. Depersonalization is a threat to an ethical system, perhaps especially an ethical system involving human-environment relations, as we have seen. Thus, the ethical position summed up in "Judge not, lest ye be judged" (Matthew 7:1) is both widespread and pragmatically well grounded.

Real-world moral codes are all contractarian in the sense that they are social institutions worked out through negotiation. It is safe to say that no one in premodern times actually sat down to draw up a contract. Hume was right: family and kinship, not formal contract, was the source of moral society. However, there is a sense in which Hobbes's "social contract" (Hobbes 1950 [1657]) tale is a realistic fable. Since neither "family values" nor "moral intuitions" are complete guides, a society must have a set of institutions, worked out through mutual accommodation, mutual commitment, and mutual negotiation, that end "warre" by laying out rules for "peace." In modern terminology, they convert a sort of worldwide Prisoner's Dilemma into an assurance game. They allow people to exchange and cooperate long enough to develop assurances of reasonable dealing. Social behavior thus arises out of individual exchanges of goods and information nested in an emotional and social context of kinship and friendship networks. In other words, society arises when individuals, necessarily included in families (at least as children), work and negotiate together to form institutions, which then reshape their societies, or even create new societies.

The belief that cultures (at least traditional cultures) had rigid values systems, to which everyone conformed, has turned out to be false (see Bourdieu 1978, 1990—or any modern ethnography). This is fortunate; it was a depressing and totalitarian view. In reality, all social groups deal with dissent, debate, argument, and a plurality of values systems. Some deal better than others, but all face the same irreducible tendency of humans to disagree about both basic principles and immediate applications. A moral code need not be perfectly consistent and proof against all criticism. It need only hold society together. It is an institution, one of whose functions is to make transaction costs lower (North 1990). Morals are cheaper than lawsuits; Japan, held together by a widely shared ethical code, is said (at least in folklore) to have fewer lawyers than the Bay Area of California, where self-interest and diversity prevail.

UNIVERSAL MORALS

No moral rule is completely universal, but, worldwide, some moral rules seem close to universal (Brown 1991; Goldschmidt 2005). Shwedet (1991; Shweder et al. 1997) described five dimensions of morality: ethics of the individual (harm vs. help; autonomy); communitarian values (hierarchy; ingroup/outgroup; and divinity (purity). (See also Gigerenzer 2007:187). Another way of classifying codes follows the thinking of Jonathan Haidt and colleagues (2006, 2012; Graham et al. 2011). These sources broadly agree that meanness, selfishness, injustice, rudeness, and cowardice are widely condemned. Sloth and self-indulgence are less widely devalued, but rarely praised. These tend to be defensive reactions. Cowardice certainly is. Mean, selfish, unjust, and biased behaviors also involve defensive aggression. They are almost always the aggression of the weak, scared person who feels trapped and cornered.

Societies are generally ambiguous toward competition, independence of mind or conversely overdependence, originality, fun, pride, ambition, humility, religious faith, and sexual morality. All these can be considered good or evil, depending on the society or on how they are actually used.

One dramatic change has been the downfall of slavery. Until the late eighteenth century, slavery was universally accepted without question in all civilizations and most simpler societies that had any hierarchy to speak of. Many isolated individuals came out against it, but no organized opposition surfaced. Even revolted slaves usually accepted the system, often taking slaves of their own. Finally, some Quakers decided in the late eighteenth century that it was unacceptable. The idea spread slowly. Even John Stedman, who provided the classic and horrific account of slavery in practice (Stedman 1988 [1806–1813] did not question the institution until he met Quakers in London after his book was completed. However, once the Quakers raised the issue, antislavery propagated fast. Serious antislavery movements began in the 1770s. Within a century, slavery was eliminated almost everywhere. The progress of capitalism, which substituted more productive and manageable proletariat labor for forced and inefficient slave labor, explains a large (if debatable) amount of this change. Slavery persists today in out-of-the-way corners of the world, and is still accepted there in spite of being technically illegal. The fall of slavery was thus due to Christianity and capitalism, two forces now associated in many quarters with all things evil. An ironic sidelight.

THE BACKSTORY OF ETHICS: ETHICAL PHILOSOPHY FOR EVERYDAY USE

Most current Western secular ethical philosophy can be divided into two camps: Kantianism and utilitarianism. These roughly map onto a more basic divide between ethics that are deontological (given by God or by logical inevitability) or assertoric (simply asserted, without ultimate proof but hopefully with rational justification). In fact, people combine these, and often do good simply through inaction (Gawronski et al. 2017)—they abstain from wrong when not certain of the situation, or when they *are* certain of it and do not like what they see. The present book is written from a position that bases morality on one deontological principle—helping is better than harming—and deduces everything else from it by largely utilitarian consequentialist thinking.

Kantians hold that humans should never be treated as means, but only as ends; that there are absolute (deontological) standards of ethics and morality; and that these absolutes are binding on all persons at all times (Kant 2002; Korsgaard 1996a, 1996b). For instance, Immanuel Kant defended a strong position on honesty: it is binding, and an individual cannot lie. Kant also privileged the individual. Respect for the individual and his rights (sic; Kant was equivocal about women's status) took precedence over communal goals. Individuals were always to be treated as ends, never as means.

Kant advocated institutions that would guarantee freedom and fairness beyond the immediate community. A rather cynical individual in a hard time and place, he worked to ground Christian morality is a more harshly realist view of the world. Cold logic and some degree of political realism, not love for all, grounds his Christian values. Kantian ethics seem best at dealing with justice issues; John Rawls's justice-as-fairness morality (1971) has a Kantian base and thus a Christian one. Rawls has been accused, not without basis, of sneaking Christianity into a supposedly secular ethic.

Kant deduced these absolutes from his version of the Golden Rule: "Act in such a way that you can wish your maxim to become a universal law (irrespective of what the end in view may be)" (Kant 2009:52). This principle, however, is highly problematic. The Golden Rule has not done well lately, largely because people don't keep it, but partly also because people want different things. The most intractable problem is logical, but a close second is the practical one of sheer human difference. Roger Williams, in *Biochemical Individuality* (1956), showed that each human is not only psychologically but also biologically and biochemically unique. This makes it impossible to live by the Golden Rule: one would have to deal with people ranging from devotees of Brussels sprouts to outright sadomasochists. What works for some does not work for others. Kant argued that one simply "extracts the maxim" from such questions, and does what is best for all, in which case the basic rule is altered. Kant's advocacy of absolute honesty would be impossible in any normal society. One does not answer "How are you?" with a full symptomatology, nor does one answer accurately when a female friend asks if she looks fat. No one is ever surprised to learn that Kant never married.

Two Kantian points basic to further arguments are *we're all in this together* and *my rights stop where yours start.* These may be "folk Kantianism," but they follow directly from Kant's respect for other persons, and from the Golden Rule. In Kantian logic, others are always ends, never means (though Kant did recognize such partial exceptions as the fact that soldiers have to die in defensive wars). These guiding principles also "pay off" in utilitarian calculus, but they are Kantian formulations.

John Rawls, Christine Korsgaard (1996a, 1996b), and other modern Kantians or quasi-Kantians also maintain a focus on individual rights. Rawls, in *A Theory of Justice* (1971), derived a Kantian goal—fairness—that is absolute and should be met 100 percent, but that can also be approximated with much good result. The closer we get to perfect fairness, the better off we all are; it is a process goal. Rawls postulates a rational individual behind a veil of ignorance. This individual is assigned to construct a world in which he (sic) would be happy. (Rawls has been criticized for a traditional-male view of morals; he partially corrects this in later works; see Rawls 2001.) He would have to build self-respect into it, as well as fairness and equal opportunity for all, because he would not know where he would wind up. There is much to be said for this view as one basis for morality. It foregrounds social justice and defines it the way most of us instinctively define it: as basic fairness, in the sense of equality of opportunity and equality before the law and before the social body.

However, Rawls argued from a highly individualist, almost Hobbesian position: Morality as devised by a detached observer "behind a veil of ignorance," figuring out what rules society should have such that he or she would be least badly off no matter where he or she wound up. This neatly allowed Rawls to construct a morality on the basis of individual rational choice. People do not need to be "good" or self-sacrificing. They need only be rational about what they want of the social order—assuming they could be anywhere in it. Rawls's humans are isolated. They are also emotionless; they are without jealousy or envy, for example. His ideals are unworkable for actual humans, with their irrational hates and self-sacrifices. Since morality is about regulating social interaction in a warmly emotional, compulsively social species, a morality developed for coldly rational beings cannot be quite adequate.

This gives one advantage to the Kantians, with their often-passionate commitment to absolutes.

"Justice as fairness . . . would seem to include only our relations with other persons and to leave out of account how we are to conduct ourselves toward animals and the rest of nature" (Rawls 1971:17). Since Rawls wrote this, justice-as-fairness has been generalized to apply to at least some environmental concerns (Rawls 2001), but few would deny that it needs some serious supplementation. Putting oneself behind a veil of ignorance does not help decide such questions as fur trappers vs. fur-bearing animals. If one expands the veil of ignorance to make one ignorant of what species one is in (Attfield 1991), one will probably decide for the animals, since there are more of them and they die immediately and horribly. But then the trappers starve. If one decides for the trappers, the fur-bearers die. A general conclusion follows: From an environmental point of view, justice is a necessary precondition to dealing with the real questions, not the final answer.

Rawls's "rational person" behind a "veil of ignorance" is also a bit unrealistic. The theory appears to be based on the idea of trial by jury, and to share its problems in this modern world of all too abundant information on every case. Rawls admits that the problem of the mentally incompetent is hard to handle under his theory (Rawls 1993:272). Perhaps Kantian ethics fit troubled, harsh times, and utilitarian ones go with expansive, hopeful periods. This would account for the shift from Millian utilitarianism to a Kantian concern with individual harms in the contemporary United States. This shift has led to better protection. Unfortunately, ruling out even the least harm, no matter how huge the benefits, has led to such things as the end of playgrounds and outdoor games in schools. (Some child might get hurt—no matter that literally tens of millions receive major benefits.) Meanwhile, as people lose control of their lives to giant corporations and government agencies, they desperately assert what control they have, by "suing the bastards." More seriously, Kantian ethics can serve as excuses for totalitarianism. The dictator need only maintain that he has special, often divine, access to the absolute principles. Moses and his Ten Commandments can be brought in as justification. Such appeals to special revealed wisdom are common stock among dictators everywhere (Ben-Ghiat 2020a; Dikötter 2019).

The counter to Kantian deontological ethics is utilitarianism. Utilitarians hold that the ultimate guiding principle for action should be Jeremy Bentham's rule of "the greatest good for the greatest number over the greatest time" (Mill and Bentham 1987; see also Brandt 1979). Bentham and Mill, who appear to have been more hopeful individuals than Kant, grounded ethics in rational self-interest, making popular the concept of "utility" as a self-interested goal. Mill's ethics owe a lot to Christianity too, and a great deal to the Celtic and Germanic tribal ideals of freedom and equality that kept cropping up irrepressibly throughout North European history. The cold utilitarian calculus, however, is not well suited to the human animal, which is wired to be warm, generous and kind to immediate family and friends, not so much so to the distant (Moll and de Oliveira-Souza 2008). Cold calculation to sacrifice one for the good of many is necessary in war, and is done, but no one enjoys it, and doing it outside of a conflict situation is truly difficult.

Bentham's "the greatest good for the greatest number" was found in Jeremy Bentham's writings, apparently after he died (Sidgwick 1902:244). Bentham did not add "over the greatest time," as later writers did, but Bentham apparently meant this too. Bentham also ruled "everybody to count for one, and nobody for more than one" (Sidgwick 1907:417). This sneaks Rawlsian fairness into the ethic. Like the privileging of helping over hurting, this is a concession to deontology. It would seem that pure utilitarianism, like pure deontology, does not work well for anyone.

Henry Sidgwick's utilitarian classic, *The Methods of Ethics* (1907), equated good with happiness, on the theory that no one has any better way to judge it. Sidgwick eliminated Darwinian evolution as a source of ethics. The "struggle for existence" (the right of the strong to do anything they want to the weak) and "preservation of the species" simply do not give adequate philosophical grounds for ethics. (Sidgwick 1907; he was unfair to Darwin; Spencer was the guilty one here, while Darwinian theory allows dogs, chimpanzees, and people—among other animals—to have some biological underpinning for morality.)

Sidgwick tried to establish utilitarianism at the expense of intuitionism; he showed that our ethical intuitions are inconsistent, incoherent, and unclear. He knew enough about other cultures to realize that they had very different standards. He did not know quite how bad it could get. The Aztec's intuition told them it was necessary to sacrifice children and captives to the gods. In the early 1940s, the best intuitions of several million Germans, Rumanians, Poles, Italians and others, were that truly ethical behavior consisted of exterminating Jews, Roma, mentally ill persons, and the congenitally handicapped or physically challenged, to say nothing of political dissidents and religious leaders. Germany's leading philosophers, such as Martin Heidegger, gave their active support to this cause (Sluga 1993).

However, by focusing on "happiness," Sidgwick merely took another step down a path of infinite regression. Intuitions (!) of what makes people happy are then the guide. Sadists, rapists, and vandals have debatable ideas of happiness and the Good. Sidgwick partially countered such claims by strongly advocating individual rights and a sort of society-wide cost/benefit accounting of happiness, but this, again, sneaks Kantian justice into the picture. The "one for one" rule eliminates the charge that utilitarianism would hold a nation successful if the dictator is supremely happy and everyone else miserable. This is a common Kantian charge against utilitarianism. In fact, it is true of one type of utilitarianism: the libertarianism of the post-Nietzschean Ayn Rand and some other economic thinkers.

The key argument for utilitarianism is that it is the only ethic that tests all actions against actual human welfare. All other systems end by privileging abstract ideals and sacrificing humans to them. Utilitarianism was something of a world-rulers' ethic, a true child of the British Empire; it was something you could impose over all those local cultural systems. They could keep their moralities, but "practical" and "reasonable" considerations were imposed. As such, it has been criticized for indifference to culture and nature (See Elliott 1995). The attacks are not without reason. A narrowly construed utilitarian calculus would reduce nature to more groceries. However, utilitarianism has not usually been that narrow (Sidgwick 1907 reports that he and other utilitarians have defended animal welfare), and at least utilitarianism offers something of a beginning. Richard Brandt (1979, 1996) and R. Hardin (1988) have done much to rehabilitate utilitarianism as a general and environmental philosophy.

Theoretically, a utilitarian could argue that enormous "good" to one person would justify imposing appreciable suffering on many, or slight good to many would justify imposing enormous suffering on one. Indeed, all societies do impose enormous suffering and unfreedom on some individuals who reduce others' welfare and are thus considered "criminals" or "lawless" (see Hardin 1988). More serious, and all too common in this world of ours, is for a society to impose terrible suffering on one group—the poor, the nonwhite, the young, the old, the religiously different—in the belief that it will benefit the majority. This prejudicial behavior is invariably justified on utilitarian grounds, naming specific benefits for society. Either helping the weak is a "waste of money" that could be better invested elsewhere, or cutthroat competition (resulting in immiseration of the poor) is necessary to progress, or, at worst, that these people are "inferior" and need to be "kept in their place" for social order. The utilitarian calculus in question very rarely survives unbiased scrutiny, but what if it does survive in some particular case? Does that make discriminatory laws ethically right? Obviously not. Here moral persons really can rely on intuition, because it tells them that there is a more basic definitional issue here. The absolute moral injunction against treating whole groups prejudicially is a qualitatively different thing from the sordid practical reason that might make people want to discriminate. These issues are powerfully raised and addressed in their environmental applications by Robert Bullard (1990) and the environmental justice literature stemming from his work (E. N. Anderson 2010).

Similarly, a utilitarian ethic could become a rigid totalitarianism by finding "the good" and forcing it on everyone. Humanity is spared from this as a realistic option by the noncomparability of values and the lack of information about the "perfect good." This has not stopped dictators from trying their best to justify tyranny in precisely these terms. The fact that utilitarianism can be credibly bent to this end, even though dishonestly, is a problem for the utilitarian ethic. Thus, both assertoric and deontological ethics can be bent to the worst uses. It should be emphasized yet again that Kant, Mill, and Sidgwick were among the loudest and clearest voices ever raised in defense of personal liberty and social benefits to all. Their example speak louder than their precepts.

Arguably the worst problem with utilitarianism, especially vis-à-vis Kant, is that utilitarianism assumes that people can rationally calculate their own and others' best interest. Utilitarianism depends on a Lockean psychology that holds people are good information processors and learners. They can maximize their utility or happiness, or, following Mill, they can at least do better at it than anyone else can. This bears some elaboration. Robert Zajonc (1980) pointed out some time ago that humans react to stimuli, and evaluate them as "good" or "bad," "positive" or "negative," before they are aware of them. The first thing humans do, when noticing something, is rapidly and subconsciously evaluating it. This quick, pre-attentive check allows them to decide whether they want to notice it—that is, to bring it to conscious awareness.

In fact, people are generally unaware of their most pernicious biases, and are not reliable judges of how to reach their own best futures (Kahneman 2011). Particularly shaking to moral groundings are two truths. First, people often pretend to "enjoy" things they actually hate, simply to get social approbation. This sustains pop music and lawns, among other things. Much "luxury" is miserable. This is not to deny the ironic message of *The Fable of the Bees* (Mandeville 1988) that luxury sustains the economy by creating work. Indeed it does. The question arises only when luxury consumption destroys more than it creates, or when it destroys irreplaceable and valuable resources for transient benefits.

Second, people often sacrifice their own welfare, and even harm themselves terribly, if they can hurt opponents in the process. Suicide bombers are the most conspicuous case, but it goes on down to the lowly level of drivers who incur tickets for acting out "road rage." This constructs into the monstrosities of fascism. Kant believed more in rationality than we do today, but he was acutely aware of human information processing problems and social pressures, and took account of them. This is one bit of factual undergirding of his deontological ethics (Kant 1978).

Even if we allow rational calculation to mature, educated adults, what of young children? In practice, they have to be raised in a deontological world, and not a Kantian one of sweet reason, but an "irrational" one of "because I say so." Even parents who idealize learning through experience, natural curiosity, and situational morals draw the line when the child hits other children or steals the grocery money or starts running into a busy street. Good utilitarian parents try hard to explain why these are bad things to do, but ultimately they have to teach the child absolute rules, just as Kantians do. Moreover, the peer group insures that children learn many cultural rules as absolutes. These carry over into adult life, reason or no.

More important, there are some things that are so devastating to society as a whole that they have to be forbidden, even though they might make utilitarian sense for a lot of people for quite a long time. Slavery, armed robbery, aggressive war, genocide, repression of freedom of conscience, and other abridgments of others' rights have all seemed like excellent ideas in many societies over many centuries. In the end, they cost too much. Thus, they are condemned in the last analysis for utilitarian reasons—by Kant himself, among others. (Appeal to human flourishing is a thread running through all his writings.) Kant knew that in real-world societies, this final cost never appears till too late; the societies in question have institutionalized the evils, and kill anyone who challenges them. But the evils are also unacceptable because they trample on humans. They use humans as means (at best) rather than ends. Thus they have to be absolutely banned for Kantian reasons, long before their utilitarian evils appear.

Real-world societies that have eliminated slavery, repression, and so on have done so for both Kantian and utilitarian reasons. Modern utilitarians usually argue, therefore, that what is needed is not individual rationality, which easily declines into greed, but open and free dialogue and negotiation, to allow all positions due consideration. In fact, this was the basic reason why both Kant and the utilitarians were among the early champions of freedom—especially freedom of speech, press, and conscience. Neither deontology nor utilitarianism solves the basic problems; negotiation must do it (Habermas 1984).

The ideal example of a principle that satisfies both is the precautionary principle (Cooney and Dickson 2005 provide ecological applications; see also E. N. Anderson 2010; Cranor 2011). Kantian in origin, it requires utilitarian assessment. The only problem with it is that both sides of a controversy can use it. Global warming debates in the early 2000s pitted those who feared the dreadful effects of global warming, in the far future, against those who feared the dreadful effects in the immediate future, or even in the present, of economic chaos caused by sharply cutting fossil fuel use. Both sides pleaded the precautionary principle—one in regard to future humanity, the other in regard to immediate economic life. The world's most serious problem now is that too many people, left to themselves, not only want above all to hurt those that they perceive as potential threats, but tend to think of this as the highest moral good.

INTERACTIVE ETHICS

The post-Kantian philosopher and Jewish theologian Emmanuel Levinas worked out a system of ethics based on the importance of individuals interacting, an extension of Kant's taking everyone as ends rather than means (Levinas 1969, 1985, 1989, 1991, 1998a, 1998b, 1994). He realized that, if interaction and evaluation are *prior* to knowing and (consciously) being (and they are), then *ethics is prior to philosophy*, and *ethics is interactive, not individual*. This would not be "ethics" in the textbook sense—rational rules of conduct—but the real ethics and morals that govern our dealings with other people. Minds are literally created by intense, emotional interaction with those others (Mead 1964). Newborn infants understand helping, harming, and responsibility before they can "think" in any meaningful sense. Cogito, ergo sum is the end point in a long process. No wonder Descartes went so wrong (Damasio 1994). Every higher animal is living proof. He had forgotten that far more intense, searing, and deep physical and emotional experiences came before the rational, self-conscious, self-reflexive thought that he meant by cogito (Zajonc 1980). The very core and basis of those blazing experiences that form human lives are the experiences of help, harm, care, recognition, sociability, love, warmth, anger, forsakenness, and, perhaps most formational to selfhood, the anxiety of abandonment. From the fear of being alone and the warmth of active, warm interest in each other, infants construct a world.

Therefore, in its very beginning, before they have even the slightest idea of anything else, they live in and by social ethics. Ethics begins as lived experience—not as rules deduced rationally from dispassionate knowledge. Instead of ethics being deduced from philosophy, philosophy is deduced from ethics. A more skeptical reader may suspect that philosophy is all too often faked up by someone wishing to *avoid* ethics. Heidegger and Ayn Rand were not the first or the last persons to use philosophy to argue themselves out of acting like decent human beings.

Ever since Hume, philosophers have known that one cannot deduce an "ought" from an "is." Whence, then, *can* people deduce an "ought"? Only from spontaneous social nature: from the immediate sense of empathy with the Other, of understanding of his or her joy or pain and our own responsibility for increasing the joy and alleviating the pain. We cannot avoid choosing whether to be helpful or cruel. We know perfectly well what our more serious actions do to the Other, and we know we are responsible for the choice. From this comes our general decisions to be good or evil, supportive or sadistic. From these decisions, in turn, come moral laws of various types. Thus Levinas escaped the uncomfortable need of deontologists and utilitarians to regress to moral instincts in the end. He simply recognized the fact and started from there.

For Levinas, the key words are *responsibility* and *interest*. He meant being interested in others, not money added to capital. He reminds us of etymology: responsibility is the ability to respond. Interest is Latin: *inter est,* "being between." This does not imply a particular content to morality. It merely provides a grounding for moral codes. Societies must construct their own moral codes. This is where the debates come in: Kantian versus utilitarian, puritanical versus liberal, and so on.

For deeply religious Jews like Levinas, the priority of emotional, supportive interaction is enough to make us infinitely responsible for the Other. More skeptical readers, and those from other religious traditions, may need further justification and elaboration. Levinas's perception implies that we must combine utilitarian and deontological approaches rather than treat them as mutually exclusive. Levinas was a Jewish theologian as well as a phenomenological thinker: a Rabbinical Kantian. His position was reasonably close to that of Martin Buber (1947), but there are important differences. In his own words, he "attempted a phenomenology of sociality based on the face of the other . . . " (Levinas 1998a:148).

Levinas was motivated partly by a felt need to justify his Jewish ethics with phenomenology after Martin Heidegger made the latter a Nazi philosophy. Levinas was apparently unaware of the degree to which Heidegger was a committed, enthusiastic Nazi to the last (cp. Levinas 1998a:116 with Bourdieu 1991, Sluga 1993), but he knew enough to realize he had to devise a new phenomenological ethic that could not be coopted for mass murder (Levinas 1969:45–46; 1998:103–21). Unlike some modern apologists for Heidegger, Levinas knew that Heidegger's philosophy was integral to his Nazism, and not a separate part of Heidegger's thought. So Levinas sought to refute Nazi ideas, notably the submission or submerging of the will into the vast will of the power State (Levinas 1969:120).

Heidegger was not just a "good German"; he was an active developer of the Nazi worldview, and he became, so to speak, the Nazis' primary philosopher—a pet who was docile on a short leash or yapping at strangers—and he remained loyal to Nazism to the last. The claims that one can separate his philosophy from his Nazism are hopeful nonsense. He made it clear that he made no such separation. Heidegger's background and personal quirks explain some of his attraction to Hitler (Bourdieu 1991). Heidegger (following, in some measure, Nietzsche) privileged the lone individual, his authenticity, his will, and his power and control. (The male pronoun is used deliberately here.) This viewpoint was all too congruent with the *Triumph des Willens* (to remember the title of Leni Riefenstahl's brilliantly sickening film). The core philosophy of Nazism was one of the autarkic, authentic Will constructing a world through its power and control. Paradoxically, this led to a culture of blind obedience, and, ultimately, to one of mass extermination. Heidegger was more than willing to live with all these things.

Hence the need Levinas felt to construct a phenomenology that held inter-action and person-person relationships to be prior to Dasein and its ilk. To save phenomenology, Levinas combined it with Jewish ethics, and came to a powerful and radical vision. Levinas maintained that humans find their very selves in interaction with others. To this point, he followed well-known findings in social psychology. Martin Buber created a theology based on the relationship of I and Thou—of human and divinity. Social psychologists such as Ellen Berscheid have proposed "a science of interpersonal relation-ships" (Berscheid 1999:260). This is no new field; it was invented by the great German social scientist Wilhelm Dilthey (1985). It was transmitted to psychology by his student George Herbert Mead (1964). It was based on Kant (perhaps most directly Kant 1978), and forms part of a phenomenological humanism known as "neo-Kantianism."

Levinas pointed out that this makes other people literally infinitely impor-tant to us. Our very selves, our very being, depends on others. Unbarriered, unchecked experience of self (to say nothing of others) opens the world—we contact "totality and infinity" (Levinas 1969) by our experience of others. This is truly seeing the face of the other, as opposed to simply looking at him or her. Of course we can "see" in contemplation, without even having to be looking at that other presence. Yet this makes us individuals and keeps us so: "the idea of infinity, revealed in the face, does not only *require* a separated being; the light of the face is necessary for separation" (Levinas 1969:151). We are unique individuals, experiencing each other and learning from that. There is no isolation, but there is no group-mind or group-will either.

It is therefore reasonable to find what we actually do find: a spontaneous sense of caring and responsibility toward others. Here, Levinas has evidently been influenced, directly or indirectly, by sociology and anthropology. He was writing before the recent discoveries in primate studies that show a real if rudimentary morality in chimpanzees and bonobos (de Waal 1996); this work dramatically confirms Levinas's guarded claims. The infinite, or at least unbounded, importance of others is a rational corollary of our recognition of their importance to us. It is also an emotional response to those who make, shape, determine, and validate ourselves and our worlds.

Of course, such spontaneous feelings are not adequate in themselves, or we would be as happy as bonobos, with their policy of "make love, not war" (de Waal 1998). Kant grounded ethics in reason (cf. Grenberg 1999). Levinas takes us farther. He sees the experience of the other person as a far more shattering thing than Kant ever described. For Levinas, it is something like a mystical enlightenment. Clearly, he agrees with Kant that people are ends, not means. But they are the ends of a more brilliantly intense program. From this, the reason naturally infers a greater importance to humans. They are not just the ends of action; they are the very essence of ourselves, our lives, and our meanings as people.

This ethic solves the major environmental problems. Clearly, humans depend on the environment, and the human life support system cannot be ruined—that would destroy other people. But, more to the point, humans are not the only "others" out there. We owe a great deal to the environment. It, too, defines and creates us. It, too, presents itself to our clearest sight with mystical intensity. We have to save it. That is a paramount end of human action, and it eclipses all other imperatives save the imperative to care about and care for other humans. It also follows that preserving the environment from destruction is necessarily more a concern than preserving minor comforts and luxuries for a few humans. This follows both because the environment has its own importance and value, and because a really healthy environment is necessary for human survival. It is not moral to destroy the livelihood of millions to provide a few luxuries for a few hundred.

Clearly, again, humans near to us are more directly important than humans we never meet; but even the latter are of total concern, because as humans we are totally personally involved in humanity. We have to care about starving children in Bangladesh and about Ukrainians butchered in Putin's war. But we also need to care about rainforests and fish, because we are totally personally concerned with their lives. This realization would bring us close to Native American environmental ethics, which recognize trees, animals, mountains, and waters as persons—other-than-human persons and needing a different type of interaction, but persons nonetheless. Levinas speaks of face-to-face encounters as the basic human act. The "naked face"—the face we see when we drop barriers and defenses, and actually look at and encounter the person in front of us—is the "other" in pure, immediate form. Indeed, anyone who looks without defenses or distancing at another person cannot help being absorbed in the emotional tides that sweep through the mind.

It seems that biology gives us some "oughts." When we see anything, no matter how trivial, we automatically evaluate it as good or bad (Zajonc 1980; cf. Damasio 1994). Some degree of rudimentary morality thus inheres in all perception. Certainly, judging people as good or bad is an obvious given of the human condition. People do it all the time; they cannot help it. We may not be able to deduce "ought" from "is" by rational logic, but we do it anyway, quite automatically.

From the perception that the other is boundlessly important to us follows a great deal of moral concern. Levinas cautiously stops short of getting into difficult cases. He condemns violence and genocide, but he does not talk about everyday questions or about the environment. Reading Levinas through the lenses of Mead, Damasio, and de Waal is thought-provoking indeed. One must conclude that humans are moral animals far more than they are rational animals. People want social goodness—in others even if not in themselves. Even sociopaths and psychopaths know that they can exist only in a world where most people are good enough to be taken advantage of without their taking revenge. As noted earlier in this book, psychologists find that most people are never happier than when they are doing good to others (Lyubomirsky 2007, 2014). They feed the stranger and send money to orphanages halfway around the world. The curmudgeons among us show signs of brain damage or abusive childhoods, just as even the most loving dog can be whipped to savagery.

Levinas could argue that the worst evil comes from an odd mix of good and cruelty. It is the evil of "for your own good," on which Alice Miller has cast so pitilessly brilliant a light (Miller 1990). Such oppressive goodness ranges from mere parental ignoring of a child's cries to the massacre of six million people to "purify" the world for the rest. From parents to tyrants, from inquisitors to deans, wounded humans in authority are most sadistic when they seem most genuinely convinced that they are doing right (this brings back the underpinning of truth in Fiske and Rai 2014). Truly, humans are a moral animal, and they can be truly vicious only when they can argue themselves into thinking they mean well. Few observations could be more sobering.

This puts Levinasian ethics into something of a bind. We are infinitely responsible for the other, but must be infinitely careful not to let our responsibility get out of control. Infinite responsibility means everything it says: we have to be responsible not only for the other person, but, still more, for ourselves in the interaction. Paraphrasing Dostoevsky, he says "All men are responsible for one another, and 'I more than anyone else'" (Levinas 1998a:107). Thus, interaction becomes a complex and charged invocation, a "religion" in concentrated form (Levinas 1998b:7). Love and mercy follow, and justice should theoretically grow from them (Levinas 1998b:108). For Levinas, love is not the rather banal amour, but something like a sacred flame—people being open with each other and thus totally personally involved with each other.

Naturally, in such an interactive world, people will want to relieve the suffering of others, and this is the base of Levinas's working ethics. He never developed an ethical code in any cut-and-dried sense, but left it to humans to work out their own. He was concerned with the phenomenological grounding of ethics, not their specifics. Almost all he has to say about that is a quote (used as an example, at that—not as a commandment) about feeding the hungry (Levinas 1969:201). However, he is explicit about the beginnings of ethical life. As we have seen, he starts with responsibility. He works outward from that to a "help, not harm" ethic. He expects people to work out their own salvations from those grounding principles.

Social cognition, however, is naturally based on an interactive approach, and is our source for much of what follows; see reviews in the special issue of *Social Cognition* (vol. 17, issue 2, 1999; on interactive aspects of morals, see Damon 1999; Kohlberg 1983; Kagan and Lamb 1987). Some might see hyperbole in Levinas's "infinity," and prefer to read "large and unbounded." But even if our interactive experience requires only some large and unbounded share of responsibility, it still is so rich, complex, and foundational that the amount of responsibility must be very large, and must grow with further interaction. Usually, interaction means the kind of involvement that leads to love. Sometimes it produces hate, but we are still responsible. Sometimes the responsibility is of a hard kind—we are forced to kill or destroy that with which we interact. Killing in self-defense is only the most dramatic such case. Even eating bread takes the lives of countless wheat seeds, and of insects that inevitably were mixed in with them; vegetarianism is no easy out.

An inevitable corollary of his view is that we have an actual moral charge to be as open to experience and interaction as we can be. This does not mean sensation-seeking. It means opening ourselves to really seeing the other, face to face (Levinas 1998a). If we are to have an environmental ethic, we have to begin by seeing—actually *seeing*, not just looking at—the warblers, walnuts, and waters around us. It may be a less intensely and totally involving vision than that which we have when we actually *see* a fellow human being, but it is vitally important.

This involves two things. First, we have to cut the social and personal barriers that keep us from such clear sight. This cut requires at least some serious consideration. Second, we have to do the looking—to see those others who are truly and infinitely important. Usually, we see daily trivial problems and worries. At best, we see abstractions and simplified representations. Following Levinas takes serious moral discipline; we have to cut the old simplifications that blindfold us with indifference, and see the brilliant lights around us.

Such experience is reminiscent of Daoism and Zen, which teach the same opening to the world through meditative or contemplative clear sight. Indeed, there is a great deal that is parallel. (One source of the similarity lies in the Hasidic teaching stories that Martin Buber made famous; they were greatly influenced by Asian traditional religious teaching stories.) The difference lies in two things. First, Levinas does not build from a long meditative discipline that guides the looker to a certain sort of experience. He starts with the newborn baby (if not before), and looks at the whole development of interaction, from raw new experience onward. Second, he does not construct his experiences into a remote, otherworldly code that idealizes isolation and inner experience. He constructs it into a warm, directly human, totally engaged ethic of helping people.

Levinas himself lived a remote, philosophic lifestyle. Yet the revelation of Levinas's ethic is that one can go directly from clear sight of the world to caring and engaged behavior in the world. This may be no more than a sophisticated version of what all normal parents know by experience, at least about their children. Levinas assumed an impassioned but rational observer. He was aware that people are creatures of emotion, sympathy, and reason, and that all of those things are linked. If he had known of Antonio and Hannah Damasio's work he might well have incorporated it in his philosophy. Levinasian selves—the I and the other—are rational-emotional beings. The system has a place for feelings—indeed, is based on them. In this it differs from the cold and inhuman "reason" and the long, arid deductive chains that seem so sadly endemic to Western philosophy. Levinas's philosophy is a philosophy for living beings.

A corollary of Levinas's ethic is that we should see a full range of emotions as not only desirable but almost necessary to the human enterprise. In particular, we need to cultivate those emotions that are not barriers and defenses erected as a way of dealing with hurt and fear. Hurt and fear are natural enough; the point is to find rational or at least natural ways to cope with them. Once we drop barriers and defenses, we have dropped hate, cruelty, and prejudice, since these are (or are based on) defenses against fear. We can confront the natural world with warm interest and enthusiasm. We can contemplate it with the calm intensity of the Taoist poets and Zen artists. We can engage in it with the passionate and complex emotions that animate the Maya when they deal with their beloved and demanding forest, or the American small farmers of Aldo Leopold's vanished era. Levinas can be used as the charter for meditative discipline and for walking in woods and mountains, as well as for action on the humane front.

From this we can deduce Kant's categorical imperative and its variants and relations, from the Golden Rule itself to the recent ethical statements of Kantian philosophers such as Christine Korsgaard. But, following another fork, we can deduce utilitarian ethics. If we *see* those others—human or nonhuman—we naturally care about them and want to help them. From this comes the sense of consequences that we need to construct utilitarian or consequentialist morals.

Interaction brings us in touch with infinity. If our eyes are open, we see that the other is infinitely worthy of care and cherishing, and we have an open-ended responsibility to that other. That being sensed, we naturally love and care for the other, or at least for the world in which we interact. Reason extends the emotional message to a general, operational plan. Caring entails a help-not-hurt ethic—an ethic based on helping others and minimizing harm to them. This leads us to extend care logically. We are led to help, and to reduce harm, even though sometimes we have to hurt to help. We can calculate these things both empirically and logically. We are thus no longer dependent on raw experience and raw caring. Even when we are not in a Taoist meditative state of total openness to experience of the flower or leaf, we can figure out how to enjoy the flower without killing it.

It also implies tolerance, in all senses: putting up with the other, except in so far as he has to be stopped from doing harm; and also profiting from others' experiences, even if those experiences are new and strange to us. Again, the logic of caring and responsibility has taken us beyond the raw feeling, into a realm where we can calculate behavior rationally. We are led to figure out how much to tolerate, and how much to learn from others. The basic rules of responsibility to others preclude some types of tolerance: tolerance for genocide, for oppression, for prejudice-based hate, for instance. We are enjoined to oppose these to the last fiber of our being. Tolerance for massive or unnecessary damage to the environment is obviously in the same category, for the same reasons. Moreover, this means that valuing diversity is a foundational principle—for far more basic and important reasons than the utilitarian ones. We must experience, as thoroughly and directly as possible, all that the other can give to the world. This entails sympathy, charity, and mutual appreciation as absolute moral imperatives, and ones that are particularly crucial to the whole system.

Once we define terms through logical extension of caring and tolerance, we can build a structure by a utilitarian calculus of helping and not harming. We will look to maximize mutual aid and minimize harm. It is in this realm that we locate the general policy of minimizing government role in production while maximizing its role in protection, and of giving maximal control and decision power to the people actually using the resource. These become general rules of thumb because they work—not because they are absolute moral charges derived from Kantian imperatives.

The circle has to be completed. The final step is to check our utilitarian calculations against our own direct, impassioned, open experience. It is all too easy to follow a logical path to an insane conclusion. No doubt every evil has been justified at some point or other by recourse to moral arguments, often both utilitarian and Kantian. When we reach a point of doubt, the appropriate behavior is to sit down and look at the world again—dropping prejudices and logical extensions long enough to see that other, that being for whom we are responsible. When we see him, or her, or it, face-to-face, we have the space to reconsider. This passage, however, shows one limit of Levinas's philosophy:

it assumes that the thinker is a reasonably normal, caring, rational human. It does not work at the social level in a world where deranged psychopaths routinely take over countries, start wars, and murder millions. That world will have to be regulated by cold law.

A morality based on love might work if everyone could love everyone else. This being dubiously achievable, the best we can seriously hope for is a morality based on care. Even this may be too much, at least if caring is a warm, deeply felt emotion. Cool caring—responsibility, civic duty, consideration for others' rights—is perhaps the best we can hope for in these parlous times. But we can hope for that. The corollaries include personal courage, the only real security; real enjoyment, without puritanism or conformity hindering it; and really rational action. The time for quietist retreat is long past. Hermits and divines in previous eras could retain their integrity and shine as examples. Today, there is no escape, and we have to stand and work actively to help.

MORALS INTO ACTION: WORKING WITH IDEAS

Sophisticated morality from religion and philosophy is needed, though intuition and childhood interaction do so well, because there are always exceptions: people born sociopathic or psychopathic. Much more common is the problem of the natural human tendency to overvalue one's own immediate concerns. Sometimes, even unselfish concerns get too much play. The most dedicated, selfless, ethical persons can, with the best will in the world, feature their personal crusades at the expense of all else.

Formal morality deals with another human curse: blame. People attribute intention to everything, even the weather. They are particularly prone to attribute evil intentions to everything and everybody that seems to oppose their preferred interests. This lies behind a great deal of fascism. When people attribute bad things to innocent others, morality is needed. Also, people often act impulsively, without thought, especially on fear, anger, and hate. The need to control this has been perhaps the most widespread justification for ethical rules.

Humans feel a strong sense of outrage—of deep *wrong*—when the most trivial and silly social codes are violated. There are countless proper souls who are more outraged over seeing someone use the wrong fork, or wear ill-matched clothes, than over the deaths of millions in Africa. Apparently, this part of the moral sense has more to do with social-membership and class markers than with deeply meaningful rights and wrongs. Massacres and genocides often turn on trivial differences in religion, language, and culture. Edward Gibbon's famous example was the war over *homoousia* versus *homoiousia* that nearly destroyed the Roman Empire (Gibbon 1995:vol. 3, p. 787). Christians, supposedly peaceful, were fighting over obscure and trivial doctrinal matters that not even the priests understood.

Finally, there are, inevitably, times when moral rules come in conflict. Conflicting loyalties, and real moral dilemmas, are daily occurrences in many lives. Many will remember, from introductory philosophy, Lawrence Kohlberg's (1983) story of Heinz and the medicine: His wife is deathly sick and he has no money, so must steal the medicine or watch helplessly while she dies. Almost everybody says "Steal it!" But a good philosophy professor will go to ask: What if his wife is only badly sick, not on death's door? What if Heinz has the money but has to trade off food and rent? That gets to the real choices that require moral philosophy.

Humans have a deep, intuitive, innate moral sense. But this sense is not always a good guide to ethics. On the other hand, it is inevitably there, a powerful, deep-rooted, emotional force that is absolutely essential to human moral behavior. One cannot predict from any economic data the content or shape of moral codes. We know only that there will be *some* code.

Aristotle was already quite conscious of intuitionist ethics (Aristotle 1955:89). Along with later writers, he tried to maintain that people really want to do each other good, but sometimes need to have this urge jogged. Hopeful writers of a later age tried to maintain that everyone really wants to be good to everyone else. Henry Sidgwick, dean of English ethicists, was one such (Sidgwick 1907:501), but even he had to admit many people were a bit undeveloped in that regard (Sidgwick 1907:502—yes, the very next page). Aristotle, writing for aristocrats, could finesse this by saying that people who did not want decent civic values were coarse, low, or sick. We cannot sustain that claim. They are too often our rulers.

Derek Parfit (1989) pointed out that even one's "self" is a problematic concept. He showed (following Hume) that the only clear, consistent, infallible way to run your life is to do exactly what you want to do right now—the ultimate in short-term, narrow strategies. This may be clear and consistent, but it will not do for an ethic.

There are total skeptics, as well as post-Nietzscheans, postmodern amoralists, and other rejectors of any moral charge. The skeptical position is not a mere analytic abstraction. In the modern United States, even family morality has widely broken down (in spite of rigorous laws); what hope is there for the great family of Gaia? Kant might say we need morality to control both external negation leading to general indifference, and internal negation leading to malicious destruction.

Humans are also capable of nastiness and cruelty inconceivable to a chimpanzee or macaque. Moral intuitions are not, by themselves, adequate guides to prosocial behavior. Too often, morals are outright destructive. Revenge, feud, and oppression of minorities are often considered to be moral imperatives. Particularly striking is the horrific treatment of women in a vast number of societies around the world (Margolis 2021). These various evils prove our social nature, for our most horrible acts (war, genocide, political and religious repression) are done collectively to collective "enemies." The most evil human acts often require the most loyalty and cooperation, as in the case of the Nazi atrocities. People being social animals, the irrationally social individuals win out in society. Recall that a world of rational individual choosers in the classic Hobbesian sense would be defeated, one by one, by even a pair of "irrationally" social humans that could cooperate to take them on one at a time.

A real-world case of social irrationality is presented by voting. Notoriously, it is irrational to vote; the chances of one's vote making a difference are often less than the chances that one will be killed in a traffic accident while driving to the polls. Therefore, the rational people who do not vote find themselves ruled by the less rational. Admittedly, this explains all too much about the observed functioning of the United States. However, even this beats totalitarian systems, in which one or a few persons, inevitably less than perfectly rational, make all the key decisions.

So instinct and emotion may ground morality, but the final elaborate moral codes of a society are social contracts in a solid Hobbesian sense. People draw up codes through conscious practice. Codes are not carefully planned. Those that are never seem to work. Codes actually happen through constant practice and renegotiation (Bourdieu 1978, 1990; Giddens 1984). Another corollary of these findings is that morality needs to be represented in an emotionally compelling way. Since humanity began, this issue has been resolved through religion. A rational morality is sold by irrational but compelling beliefs, images, symbols, allegories, and artistic glories (Durkheim 1995). God or gods provided the foundation in past ages, but any comparative scrutiny of sects shows that people develop all manners of moralities, up to and including Hitler's Nazism, and then claim God or the gods revealed those. Even within small traditional communities, morality, and consequently religion, changes fast. This gives no consolation to those claiming morality is divinely revealed. Religion continues to be highly effective in such moral matters as conserving nature, as shown by the research of Leslie Sponsel (2012) and others (Johnston 2013; Kent 2013), but also by the worldwide attention given to Pope Francis's encyclical *Laudato Si* (2015).

Alexis De Tocqueville pointed out that "those who prize freedom only for the material benefits it offers have never kept it long" (de Tocqueville, quoted in Elster 1993:145). The same is obviously true of almost any other good, as de Tocqueville would surely have agreed. It is certainly true of conserving nature. When that is done for purely economic reasons, the result is rarely good. Lovers of forests, fish, and mountains have generally been the leaders; responsible citizens concerned about humanity or community have been most important of all; narrow economism rarely saves anything by itself (cf. Elster 1993).

In fact, jogging people into thinking of their moral acts as self-interested or financially motivated usually makes them less moral (Bowles 2006). Experiments and surveys from all over the world show that people will usually act fairly decently, and that getting them to think "money" will change this. Rewarding people financially for being good can be highly counterproductive, as many parents know (often to their sorrow).

Ideally, societies allow people to try to bring social codes into accord with their own basic moral views, as these develop through personal experience. People self-consciously abstract moral principles from their life experiences, and negotiate morality in their lives and communities on the basis of this. The Kantian loner who reasons out his morals in splendid isolation is an ideal type, not a reality, as Kant knew perfectly well (Kant 1978; and, following him, Rawls 1971).

Chapter 7

Sustaining Social Harmony

THE VALUE OF MORAL ACTION

The key point of this book is that mass violence and hatred do not just happen. They come directly from hatred, which in turn comes from fear and defensiveness, often occasioned by lack of control and by rivalry with structural-opponent groups or outright enemies and competitors. This fear and hate is then exploited by power-hungry leaders, and, above all, the conservative and reactionary interests that fund them and their movements. Money is used to whip up hate, and the leaders who channel it commit genocide when they have the power and are challenged.

The cure is reasonable self-control, self-reliance, and confidence, but also respect and responsibility in the face of others and inevitable differences and conflicts. The good wolf is fed by putting up with these and dealing rationally with them. The bad wolf is fed by petulance and spite toward even one's nearest and dearest, which inevitably leads to even greater malevolence toward rival groups.

More to the point, though, organized political violence and hatred require a great deal of money, donated to or spent on rabble-rousing politicians. Tracing the money to its source, and blocking that, is the most important single thing in stopping fascism and extremist violence. One basic home of violence, cruelty, and bad wolves is the extractive estate or industry owned by rich landlords (or resource-lords or rentiers) and worked by landless laborers without rights. Another is the munitions and "defense" industry. The first need in helping the world is to eliminate such social formations. The next is to level up the oppressed, such that everyone in society has equal rights before the law. None should be denied appeal and recourse. In the United States today, much of the economy is owned by billionaires who are far above the law—even in the extremely rare event that they are found guilty of something, they get a nominal fine, not prison. Normally, the cost of bringing them before justice is impossibly high for any authority, even the United States Department of Justice.

Work in the giant primary-production enterprises, since ancient Egypt and Mesopotamia, has been done by servile labor. Today, it is often done by noncitizens, very often undocumented immigrants. They have no enforceable rights, no appeals, and no hope if caught. They are thrown in cells and then deported. They had some rights before Trump, but now have none that can be enforced. This is a formula for continued increase in fascist rule in the country.

One direct and immediate intervention needed is blocking the funding of extremist and exclusionary movements. This would involve reversing the "Citizens United" decision of the Supreme Court, and then requiring disclosure of funding sources, especially hate groups, and restriction of campaign spending to reasonable levels. Second comes voting and otherwise working against the rise of clearly psychopathic or rabble-rousing leaders who exploit hatred. Third comes systematic and thorough refutation of public lies of the Fox News type. Laws against fraud and false advertising should be deployed, but the lies should be countered with truth, rather than suppressed. Freedom of speech must be defended, but freedom to spend billions bankrolling hateful lies runs close to violating fraud and misrepresentation rules, and certainly leads to violence. Fourth would be restrictions on lobbying and outlawing the revolving-door practice of moving lobbyists and corporate managers into regulatory positions, then letting them return to lobbying and managing. Fifth comes ending subsidies to reactionary corporations, always a difficult process but possible (Inchauste and Victor 2017 provide many plans). These plans are obviously targeted at the current United States, but they work with appropriate adaptations anywhere. Basically, the idea is to do everything possible to defund the extremists.

Outlawing the bad, specifically economic ones, is more important than helping with good things. Helping the good leads too easily to subsidies, and on to unfair and unequal treatment that corrupts the best of the good. Even so, we have to forge ahead on both fronts. Fighting the lies involves more than disproof and shutdown. It requires a counternarrative, to carry the argument for responsibility and the public good. Classically, religion and patriotism held this function, but they are in a shaky state now. Leaving nationalist ideas to the evil leaders has been a disastrous mistake. Reviving true patriotism—loyalty, but taking that to mean doing everything to get the country back on the right track when it goes wrong—seems inescapable.

Doing good—helping and caring—should be as profitable as possible to as many people as possible, and vice versa for harm. Rewards need not be financial. Social approbation should go to doing good, but in the modern

United States attention and respect tend to go to troublemakers at all levels. The deontological calculus suggests that people should develop a morality of doing good and being responsible. The Chinese tried that too, with the Confucian (and later Buddhist) teaching that leaders should be moral and should be followed according to their moral level. This did not work well, so the rewards-and-punishments strategy was combined with it, officially in the Han Dynasty and widely thereafter. The rewards-and-punishments strategy failed as badly as the Confucian one when tried alone, as in the Qin Dynasty; it took both high moral suasion and low material interest to make people act civilly.

Many societies around the world have managed to be extremely peaceful. Some are traditional, with long histories of nonviolence. Others are modern nations. Some of these have long been fairly peaceful, like Switzerland, but others have earlier histories of extreme violence, such as Scandinavia and Japan. Some countries cycle from one to the other state; Japan was uncontrollably violent in the sixteenth century, peaceful thereafter until the extremely violent wars of the early to mid-twentieth century, and peaceful since. A major worldwide investigation into peaceful societies is now in progress, and will hopefully tell us how they did it (Coleman and Fry 2021).

Rich and Kavanagh recommend: "Increase transparency. . . . Elevate experts. . . . Build a diverse administration. . . . Invest in civic education and development" (Rich and Kavanagh 2020). The ethicist Peter Singer and his group have a different set of priorities: "strengthen economies, reduce inequality, improve metrics, address funding, protect identity, expedite aid, save more lives, support mental health, democratize data access, boost direct communication" (Daar et al. 2018). What is notable about these two plans is that they do not mention global warming, epidemics, fascism, or the other problems most of us would see as the desperate crises requiring attention. They are looking at the backstory: the public institutions needed to fix anything, from climate change to corruption (see also Neuborne 2019).

This is thought-provoking, but some other things would have to be done first, to allow these to be deployed. The first need is a return to truth and to the rule of law. The United States needs to restore civil discourse, freedom of speech, freedom of religion, separation of powers, separation of church and state, balance of powers, and other Constitutional guarantees that were abandoned from 2017 to 2021. This may require truth and reconciliation commissions at all levels, and a Congressional truth commission with equal numbers of Republicans and Democrats, establishing facts about key issues and stating them publicly. But above all: all nations, worldwide, must control hate money and lie money—the political donations that fuel the bigotry machine.

Our experts on evil agree that empathy is a key value (see esp. Baron-Cohen 2011; Batson 2011; Zaki 2019). It can be taught. Empathetic people can convert even hardened fascists and terrorists, as shown in careful studies (Zaki 2019). Progressive as well as right-wing social movements worldwide are meticulously documented by Chase-Dunn and Almeida (2020); there are many large movements against fascism and corruption, in almost every major nation. Erika Chenoweth has been very active in pointing out that nonviolent resistance works, and in speaking for it worldwide (Chenoweth 2021; Chenoweth and Stephan 2012). In a world where reactionary governments are heavily armed, we will have to rely on this hope, and Chenoweth tells us how to do it. An enormous study of all protest movements from 1900 to 2006 found the same: peaceful movements work if they are large and united (Dahlum et al. 2019).

Solidarity and hope are vital in politics and movements. It is actually possible, though difficult, to see "all humanity [as] my ingroup," and we can increase and develop that (McFarland et al. 2012). Scandinavia has now gotten as close to creating ideal societies as the world has come so far. They have outdone even utopian colonies by a fairly wide margin. The formula is simple: public support of everybody when it comes to necessities of life and the all-important task of educating the young, but private enterprise and considerable personal freedom for the rest of life. Science is promoted and applied.

Good comes when a few really dedicated well-meaning or inquisitive people develop really good ideas, from vaccination to women's suffrage to solar power, then build a movement around it, and then convince enough elites that it is in their immediate major self-interest to go with it. Many (if not most) elites care little about anything but their own power, so they go with ideas for progress and improvement only if they can see such interest.

Good involves maximum inclusiveness, which means excluding hate-mongers or at least shutting them down, though looking for allies everywhere else. This implies mutual aid, solidarity, and cooperation, as well as negative feedback in conflicts instead of positive unless attacked and without alternatives other than violent resistance. Mutual aid must be encouraged by constant linguistic cues. People react much better to requests to work together than to simple orders or even to information about "everyone else doing it" (or a large number of others doing it).

Evil usually comes the same way: a small group motivated by hate and desire for power starts a movement and eventually takes over. Revolutions that totally replace the elites with new leaders usually turn sour. This has been shown by the fate of religions since history began, and more recently of communism, Latin American coups, African revolts, and too many anti-colonial "liberation" movements.

Strict social and moral rules work, even if unwritten, but written and enforceable is better. Vague principles accomplish little. Much of our problem is the imperative of focusing on immediate threats above all else—all love, care, future benefits, anything. Those who feel they are downwardly mobile or threatened by other groups are going to organize evil unless they feel secure and hopeful. The fascist coalition worldwide now consists largely of people who feel they are relatively losing from today's changes. The leaders and the funders of right-wing movements are the leaders of the giant corporations that are genuinely threatened by progress: fossil fuels, the military-industrial complex, and their allies. Their troops are the traditionally religious (threatened by secularism), the less-educated working class, the rural sector almost worldwide, and many older traditional people who simply feel threatened by change. Governments and change advocates should do everything possible to reassure such people and keep them from losing out. The rural sector in particular is obviously vital to human survival, producing essentially all the food and other necessities, and losing it to the enemies of humanity is not tolerable.

The United Nations has been good about setting goals: health, labor fairness, preserving the great achievements of traditional cultures, peace, environmental protection, and others. These are what can be called "process goals" (Anderson and Anderson 2020). These goals can never be fully achieved, but every move in the direction of achieving them is beneficial. The world can never have truly perfect health, but anything that makes people healthier is a benefit. One can add integrity and considerateness. Conversely, many goals are best served by moderation, including everyday pleasures like eating, drinking, and sex, but also such civic goods as harmony. A society with too much harmony will die of stagnation and lack of innovation. Setting goals for the future depends heavily on separating process goals from moderation goals. The good is always slow in coming, by gradual steps. Learning to play a musical instrument is the model: one slowly gets better, is never perfect, but always improves. There is a folktale of a great musician who played on his deathbed, just before passing. Asked why he was still practicing on the instrument, he answered "I want to play it better."

CIVIL RESISTANCE

Erica Chenoweth (2021; Chenoweth and Stephan 2012) has described the striking success of nonviolent civil disobedience and resistant action, from street demonstrations to economic campaigns. She started as a skeptic, but found such measures worked better than violent resistance in the face of authoritarian or bigoted rule. Changes of government occurred thanks to long-running civil campaigns in South Africa, Sudan, Tunisia, and many other countries. The US civil rights movement is well known. In recent years, "maximalist nonviolent campaigns that were facing violent repression succeeded 45% of the time, while violent ones only succeeded 22% of the time" (Chenoweth 2021:92). She found by comprehensive research that it takes only about 3.5 percent of the public getting involved in active civil campaigns to achieve victory, at least if the passive noninvolved majority is tacitly behind them (Chenoweth 2021:114). The final sentence of the book says that "it works much more than its detractors ant you to know" (Chenoweth 2021:252).

They succeed best when they are really mass movements (not small-scale), consistently nonviolent (not allowing opponents to claim "riots" because of a tiny disruptive group), led by a respected group of people (not self-consciously leaderless), and above all economically targeted. Boycotts, strikes, slowdowns, sick-outs, embargoes, and similar economic measures work very well if consistent. Also effective are anti-administration disruption: burning draft cards, overloading systems with disobedient actions or even with calls and letters, and otherwise blocking administrative action at all points (Chenoweth 2021). Martin Luther King Jr. identified five critical steps: Information gathering; education; personal commitment; discussion/negotiation; direct action; reconciliation (Chenoweth 2021:72–73). Chenoweth repeatedly stresses the need for organization and leadership; spontaneous and self-consciously anarchist movements almost always quickly run out of steam and collapse.

Overall, solidarity, mutual aid, mutual support, and fairness are the great overarching values and animating ideals of civil movements of all kinds. Gandhi and King were masters of invoking and living these ideals. They are conspicuously absent from political debate today. The right hates solidarity and unity above all else, and seeks to maximize hatred and division. The rest of the political spectrum is too concerned with immediate pocketbook issues to do much with such high goals. Human survival now depends on escaping the pocketbook, which is too closely connected with environmental ruin and with racism and exploitation. Solidarity remains the basis of survival.

COMPASSION AS MORAL ACTION

Readers by now will know that humans act from deep emotional drives more than from rational self-interest or other rational considerations. Thus, political appeals to pocketbook issues, even the most compelling, necessarily fail when playing against emotionality. The right wing exploits this, whipping up hate to make majorities vote against their most urgent self-interest. This has been an astonishingly successful tactic in the United States and dozens of other countries.

Hope comes from appealing to the other end of the emotional spectrum: caring, cooperation, concern, love, affection, common decency, integrity, and help, in the face of fear and hate. Religion used to serve this function, but does less of it now, in spite of such moral teachers as the Dalai Lama and Pope Francis. It is common experience that good is done—when it is not simply part of a job—by people motivated by care and responsibility more than by people motivated by fear and anger. The fearful, angry souls more likely to be doing harm, and they abound on the left as well as on the right.

The traditional religious virtues of compassion and charity increasingly depend on private individuals. An ominous development is the abandonment of small-government conservatism. As recently as the 1920s, we were spared the worst of conservative ideas, because conservatives kept governments small. Hitler changed that, and modern right-wingers from Trump to Bolsonaro follow him. Conservatives in power now create huge governmental systems based on militarism, subsidies, surveillance, repression, and vast resources for high elites. The ordinary people pay increasing taxes, but see few services in conservative-led countries, because the tax money goes to subsidies, military, prisons, and police. This makes the ordinary taxpayers still more disaffected, and willing to vote for the right wing. Increasing taxes and decreasing services is a deadly combination, as Ibn Khaldun and many since have pointed out.

Ultimately, humanity's best hope is to unite the non-fascist majority—the vast majority of humans—behind a renewed commitment to public compassion and charity. This is necessary not only to counter outright fascist teachings such as racism and hypermilitarism, but also the arguments that "freedom" means my freedom to bully you, an argument popular with both left and right (Costello et al. 2022). The right adds the ideas that "free enterprise" means the right of giant subsidized corporations to crush small independent businesses, and "defense" means the right of big nations to invade and take over small ones on the basis of imagined threats. The communist left has tended to add the idea that "workers' rule" means rule by tyrannical apparatchiks, "public ownership" means ownership by a few oligarchs, and so on. The only way to counter arguments of these types is to argue from a position of helping all, with compassion and charity as the emotional drives behind it. This can only come from something like equality and equity; current levels of inequality worldwide simply cannot coexist with democracy, freedom, or widely shared prosperity (Piketty 2017, 2020). Inequality in wealth is bad enough, but inequality in power is worse; some is inevitable in modern society, but the current disproportion in power and control between public and private elites and the rest.

These further imply caring, civility, and considerateness, which need to be taught in school along with reading and math, and for the same reasons:

survival in the real world depends on these (Baron-Cohen 2011; Zaki 2019). Simple compliments do amazing wonders, as shown by sober scientific research; people greatly underestimate the power and value of this seemingly minor behavior (Zhao and Epley 2021).

The classic paradox of tolerance, flagged by philosophers from Plato to Karl Popper, is that it cannot extend to tolerance for intolerance. It can, actually, up to a point, but once the intolerance spills over in genocide or threats of it, tolerance has to go out the window. In the end, tolerance, like freedom, sex, and beer, is wonderful in moderation but less so the more of it we have. There are two kinds of tolerance: Putting up with people so far as possible, and at least trying to understand and deal with people one cannot put up with. Tolerating ordinary bad neighbors are in the first category, tolerating Nazis and violent racists in the second. This means, above all, countering the convenient lies that whip up motivated belief in the superiority of one's own group. It means zero tolerance for the lies that divide the good and set them against each other while uniting the bad.

JUSTICE AS MORAL ACTION

The basic opposite of evil is justice. Following John Rawls (1971), this means fairness, as well as tolerance, support, and enforcement of the peace. Recall that Rawls's idea of fairness is based on the image of a person choosing what he (sic) would choose for himself if he had no idea what he was going to become: broke, disabled, sick, powerful, rich, young or old. Observers noted that this was basically a formalization of the Golden Rule. The masculine assumption here was immediately targeted by women philosophers, who proposed that a woman's view might well run to nurturance and protection rather than dispassionate and abstract philosophy (Nussbaum 2001, but she supports Rawls's general idea). G. A. Cohen criticized Rawls's individualism, pointing out correctly that a whole society is required to implement justice (G. A. Cohen, 2000). Rawls actually admits this, but wastes little time explaining it. A group of psychologists tested Rawls's thought experiment in real-world settings, and found that thinking of oneself as being in all sorts of situations did indeed make people more fair and reasonable (Huang et al. 2019).

Amartya Sen (1998) addressed issues of social choice in connection with both utilitarian calculus and Rawls's Kantian theory, using both to escape the impossibility paradoxes of social choice. These paradoxes involve the impossibility of pleasing everyone or even knowing what everyone wants, and thus of coming to any informed conclusion about what social welfare really is or could be; the deciders themselves must be either democratic, in which case they have all manner of disparate wants, or autocratic, in which case one person (most likely a difficult individual) has to pretend to know all. Sen pointed out that with ideas of justice such as Rawls's, we can conclude that at least people are better off with food, clothing and shelter than without, and generally better without oppression and unfair treatment too, even if they may believe in a traditional religion that consigns them to a lowly place. Thus welfare can be advanced, according to available information. The implication seems to be that such information should speak to both utilitarian and deontological ethics.

Sen pointed, further, that fairness and the Golden Rule can only go so far (Sen 2009). Modern societies have to have some sort of leadership hierarchy. Societies must restrain schizophrenics and other dangerously mentally ill. We also have to deal with children, and with those whose minds have gone— people with terminal cases of Alzheimer's disease, for example. We cannot simply let them die. We must restrain psychopaths and incorrigible criminals for society's survival.

Thus, justice must be based on overall help versus hurt, *coded into law.* In a small-scale society, popular opinion can take care of it. This is where Levinasian ethics should come in. As differentiation and hierarchy increase, social regulation gets steadily more difficult. Violence and gratuitous harm increase to the chiefdom and early state level, then decrease as states get more and more differentiated and able to implement the rule of law. The ultimate opposition to evil is actively caring for people: valuing diversity, cooperating, showing loyalty and integrity, and acting for everyone's best interests.

The founding fathers' idea of freedom was more about freedom *from* than freedom *to.* Many came from backgrounds that had experienced religious repression in Europe, and a large percentage of the early settlers came to America fleeing religious persecution. (Most of the authors' own ancestors did.) Persecution on the basis of class, origin, and other personal matters was common. Many admitted that slavery was incompatible with their ideals; some had no enslaved persons, at least one freed his, and the issue caused debate and real guilt.

The United States was based on the Enlightenment ideas that *my rights stop where yours start* and *we're all in this together.* I am free to worship as I please, but not free to stuff my religion—or, for that matter, my atheism— down your throat. I am free to eat what I want, but not to force you to eat it. Especially this means protecting the weak from the strong. I have the right to avoid being forced to do what stronger people want me to do—that is the most important founding principle of the United States. Bullying is not morally right anywhere, and it is illegal here.

A more difficult issue, constantly raised in cases of public safety, is how much the government can encroach on my freedom to protect your life. This has led to fights over seat belts, gun control, masks and social distancing during the COVID-19 pandemic, vaccinations, and many other issues where a minor restriction on everyone is necessary to save the lives of the vulnerable. (Social distancing was even described as "commie," reviving a cold-war epithet used against communists.) Common sense, and universal behavior in all functioning nations, is to make people bear small costs to prevent large disasters. The most successful nations today are those that are most successful at nation-building, in the sense of true unity from diversity. The United States is moving rapidly in the wrong direction.

RESPECT AS MORAL ACTION

The core of many small-scale religions is respect: respect for people, for the environment, for all lives. The authors have encountered respect in one form or another as a core value from the Akha of south China to the Mongols, Tungus, and all Native American groups known to us. It is the key and most important of all ethics in many small-scale societies around the world. It means, focally, seeing others as they are and seeing the good and worthy in that, but also seeing the bad, taking it seriously, and working to stop it. It then means considerateness and civility, which imply reasonable, polite, low-key, understated, questioning, nondogmatic, humble, deferential, and in general bland and positive behavior. Tolerance and valuing others are also part of respect.

Ideally, it includes help: mutual aid, solidarity, lifting up, and charity. Compassion is valuable, but can become a putdown, like pity and sympathy. Building on this, another level of morality includes learning and knowledge; care and caring; the Franciscan virtues of patience, courage, wisdom, and industry; and everyday reasonable and responsible behavior. This goes onward to the personal virtues of spirituality, appreciation, awe, reverence, and the like. Respect is not adequate, however, to deal with the basic problem of taking too much offense at slights or differences. This sort of overreaction comes from fear of loss of control, so self-efficacy and self-control can cure it. No one has enough of those, so the foundation of morality involves mutual strengthening and empowerment.

The immediate opposite of evil extremism is not love or caring, but reasonableness. Nobody would create net harm if they and their society were reasonable, in the sense of able to balance benefits and costs and to stop and think before acting. The problem is that most people have that built-in babyish insecurity. Good upbringing, making them secure and self-efficacious while providing good cultural models, is the cure.

People are naturally scared of social isolation, and then go with conformity as the safest path. People are not born responsible. They start out as babies, incapable of understanding the concept. They must learn painfully to be responsible for themselves, let alone others. People do not simply self-improve, or even seek enjoyment or happiness; they go for social acceptance and approbation. They thus improve not by self-driven desire by conforming to better and higher standards, and learning to enjoy the deeper and more satisfying things their society values, at least until they get old enough to act independently for fun or benefit.

Responsibility develops only in a stable, ongoing social group with mutual respect. It is generally developed in families and then in the community. The breakdown of community in the modern world, with its mass media and giant corporations, has meant the breakdown of responsibility (see, e.g., Habermas 1984; Putnam 2000). One hopes that communities will develop, but meanwhile the schools have much to do in developing this needed quality.

STRATEGIES FOR SOCIAL HARMONY

A number of successful interventions backed and described by Rezarta Bilali and the great genocide scholar Ervin Staub (Bilali and Staub 2017; Staub 2018) involve media campaigns to promote peace, cooperation, and calm. Less successful are committees, commissions, pious hopes, and political rhetoric. Bilali and Staub provide successful plans for media interventions. When conflict happens, innate good or compassion or considerateness help, but are never enough in the long run. Society is saved only by superior third-party authority—moral, legal, or forceful—making the combatants sit down and negotiate. This requires deploying commonsense economic and political arguments, and constant pleas for solidarity. Then, damping down—de-escalation—is what works.

It also requires creating a social system without huge inequities in power or wealth, since large inequities allow evil leaders to take over and seize full power. Immanuel Kant thought that democracy, international institutions, and international economic ties and mutual dependence would bring peace (Kant 2009). A recent worldwide study showed he was right; the world needs all three (Cranmer et al. 2015).

The good wolf is a local animal, slow to act. The bad wolf unites with others in fanatical mass movements such as fascism, and can act fast. Good people are often satisfied with little, but bad people often want boundless wealth, power, and prestige. Teachers, nurses, and aid workers are ill-paid and put up with it; CEOs and corrupt politicians cannot rest, demanding more and more riches and glory.

A threat to social standing, even a tiny one, is an existential threat on many levels. The key is intervention at every point. People must learn to react calmly and rationally to insults and attacks, rather than brooding and working themselves up into fury, or, at the other extreme, trying to ignore attacks and let them go. If attacks are serious, they must be handled somehow. People must learn not to let defense move into hatred. Cowardly defensiveness and resulting overreaction to negatives is the basis of most evil, though also of much good, since people are as easily scared into doing what's right as into doing what's wrong. Cultural and social pressures make the difference.

Above all, they must learn not to displace hatred onto scapegoats—the real problem behind racism, religious bigotry, and most other forms of hate. Finally, if they are hopelessly lost in racism and bigotry, they must be prevented from acting it out. No hate-driven violence or prejudicial behavior can be accepted. Every functional society must recognize those four intervention points and do everything possible to resolve tensions and conflicts at every point. This requires a general morality of caring, civility, considerateness, and responsibility. It also requires rational consideration at every point. A corollary is the need to respect every individual, and see people—following Kant—as always ends, never means.

In order upward, the effective ways of changing behavior are rational argument, money, law, public opinion/conformity, praise/adulation, real leadership, and ostracism (or threat of it). One problem in the United States now is that prestige comes from being as extreme as possible, whether right or left, and reasonableness is attacked savagely.

"Because conflict is unavoidable, forgiveness is crucial for maintaining social relationships. People must be able to move past negative motivations if they are to retain their valuable social partners" (Forster et al. 2020:862). Forgiveness of intimates or distant contacts includes not just words, but actions showing restored friendship and good wishes. It involves moving along a continuum from breakdown of relationships to returning to good will (Forster et al. 2020 provide a measure).

EDUCATION FOR SOCIAL HARMONY

In the end, only education can save us, which is frightening given the current dismal state of funding in that area. Public and private, formal and informal, in school and out of it, education must be decently funded or civilization does not survive. Since emotions tend to get out of control, we need to have social and educational controls accordingly. Raising problem children has led to better insights into all child-rearing (Greene 2016). The key to all is teaching children to avoid cowardly defensiveness; they must deal with attacks, threats, and stress by more rational means.

They also need to have their natural interest in the world encouraged and empowered, rather than shot down by endless drills and standardized tests. They need to be empowered in seeking beauty and excitement and quality in life. Otherwise, they become discouraged and fail to work for a better world.

This brings us back to Mencius, who pointed out repeatedly that only education can bring out the good in humans and prevent the bad from taking over. Education must focus on individuals taking responsibility for collective well-being. Children in Confucian societies are trained in this from birth onward, with no new rights coming unless the child also takes on new responsibilities for self and society. With maturity, the growing person finds meaning in work and love. Desperately needed is a return to serious teaching of history and civics. We also need education on the environment (Louv 2005).

Good wolves also delight in and learn from intense experiences of beauty, joy, and delight, as well as in enduring hardship and winning over hard times. The arts, within living memory, were shared within communities and held them together by engaging people's emotions and allowing them to celebrate as groups. This function has been almost lost, as arts have been taken over by giant corporations and deployed to make people even more passive and alienated than they are already. This has been one of the more destructive aspects of modern civilization. It guts communities and replaces vital self-expression with mindless conformity or snobbism.

Also key is dealing with hateful lies and why they are so plausible. They are tailored to fit cultural stereotypes and expectations, but basically to speak to cowardice and greed. Teaching children to read media critically, and to recognize hateful lies, is now the most important thing for schools to do. Schools need to manage peer contacts—healthy groups vs. drug gangs. They need to teach the truth about nature and science, but also morality and values, and also the truth about giant corporations and subsidies.

Schools seriously need counselors. ENA's junior high school produced a mass murderer, a poor lonely mentally ill boy who was bullied and otherwise left to his fantasies. Even the slightest intervention would have prevented him from killing several neighbors. Both authors knew mentally deficient (probably brain-damaged) and autistic children, who, again, got no attention except bullying. They did not turn out well. School counseling is not a luxury, as it is treated in America these days. It is necessary for a functional society.

Children, as they grow, increase and develop their wants and needs. They need more control of their lives. Usually, in the nature of things, they want to take on more than they can handle, and to want privileges without the responsibilities. Good education requires responsibilities to grow in step with privileges. At the very least, education should focus on teaching children to be respectful of all people and all living things; responsible to each other and the world; and reasonable in the face of a world going mad.

In the end, what saves children is self-confidence, which has to be from 1) parents being supportive, not making things easy not overcorrecting; 2) decent peers, not racists and bigots; 3) gradual learning of how to socialize, deal with problems and cope with inadequacies; 4) actual achievement at something; 5) learning limits, accepting them, working within or around them.

One realm of social good involves the arts, individual spirituality, and other self-enrichment. This can potentially lead to snobbism and exclusion. A second type of good has a much better track record. It is the good that can ideally lift all boats: basic science, economic and technological progress. It benefits everyone, on average, but does not change the wealth distribution in society. In fact, it often allows the rich to grind the poor down even further. Agricultural progress, for instance, often makes landowning and development attractive to large-scale interests, and they may move in to dispossess small farmers and destroy local rural communities.

A third type is the widest and most general—the type that people usually mean when they talk about morality and ethics: decent treatment of people, mercy, friendliness, caring, compassion, respect, responsibility—all the things that help society in general and help everyone in it. This is what religions usually highlight: Christian love for all, Buddhist compassion, Confucian (and general Chinese) responsibility, and on through the religions.

A fourth, and the most socially beneficial, type of good is that which levels up the least fortunate members of society. The most obvious good of this type is universally available medicine, including public health, which benefits everyone but most benefits the sick and unfortunate. More pervasive and ultimately more important is what we broadly call civil society: justice, fairness, equality before the law, civil rights, basic public education, common civility and considerateness, and a culture of opportunity. It focuses on empowering people, which benefits everyone but particularly those who are down relative to the rest. It involves community development, environmental protection. It can be legislated, but only to a certain point. Beyond simple civil rights laws, it must be maintained by a culture of individual and interpersonal responsibility, comparable to that of old-time folk communities, but much more strong, resilient, and informed.

Individuals who have recently stood up under extreme repression in Turkey, Hong Kong, Russia, and elsewhere turn out to be intensely moral people in highly moral networks, willing to suffer a great deal for very small expected returns (Ayanian et al. 2021). Religion should produce good people, and indeed there is a long and honorable record of country preachers, spiritual fathers and mothers, and theologians, but they are overshadowed by a dreadful list of sadists, bigots, pederasts and other sex perverts, tyrants, and above all persecutors of "heretics." Crass missionaries have made a worldwide saying of "when the white people came, we had the land and they had the Bible. Now they have the land . . . and we have the Bible." Inquisitions and religious pogroms generally show humanity at its very worst. Making religion serve good rather than evil is a program in itself. Children, need to learn sociability, social help, and spirituality as they learn music: by slow incremental stages, with diligent and serious guidance and practice at every step. Most of all, they need to learn and develop independence, self-reliance, and self-control. With those, they will not only live better; they will have less felt need to control others.

SUMMARY OF THE GOOD

Thinking back to the summary of the wellsprings of evil, we can oppose the wellsprings and progress of good. We define good as helping and not hurting. Since evil begins and ends with judging some unworthy, the basic good is inclusiveness, expressed in mutual aid, solidarity, and cooperation. The social opposite of racism, regionalism, gender bias, religious bigotry, and the rest of the hatreds is solidarity. The only hope for working people confronted with giant corporations and cruel rulers is, as always, "solidarity forever." The only hope for dealing with elites who see the world as a zero-sum game that they play against workers and public interests is the same. The zero-sum mentality and the divisive rhetoric simply must be replaced, somehow, by the realization that we are all in this together and rise or fall together.

Love for all beings is the Buddhist ideal, but is impractical, if only because love of violent fascists should be very limited. Wide tolerance and proper evaluation of all beings and ideas is an actual need. So is active support and empowerment for the less fortunate, leveling them up to full social life. So is de-escalation and conflict resolution, including forgiveness. This requires an economic system based on positive-sum games in so far as possible, and certainly a system based on many small firms or actors instead of a few huge ones or (worse) a single giant firm. Finally, and most important, in a world with much evil, is teaching and modeling how to defend legitimate personal interests without overreacting and causing unnecessary harm.

The 90 percent of people who inclined to act with care and goodwill should be educated and encouraged to do so. As many jobs as possible should be created that make that behavior actually pay. We need more teachers, nurses, social workers, gardeners, artists, therapists. We need fewer professional hatemongers and distorters of the truth. For the other 10 percent, only condign and rigorously enforced laws will do any good. There is no possibility of abolishing the state, weakening law enforcement, or living in self-regulating communes. The inevitability of pathologically disturbed people, hard or impossible to reach, always destroys them in the end. The major need of the world now is enforcing those laws against the great malefactors as severely as we do against the petty ones. Global cooperation must expand to the point at which it can stop great evils: aggressive war, deliberately induced famines, murderous multinational corporations, giant dam projects that destroying ecosystems and other global crimes.

FINAL THOUGHTS

The survival of the human race now depends on salvaging civil democracy. It must stop the slide of the world downward into fascism. With fascist governments triumphant and entrenched in all the larger countries, and rising in power from Brazil and Turkey to China, Russia, and the Middle East, the remaining democracies must unite to turn the world around. They must join forces to stop fascism, global warming, biodiversity loss, and inadequate responses to pandemics. The giant multinational primary-production corporations are largely backing the fascists with enormous wealth and political power, seeking to divide the rest of us.

We began this book with four questions: First, why do people easily fall into hatred and bigotry? Second, who has exacerbated this over time, arousing and mobilizing hate for their own ends? Third, how does the result of this mobilization play out over time? Fourth, and most important, what can be done about it? The answers to these questions have not been simple. Humans seem to fall easily into group hatred, specifically of rival groups, and above all toward weaker rivals who can be scapegoated and eliminated. Those who exacerbate these tendencies are would-be leaders and rulers who find setting groups against each other to be the easiest and most persuasive way to succeed. The mobilization comes through extremist ideologies, war, genocide, and crime and corruption by those who can defy law. The cure must lie in fighting all of those tendencies at all stages: calling out the lies, stopping the funding, controlling would-be leaders, and above all restoring tolerance, fairness, respect, responsibility, and the other values of worldwide traditional morality. Without these steps, hatred and genocide will prevail. We are all called to strive for and sustain social harmony.

Appendix

SAUCIER AND AKERS'S LIST OF
DISCOURSE BY GENOCIDAL RULERS
(SAUCIER AND AKERS 2020:88–90)

"Tactics/excuses for violence, dispositionalism/essentialism, purity/cleansing language, dehumanization, dualistic/dichotomous thinking, internal enemies, crush-smash-exterminate-eliminate [language], group or national unity, racialism in some form, xenophobia/foreign influence, uncivilized or uncivilizable, attachment/entitlement to land, body or disease metaphor, revenge or retaliation language, traitor talk (treason, treachery, etc.), conspiracy, subversion, something held sacred, nationalism/ethnonationalism, threat of annihilation of our people" (p. 88)."placing national security above other goals," wanting to move fast and thoroughly, and thinking "individuals must suffer for the good of the collective" are also common (p. 90). Major emphasis on idea that every X is an X and nothing but an X.

Bibliography

Aalerding, Hillie, Femke S. Ten Velden, Gerben A. van Kleef, and Carsten K. W. De Dreu. 2018. "Parochial Cooperation in Nested Intergroup Dilemmas Is Reduced When It Harms Out-Groups." *Journal of Personality and Social Psychology* 114:909–23.

Abrams, Lindsay. 2015. "Big Oil's Decades of Deception: Report Reveals that Exxon's Known the Truth about Climate Science since 1981." *Salon*, July 8, http://www.salon.com/2015/07/08/big_oils_decades_of_deception_report_reveals_that _exxons_known_the_truth_about_climate_science_since_1981/.

Abramson, Seth. 2020. *Proof of Corruption: Bribery, Impeachment, and Pandemic in the Age of Trump*. New York: Macmillan.

Acharya, Avidit, Matthew Blackwell, and Maya Sen. 2018. *Deep Roots: How Slavery Still Shapes Southern Politics*. Princeton: Princeton University Press.

Ahmed, Nafeez. 2019. "How US Climate Deniers Are Working with Far-Right Racists to Hijack Brexit for Big Oil." *Le Monde Diplomatique*, June, https://mondediplo.com/outsidein/brexit-climate-deniers.

Akçam, Taner. 2012. *The Young Turks' Crime against Humanity: The Armenian Genocide and Ethnic Cleansing in the Ottoman Empire*. Princeton: Princeton University Press.

Alexander, Marcus, and Fotini Christia. 2011. "Context Modularity of Human Altruism." *Science* 334:1392–94.

Allport, Gordon. 1954. *The Nature of Prejudice*. Cambridge, MA: Addison-Wesley.

Alvarez, Alex, and Ronet Bachman. 2016. *Violence: The Enduring Problem*. 3rd edn. Sage.

Ames, Daniel, and Susan T. Fiske. 2015. "Perceived Intent Motivates People to Magnify Observed Harms." *Proceedings of the National Academy of Sciences* 112:3599–605.

Anderson, Barbara A., E. N. Anderson, and Roseanne Rushing. 2004. "Violence: Assault on Personhood." In *Reproductive Health: Women and Men's Shared Responsibility*, Barbara A. Anderson, ed. Sudbury, MA: Jones & Bartlett, 163–204.

Anderson, Benedict. 1991. *Imagined Communities*. 2nd edn. London: Verso.

Anderson, Carol. 2019. *One Person, No Vote: How Voter Suppression is Destroying Our Democracy*. New York: Bloomsbury.

Anderson, E. N. 1978. *Fishing in Troubled Waters*. Taipei, Taiwan: Orient Cultural Service.

———. 2005. *The Political Ecology of a Yucatec Maya Community*. Tucson, AZ: University of Arizona Press.

———. 2007. *Floating World Lost: A Hong Kong Fishing Community*. New Orleans: University Press of the South.

———. 2014. *Caring for Place*. Walnut Creek, CA: Left Coast Press.

———. 2019. *The East Asian World-System: Climate and Dynastic Change*. Cham, Switzerland: SpringerNature.

Anderson, E. N., and Barbara A. Anderson. 2013. *Warning Signs of Genocide*. Walnut Creek, CA: AltaMira.

———. 2017. *Halting Genocide in America*. Chesterfield, MO: Mira Publishing.

———. 2020. *Conforming to Genocide: The Wolf You Feed*. Lanham, MD: Rowman & Littlefield.

Anderson, Perry. 1974. *Lineages of the Absolutist State*. London: NLB.

Arendt, Hannah. 1963. *Eichmann in Jerusalem: A Report on the Banality of Evil*. New York: Viking.

Aristotle. 1955. *The Ethics of Aristotle*. Tr. J. A. K. Thomson. Harmondsworth, Sussex: Penguin.

Armiak, David, and Alex Kotch. 2020. "ALEC Leading Right-Wing Campaign to Open the Economy Despite Covid-19." Center for Media and Democracy, April 30, https://www.exposedbycmd.org/2020/04/30/alec-leading-right-wing-campaign -to-reopen-the-economy-despite-covid-19/?fbclid=IwAR099hffaC0qOgrDyk5Ff -J1seigetZT3TzgRZeM_jZzmFuBJCBHPpqWONU.

Arrian. 1831. *Arrian on Coursing*. Translated and annotated by, "A Graduate of Medicine" [William Dansey]. London: J. Bohn.

Artaxo, Paulo. 2019. "Working Together for Amazonia." *Science* 363:323.

Arzheimer, Kai. 2017. "Explaining Electoral Support for the Radical Right." In *The Oxford Handbook of the Radical Right*, Jens Rydgren, ed. Oxford: Oxford University Press, 1–29.

Atherton, Olivia, Katherine M. Lawson, and Richard W. Robins. 2020. "The Development of Effortful Control from Late Childhood to Young Adulthood." *Journal of Personality and Social Psychology* 119:417–456.

Atran, Scott. 2010. *Talking with the Enemy: Faith, Brotherhood, and the (Un)Making of Terrorists*. New York: HarperCollins.

———. 2019. "Transnational Terrorism, Devoted Actors, and the Vitality of Cultures." In *Handbook of Cultural Psychology*, Dov Cohen and Shinobu Kitayama, eds. New York: Guilford Press, 822–56.

———. 2021. "The Will to Fight." *Science* 373:1063.

Attfield, Robin. 1991. *The Ethics of Environmental Concern*. Athens: University of Georgia Press.

Atwood, Margaret. 1998. *The Handmaid's Tale*. New York: Anchor Books.

Auzanneau, Matthieu. 2018. *Oil, Power, and War*. Tr. John F. Reynolds. White River Junction, VT: Chelsea Green. Fr. Orig., *Or noir*, Editions La Découverte, 2016.

Ayanian, Arin H., Nicole Tausch, Yasemin Güülsum Acar, Maria Chayinska, Wing-Yee Cheung, and Yulia Lukyanova. 2021. "Resistance in Repressive Contexts: A Comprehensive Test of Psychological Predictors." *Journal of Personality and Social Psychology* 120:912–39.

Bachman, Jeffrey. 2020. "Four Schools of Thought on the Relationship between War and Genocide." *Journal of Genocide Studies* 22:479–501.

Bandura, Albert. 1982. "Self-Efficacy Mechanism in Human Agency." *American Psychologist* 37:122–47.

———. 1986. *Social Foundations of Thought and Action: A Social Cognitive Theory.* Englewood Cliffs, NJ: Prentice-Hall.

———. 2016. *Moral Disengagement.* New York: Worth Publishers, Macmillan Learning.

Banerjee, Neela. 2017. "How Big Oil Lost Control of Its Misinformation Machine." Inside Climate News, Dec. 22, https://insideclimatenews.org/news/22122017 /big-oil-heartland-climate-science-misinformation-campaign-koch-api-trump -infographic.

Barasch, Alixandra, Emma E. Levine, Jonathan Z. Berman, and Deborah A. Small. 2014. "Selfish or Selfless? On the Signal Value of Emotion in Altruistic Behavior." *Journal of Personality and Social Psychology* 107:393–413.

Baron-Cohen, Simon. 2011. *Zero Degrees of Empathy: A New Theory of Human Cruelty.* London: Allen Lane. (Published in the United States as *The Science of Evil: On Empathy and the Origins of Cruelty.* New York: Basic Books.)

Barragan, Rodolfo Cortes, and Carol S. Dweck. 2014. "Rethinking Natural Altruism: Simple Reciprocal Interactions Trigger Children's Benevolence." *Proceedings of the National Academy of Sciences* 111:17071–74.

Bartlett, Steven James. 2005. *The Pathology of Man: A Study of Human Evil.* Springfield, IL: Charles C. Thomas.

Bassin, Ian, and Justin Florence. 2020. "How the U.S. Can Stamp Out Trumpism." *Los Angeles Times*, Nov. 27, A11.

Batson, Daniel. 2011. *Altruism in Humans.* Oxford: Oxford University Press.

Baumeister, Roy. 1997. *Evil: Inside Human Violence and Cruelty.* San Francisco: W. H. Freeman.

Beals, Alan R., and Bernard J. Siegel. 1966. *Divisiveness and Social Conflict: An Anthropological Approach.* Stanford: Stanford University Press.

Beauchamp, Zack. 2018. "Study: 24 Million Americans Think Like the Alt-Right." Vox, Aug. 10, https://www.vox.com/2018/8/10/17670992/study-white-americans -alt-right-racism-white-nationalists.

Beck, Aaron. 1999. *Prisoners of Hate: The Cognitive Basis of Anger, Hostility, and Violence.* New York: HarperCollins.

Beckwith, Christopher I. 2015. *Greek Buddha: Pyrrho's Encounter with Early Buddhism in Central Asia.* Princeton: Princeton University Press.

Bekoff, Marc, and Jessica Pierce. 2009. *Wild Justice: The Moral Lives of Animals.* Chicago: University of Chicago Press.

Bélanger, Jocelyn J., Julie Caouette, Keren Sharvit, and Michelle Dugas. 2014. "The Psychology of Martyrdom: Making the Ultimate Sacrifice in the Name of a Cause." *Journal of Personality and Social Psychology* 107:494–515.

Bellah, Robert, et al. 1996. *Habits of the Heart: Individualism and Commitment in American Life*. 2nd edn. Berkeley: University of California Press.

Bellant, Russ. 1990. *The Coors Connection*. Cambridge, MA: Political Research Associates.

Belsky, Jay, Avshalom Caspi, Terrie E. Moffitt, and Richie Poulton. 2020. *The Origins of You: How Childhood Shapes Later Life*. Cambridge, MA: Harvard University Press.

Ben-Ghiat, Ruth. 2020a. *Strongmen: Mussolini to the Present*. New York: W. W. Norton.

———. 2020b. "Trump's Formula for Building a Lasting Cult." *Los Angeles Times*, Dec. 9, A13.

Benner, Aprile D., Yijie Wang, Yishan Shen, Alaina E. Boyle, Richelle Polk, and Yen-Pi Cheng. 2018. "Racial/Ethnic Discrimination and Well-Being During Adolescence: A Meta-Analytic Review." *American Psychologist* 855–83.

Bergh, Robin, and Nazar Akrami. 2016. "Generalized Prejudice: Old Wisdom and New Perspectives." In *The Cambridge Handbook of the Psychology of Prejudice*, Chris G. Sibley and Fiona Kate Barlow, eds. Cambridge: Cambridge University Press, 438–60.

Bergh, Robin, Nazar Akrami, Jim Sidanius, and Chris G. Sibley. 2016. "Is Group Membership Necessary for Understanding Generalized Prejudice? A Re-Evaluation of Why Prejudices Are Interrelated." *Journal of Personality and Social Psychology* 111:367–95.

Berscheid, Ellen. 1999. "The Greening of Relationship Science." *American Psychologist* 54:260–66.

Bilali, Rezarta, and Erwin Staub. 2017. "Interventions in Real-World Settings: Using Media to Overcome Prejudice and Promote Intergroup Reconciliation in Central Africa." In *The Cambridge Handbook of the Psychology of Prejudice*, Chris G. Sibley and Fiona Kate Barlow, eds. Cambridge: Cambridge University Press, 607–31.

Bonanno, George A. 2004. "Loss, Trauma, and Human Resilience: Have We Underestemated the Human Capacity to Thrive after Extremely Aversive Events?" *American Psychologist* 59:1:20–28.

———. 2021. *The End of Trauma: How the New Science of Resilience Is Changing How We Think about PTSD*. New York: Basic Books.

Bonfil Batalla, Guillermo. 1996. *Mexico Profundo: Reclaiming a Civilization*. Tr. Phillip Adams Dennis. Austin: University of Texas Press.

Bourdieu, Pierre. 1978. *Outline of a Theory of Practice*. Cambridge: Cambridge University Press.

———. 1990. *The Logic of Practice*. Stanford: Stanford University Press.

———. 1991. *The Political Ontology of Martin Heidegger*. Tr. By Peter Collier. Stanford: Stanford University Press.

Bowles, Samuel. 2006. "Group Competition, Reproductive Leveling, and the Evolution of Human Altruism." *Science* 314:1569–72.

———. 2009. "Did Warfare among Ancestral Hunter-Gatherers Affect the Evolution of Human Social Behaviors?" *Science* 324:1293–98.

Bowles, Samuel, and Herbert Gintis. 2011. *A Cooperative Species: Human Reciprocity and Its Evolution*. Princeton: Princeton University Press.

Boyd, Robert, and Peter Richerson. 2005. *The Origin and Evolution of Cultures*. New York: Oxford University Press.

Boyer, Pascal. 2018. *Minds Make Societies: How Cognitions Explains the World Humans Create*. New Haven: Yale University Press.

Brandt, Richard B. 1954. *Hopi Ethics: A Theoretical Analysis*. Chicago: University of Chicago Press.

———. 1979. *A Theory of the Good and the Right*. Oxford: Oxford University Press.

———. 1996. *Facts, Values, and Morality*. Cambridge: Cambridge University Press.

Bregman, Rutger. 2020. *Humankind: A Hopeful History*. New York: Little Brown.

Britt, Lawrence. 2003. "Fascism, Anyone?" *Free Inquiry*, Spring, 20.

Brooke, John L. 2014. *Climate Change and the Course of Global History*. Cambridge: Cambridge University Press.

Brown, Donald. 1991. *Human Universals*. Philadelphia: Temple University Press.

Browning, Christopher R. 2018. "The Suffocation of Democracy." *New York Review of Books*, Oct. 25.

Brummelman, Eddie, et al. 2015. "Origins of Narcissism in Children." *Proceedings of the National Academy of Sciences* 112:3652–62.

Bruneau, E., H. Szekeres, N. Kteily, L. R. Tropp, and A. Kende. 2019. "Beyond Dislike: Blatant Dehumanization Predicts Teacher Discrimination." *Group Processes and Intergroup Relations*, online.

Buber, Martin. 1947. *Between Man and Man*. London: Routledge and Kegan Paul.

Buchheit, Paul. 2013. "Add it Up: The Average American Family Pays $6,000 a Year to Big Business." CommonDreams, Sept. 23.

Bullard, Robert. 1990. *Dumping in Dixie: Race, Class, and Environmental Quality*. Boulder: Westview.

Bunker, Stephen G., and Paul Ciccantell. 2005. *Globalization and the Race for Resources*. Baltimore: Johns Hopkins University Press.

Burger, Jerry M. 2009. "Replicating Milgram: Would People Still Obey Today?" *American Psychologist* 64:1–11.

Cahill, Tom. 2017. "Here's How Much Exxon Paid Republicans Who Urged Trump to Ditch Climate Deal." Resistance Report, June 1, http://resistancereport.com/politics/exxon-paid-republicans-paris/.

Callan, Mitchell J., Aaron C. Kay, and Rael J. Dawtry. 2014. "Making Sense of Misfortune: Deservingness, Self-Esteem, and Patterns of Self-Defeat." *Journal of Personality and Social Psychology* 107:142–62.

Cameron, Catherine M., Paul Kelton, and Alan C. Swedlund (eds.). 2015. *Beyond Germs: Native Depopulation in North America*. Tucson: University of Arizona Press.

Cameron, Sarah. 2018. *The Hungry Steppe: Famine, Violence, and the Making of Soviet Kazakhstan*. Ithaca, NY: Cornell University Press.

Carey, Timothy, Sara J. Tai, and Robert Griffiths. 2021. *Deconstructing Health Inequity: A Perceptual Control Theory Perspective*. Cham, Switzerland: Palgrave Macmillan (a subsidiary of Springer Nature).

Case, Anne, and Angus Deaton. 2015. "Rising Morbidity and Mortality in Midlife among White Non-Hispanic Americans in the 21st Century." *Proceedings of the National Academy of Sciences* 112:15073–83.

———. 2020. *Deaths of Despair and the Future of Capitalism*. Princeton: Princeton University Press.

———. 2021. "Life Expectancy in Adulthood Is Falling for Those without a BA Degree, but as Educational Gaps Have Widened, Racial Gaps Have Narrowed." *Proceedings of the National Academy of Sciences* 118:e2024777118.

Caspar, Emilie A., Kalliopi Ioumpa, Christian Keysers, and Valeria Gazzola. 2020. "Obeying Orders Reduces Vicarious Brain Activation towards Victims' Pain." *NeuroImage*, doi" 10.1016/j.neuroimage.2020.117251.

Castano, Emanuele. 2012. "Antisocial Behavior in Individuals and Groups." In *The Oxford Handbook of Personality and Social Psychology*, Kay Deaux and Mark Snyder, eds. New York: Oxford University Press, 419–45.

Caviola, Lucius, and Joshua Greene. 2020. "How Effective Altruists Get a Better Return." *Los Angeles Times*, Dec. 17, A11.

Charny, Israel. 2016. *The Genocide Contagion: How We Commit and Confront Holocaust and Genocide*. Lanham, MD: Lexington Books.

Chase-Dunn, Christopher, and Paul Almeida. 2020. *Global Struggles and Social Change: From Prehistory to World Revolution in the Twenty-First Century*. Baltimore: Johns Hopkins University Press.

Chenoweth, Erica. 2021. *Civil Resistance: What Everyone Needs to Know*. New York: Oxford University Press.

Chenoweth, Erica, and Pauline Moore. 2018. *The Politics of Terror*. New York: Oxford University Press.

Chenoweth, Erica, and Maria Stephan. 2012. *Why Civil Resistance Works*. New York: Columbia University Press.

Choi, Donghyun Danny, Mathias Portner, and Nicolas Sambanis. 2019. "Parochialism, Social Norms, and Discrimination against Immigrants." *Proceedings of the National Academy of Sciences* 116:16274–79.

Choi, Jung-Kyoo, and Samuel Bowles. 2007. "The Coevolution of Parochial Altruism and War." *Science* 318:636–40.

Cislak, A., et al. 2018. "Power Corrupts, but Control Does Not: What Stands Behind the Effects of Holding High Position." *Personality and Social Psychology Bulletin* 44:944–57.

Clarke, Duncan. 2009. *Crude Continent: The Struggle for Africa's Oil*. Profile Books.

Clements, Benedict, David Coady, Stefania Fabrizio, Sanjeev Gupta, Trevor Alleyne, and Carlo Sdralevich (eds.). 2013. *Energy Subsidy Reform: Lessons and Implications*. Washington, DC: International Monetary Fund.

Clutton-Brock, Tim. 2016. *Mammal Societies*. New York: Wiley Blackwell.

Coady, David, Ian Parry, Louis Sears, and Baoping Shang. 2015. *How Large Are Global Energy Subsidies?* Washington, DC: International Monetary Fund.

———. 2017. "How Large Are Global Fossil Fuel Subsidies?" *World Development* 91:11–27.

Cohen, Dov, and Shinobu Kitayama (eds.). 2019. *Handbook of Cultural Psychology.* 2nd edn. New York: Guilford Press.

Cohen, Dov, Faith Shin, and Xi Liu. "Cultural Psychology of Money." In *Handbook of Cultural Psychology,* Dov Cohen and Shinobu Kitayama, eds. New York: Guilford Press, 599–629.

Cohen, G. A. 2000. *If You're an Egalitarian, How Come You're So Rich?* Cambridge, MA: Harvard University Press.

Coleman, Peter T., and Douglas P. Fry. 2021. "What Can We Learn from the World's Most Peaceful Societies?" *Greater Good,* June 7.

Coll, Steve. 2012. *Private Empire: ExxonMobil and American Power.* New York: Penguin.

Collier, Paul, and Nicholas Sambanis. 2005. *Understanding Civil War: Evidence and Analysis.* Washington, DC: World Bank.

Collins, Randall. 2008. *Violence: A Micro-Sociological Theory.* Princeton, NJ: Princeton University Press.

Cooney, Rosie, and Barney Dickson (eds.). 2005. *Biodiversity and the Precautionary Principle: Risk and Uncertainty in Conservation and Sustainable Use.* London: Earthscan.

Cooter, Amy. 2022. "Inside America's Militias." *Scientific American,* Jan., 34–41.

Costello, Thomas H., et al. 2022. "Clarifying the Structure and Nature of Left-Wing Authoritarianism." *Journal of Personality and Social Psychology* 122:135–70.

Coulton, G. G. 1910. *A Medieval Garner.* London: Constable and Co.

Cramer, Katherine J. 2016. *The Politics of Resentment: Rural Consciousness in Wisconsin and the Rise of Scott Walker.* Chicago: University of Chicago Press.

Cranmer, Skyler, Elizabeth J. Menninga, and Peter Mucha. 2015. "Kantian Fractionalization Predicts the Conflict Propensity of the International System." *Proceedings of the National Academy of Sciences* 112:11812–16.

Cranor, Carl. 2011. *Legally Poisoned: How the Law Puts Us at Risk from Toxicants.* Cambridge, MA: Harvard University Press.

Creel, Herrlee G. 1974. *Shen Pu-Hai: A Chinese Political Philosopher of the Fourth Century B.C.* University of Chicago Press.

Crook, Martin, and Damien Short. 2021. "Introduction"; "Developmentalism and the Genocide-Ecocide Nexus." *Journal of Genocide Research* 23:155–61, 162–88.

Curry, Oliver Scott, Daniel Austin Mullins, and Harvey Whitehouse. 2019. "Is It Good to Cooperate? Testing the Theory of Morality-as-Cooperation in 60 Societies." *Current Anthropology* 60:47–69.

Daar, Abdallah S., Trillium Chang, Angela Salomon, and Peter A. Singer. 2018. "Grand Challenges for Humanitarian Aid." *Nature* 559:169–73.

Dahlum, Sirianne, Carl Henrik Knutsen, and Tore Wig. 2019. "We Checked 100 Years of Protests in 150 Countries. Here's What We Learned about the Working Class and Democracy." *Washington Post,* Oct. 24, https://www.washingtonpost.com/politics

/2019/10/24/we-checked-years-protests-countries-heres-what-we-learned-about
-working-class-democracy/?fbclid=IwAR2P8bqA29J5sLuyD71abIURr6zGz7k0c
wSWRO0G9eIp-zI2A-aUGAxuWt8&utm_source=pocket-newtab.

Damasio, Antonio. 1994. *Descartes' Error*. New York: Putnam.

Damon, William. 1999. "The Moral Development of Children." *Scientific American*, Aug., 72–78.

Dean, John, and Bob Altemeyer. 2020. *Authoritarian Nightmare: Trump and His Followers*. New York: Melville House.

De Becker, Gavin. 1997. *The Gift of Fear*. New York: Random House.

De Dreu, Karsten K. W., Jõrg Gross, Zsomber Méder, Michael Griffin, Eliska Prochazkova, Jonathan Krikeb, and Simon Columbus. 2016. "In-group Defense, Out-group Aggression, and Coordination Failures in Intergroup Conflict." *Proceedings of the American Academy of Sciences* 113:10524–29.

Dentan, Robert Knox. 1979. *The Semai, A Nonviolent People of Malaya*. 2nd edn. New York: Holt, Rinehart, Winston.

———. 2008. *Overwhelming Terror: Love, Fear, Peace, and Violence among Semai of Malaysia*. Lanham, MD: Rowman & Littlefield.

Denworth, Lydia. 2017. "I Feel Your Pain." *Scientific American*, Dec., 58–63.

De Ruiter, Jan, Gavin Weeston, and Stephen M. Lyon. 2011. "Dunbar's Number: Group Size and Brain Physiology in Humans Reexamined." *American Anthropologist* 113:557–68.

De Tocqueville, Alexis. 2002. *Democracy in America*. Tr. and ed. by Harvey Mansfield and Delba Winthrop. Chicago: University of Chicago Press.

De Waal, Frans. 1996. *Good Natured*. Cambridge, MA: Harvard University Press.

———. 2005. *Our Inner Ape*. New York: Riverhead Books (Penguin Group).

Dikötter, Frank. 2019. *How to Be a Dictator: The Cult of Personality in the Twentieth Century*. New York: Bloomsbury.

Dilthey, Wilhelm. 1985. *Introduction to the Human Sciences*. Ed./tr. Rudolf A. Makkreel and Frithjof Rodi. (German original ca 1880.) Princeton: Princeton University Press.

Dollard, John, Neal E. Miller, Leonard Doob, O. Mowrerm and R. R. Sears. 1939. *Frustration and Aggression*. New Haven: Yale University Press.

D'Souza, Deborah. 2021. "Top Donors to the Trump 2020 Campaign." Investopedia, Oct. 20.

Duckitt, John. 2001. "A Dual-Process Cognitive-Motivational Theory of Ideology and Prejudice." *Advances in Experimental Social Psychology* 2001:41–113.

Duckitt, John, and Chris G. Sibley. 2009. "A Dual-Process Motivational Model of Ideology, Politics, and Prejudice." *Psychological Inquiry* 20:98–109.

———. "The Dual Process Motivational Model of Ideology and Prejudice." 2017. In *The Cambridge Handbook of the Psychology of Prejudice,* Chris G. Sibley and Fiona Kate Barlow, eds. Cambridge: Cambridge University Press, 188–221.

Dunbar, Robin. 2010. *How Many Friends Does One Person Need? Dunbar's Number and Other Evolutionary Quirks*. Cambridge, MA: Harvard University Press.

Durkheim, Émile. 1995 [1912]. *The Elementary Forms of Religious Life*. Tr. Karen E. Fields. New York: Free Press.

Dutton, Kevin. 2013. "Wisdom from Psychopaths?" *Scientific American Mind*, Jan.–Feb., 37–43.

Eddy, Bill. 2019. *Why We Elect Narcissists and Sociopaths—and How We Can Stop.* Berrett-Koehler Publishers.

Edenhofer, Ottmar. 2015. "King Coal and the Queen of Subsidies." *Science* 349:1286–87.

Ehrlich, Benjamin. 2022. *The Brain in Search of Itself: Santiago Ramón y Cajal and the Story of the Neuron.* New York: Farrar, Straus and Giroux.

Elliott, Robert (ed.). 1995. *Environmental Ethics.* Oxford: Oxford University Press.

Ellis, Albert. 1962. *Reason and Emotion in Psychotherapy.* New York: Citadel.

Ellsmoor, James. 2019. "United States Spends Ten Times More on Fossil Fuel Subsidies than on Education." *Forbes*, June 15. https://www.forbes.com/sites/jamesellsmoor/2019/06/15/united-states-spend-ten-times-more-on-fossil-fuel-subsidies-than-education/?fbclid=IwAR1D1nxoOs1mczovgR6Xm7cWHh0aoUcM7COcc4yuAo1rAnSRKP8maHloMEA#2283014c4473.

Elster, Jon. 1993. *Political Psychology.* Cambridge: Cambridge University Press.

Enock, Florence E., Jonathan C. Flavell, Steven C. Tipper, and Harriet Over. 2021. "No Convincing Evidence Outgroups Are Denied Uniquely Human Characteristics: Distinguishing In-Group Preference from Trait-Based Dehumanization." *Cognition* 212:104682.

Falk, Dean, and Charles Hildebolt. 2017. "Annual War Deaths in Small-Scale Versus State Societies Scale with Population Size Rather than Violence." *Current Anthropology* 58:805–13.

Feagin, Joe. 2015. *How Blacks Built America.* New York: Routledge.

———. 2020. *The White Racial Frame: Centuries of Racial Framing and Counter-Framing.* 3rd edn. New York: Routledge.

Fekete, Liz. 2019. *Europe's Fault Lines: Racism and the Rise of the Right.* London: Verso.

Ferguson. R. Brian. 2015. "History, Explanation and War among the Yanomami: A Response to Chagnon's *Noble Savages.*" Anthropological Theory 15:377–406.

Fiske, Alan Page, and Tage Shakti Rai. 2014. *Virtuous Violence: Hurting and Killing to Create, Sustain, End, and Honor Social Relationships.* Cambridge: Cambridge University Press.

Forscher, Patrick S., and Nour S. Kteily. 2020. "A Psychological Profile of the Alt-Right." *Perspectives on Psychological Science* 15:90–116.

Foster, George. 1961. "Interpersonal Relations in Peasant Society." *Human Organization* 19:174–78.

———. 1965. "Peasant Society and the Image of Limited Good." *American Anthropologist* 67:293–315.

Frank, Robert H. 1988. *Passions within Reason: The Strategic Role of the Emotions.* New York: W. W. Norton.

Frank, Thomas. 2004. *What's the Matter with Kansas? How Conservatives Won the Heart of America.* New York: Metropolitan Books (Henry Holt & Co.).

Freeman, Charles. 2005. *The Closing of the Western Mind: The Rise of Faith and the Fall of Reason.* New York: Vintage.

———. 2009. *A New History of Early Christianity*. New Haven: Yale University Press.

Friedman, Ann. 2017. "Embrace the Sweet Bliss of Ignorance." *Los Angeles Times*, Dec. 20, A13.

Friedman, Lisa, and Claire O'Neill. 2020. "Who Controls Trump's Environmental Policy?" *New York Times*, Jan. 14, https://www.nytimes.com /interactive/2020/01/14/climate/fossil-fuel-industry-environmental-policy .html?fbclid=IwAR1KttMDeGql15KIlSZth-w_QgpHR_Wx86hJEcpd_yM -x1AYWdH8jYW3jBU.

Fry, Douglas P. (ed.). 2013. *War, Peace, and Human Nature: The Convergence of Evolutionary and Cultural Views*. New York: Oxford University Press.

Galtung, Johan. 1969. *Violence, Peace, and Peace Research. Journal of Peace Research*. 6(3):167–91.

Gawronski, Bertram, Joel Armstrong, Paul Conway, Rebecca Friesdorf, and Mandy Hütter. 2017. "Consequences, Norms, and Generalized Inaction in Moral Dilemmas: The NI Model of Moral Decision-Making." *Journal of Personality and Social Psychology* 113:343–76.

Gelfand, Michele, and Emmy Denison. 2019. "How Trump Weaponizes Our Fears." *Los Angeles Times*, Sept. 16, A9.

Gelfand, Michele J., and Joshua Conrad Jackson. "Cultural Psychology of Negotiation." In *Handbook of Cultural Psychology,* Dov Cohen and Shinobu Kitayama, eds. New York: Guilford Press, 650–78.

Gershoff, Elizabeth T., Gail S. Goodman, Cindy L. Miller-Perrin, George W. Holden, Yo Jackson, Alan E. Kazdin. 2018. "The Strength of the Causal Evidence against Physical Punishment of Children and Its Implications for Parents, Psychologists, and Policymakers." *American Psychologist* 73:626–38.

Gertz, Matt. 2017. "Breitbart Is Not Independent, It's the Communications Arm of the Mercers' Empire." MediaMatters, April 21, https://mediamatters.org/research /2017/04/21/breitbart-not-independent-its-communications-arm-mercers-empire /216128.

Gibbon, Edward. 1995 [1776–1788]. *The Decline and Fall of the Roman Empire*. New York: Penguin.

Giddens, Anthony. 1984. *The Constitution of Society*. Berkeley: University of California Press.

Gigerenzer, Gerd. 2007. *Gut Feelings: The Intelligence of the Unconscious*. New York: Viking.

Gilbert, Gustave. 1947. *Nuremberg Diaries*. New York: Da Capo Press.

Gilchrist, Alan. 2006. "Seeing in Black and White." *Scientific American Mind*, June–July, 42–49.

Giroux, Henry. 2017a. "The Culture of Cruelty in Trump's America." Truthout, March 22, http://www.truth-out.org/opinion/item/39925-the-culture-of-cruelty-in -trump-s-america

———. 2017b. "Trump's Neo-Nazis and the Rise of Illiberal Democracy." Truthout, Aug. 16, http://www.truth-out.org/news/item/41617-neo-nazis-in-charlottesville -and-the-rise-of-illiberal-democracy.

Goff, Phillip Atiba, Matthew Christian Jackson, Brooke Allison Lewis Di Leone, Carmen Marie Culotta, and Natalie Ann DiTomasso. 2014. "The Essence of Innocence: Consequences of Dehumanizing Black Children." *Journal of Personality and Social Psychology* 106:526–45.

Goldberg, Jonah. 2022. "France's Election Shows How Political Parties Can Fade Away." *Los Angeles Times*, April 12. A10.

Goldberg, Matthew H., Jennifer R. Marlon, Xinran Wang, Sander van der Linden, and Anthony Weiserowitz. 2020. "Oil and Gas Companies Invest in Legislators that Vote Against the Environment." *Proceedings of the National Academy of Sciences* 117:5111–12.

Goldhagen, Daniel. 1996. *Hitler's Willing Executioners: Ordinary Germans and the Holocaust*. New York: Random House.

Goldschmidt, Walter. 2005. *The Bridge to Humanity: How Affect Hunger Trumps the Selfish Gene*. New York: Oxford University Press.

Gopnik, Alison. 2016. *The Gardener and the Carpenter: What the New Science of Child Development Tells Us about the Relationship between Parents and Children*. New York: Farrar, Straus and Giroux.

Gorman, Sara E., and Jack M. Gorman. 2016. *Denying to the Grave: Why We Ignore the Facts That Will Save Us*. New York: Oxford University Press.

Graeber, David. 2014. *Debt—Updated and Expanded: The First 5,000 Years*. New York: Melville House.

Graeber, David, and David Wengrow. 2021. *The Dawn of Everything: A New History of Humanity*. New York: Farrar, Straus and Giroux.

Graham, Jesse, Brian A. Nosek, Jonathan Haidt, Ravi Iyer, Spassena Koleva, and Peter H. Ditto. 2011. "Mapping the Moral Domain." *Journal of Personality and Social Psychology* 101:366–85.

Greenberg, Karen. 2018. "The President Is Throwing the Language of Democracy Down the Garbage Chute." *Los Angeles Times*, May 18, http://www.latimes.com /opinion/op-ed/la-oe-greenberg-trump-disappears-language-20180518-story.html.

Greenblatt, Jonathan. 2022. *It Could Happen Here: Why America Is Tipping from Hate to the Unthinkable—and How We Can Stop It*. New York: Mariner Books.

Greene, Ross. 2016. *Raising Human Beings: Creating a Collective Partnership with Your Child*. New York: Scribner.

Grenberg, Jeanine M. 1999. "Anthropology from a Metaphysical Point of View." *Journal of the History of Philosophy* 37:91–115.

Grinnell, George Bird. 1915. *The Fighting Cheyennes*. New York: Charles Scribner's Sons.

Guerrero, Jean. 2020. *Hatemonger: Stephen Miller, Donald Trump, and the White Nationalist Agenda*. New York: William Morrow.

Gul, Pelin, Susan E. Cross, and Ayse K. Uskul. 2021. "Implications of Culture of Honor Theory and Research for Practitioners and Prevention Researchers." *American Psychologist* 76:502–15.

Gutmann, Matthew. 2021. "The Animal Inside: Men and Violence." *Current Anthropology* 62:S182–S192. Great, insightful review of all.

Gutmann, Matthew, Robin G. Nelson, Agustín Fuentes (eds.). 2021. Toward an Anthropological Understanding of Masculinities, Maleness, and Violence. *Current Anthropology* 62, supplement 23.

Habermas, Jürgen. 1984 (Ger. orig. 1981). *The Theory of Communicative Action*. Tr. Thomas McCarthy. Boston: Beacon.

Hahl, Oliver, Minjae Kim, and Ezra W. Zuckerman Sivan. 2018. "The Authentic Appeal of the Lying Demagogue: Proclaiming the Deeper Truth about Political Illegitimacy." *American Sociological Review* 83:1–33.

Haidt, Jonathan. 2006. *The Happiness Hypothesis: Finding Modern Truth in Ancient Wisdom*. New York: Basic Books.

———. 2012. *The Righteous Mind: Why Good People Are Divided by Politics and Religion*. New York: Pantheon Books.

Han, Xiaochun, Xinhuai Wu, and Shihui Han. 2021. "Cognitive and Neural Bases of Decision-making Causing Civilian Casualties during Intergroup Conflict." *Nature Human Behaviour* 5:1214–25.

Hardin, Russell. 1988. *Morality within the Limits of Reason*. Chicago: University of Chicago Press.

Hare, Brian, and Vanessa Woods. 2013. *The Genius of Dogs: How Dogs Are Smarter Than You Think*. New York: Penguin.

Harff, Barbara. 2012. "Assessing Risks of Genocide and Politicide: A Global Watch List for 2012." In *Peace and Conflict 2012*, J. Joseph Hewitt, Jonathan Wilkenfeld, and Ted Robert Gurr, eds. Boulder, CO: Paradigm Press, 53–56.

Harris, Judith Rich. 1998. *The Nurture Assumption: Why Children Turn Out the Way They Do*. New York: Free Press.

Harrod, Ryan P., and Donald E. Tyler. 2016. "Skeletal Evidence of Pre-contact Conflict among Native Groups in the Columbia Plateau of the Pacific Northwest." *Journal of Northwest Anthropology* 50:228–64.

Haslam, S. Alexander, Stephen D. Reicher, and Jay J. Van Bavel. 2019. "Rethinking the Nature of Cruelty: The Role of Identity Leadership in the Stanford Prison Experiment." *American Psychologist* 74:809–22.

Hays, Nicholas A., and Corinne Bendersky. 2015. "Not All Inequality Is Created Equal: Effects of Status Versus Power Hierarchies on Competition for Upward Mobility." *Journal of Personality and Social Psychology* 108:867–82.

Heinberg, Richard. 2017. "Energy and Authoritarianism." http://energyskeptic.com/2018/richard-heinberg-energy-and-authoritarianism/.

Held, Lisa. 2020. "How Four Years of Trump Reshaped Food and Farming." Civil Eats, Nov. 2, https://civileats.com/2020/11/02/how-four-years-of-trump-reshaped-food-and-farming/.

Helvarg, David. 1997. *The War against the Greens: The Wise Use Movement, the New Right, and Anti-Environmental Violence*. San Francisco: Sierra Club.

Henrich, Joseph. 2016. *The Secret of Our Success: How Culture Is Driving Human Evolution, Domesticating Our Species, and Making Us Smarter*. Princeton: Princeton University Press.

———. 2020. *The WEIRDest People in the World: How the West Became Psychologically Peculiar and Particularly Prosperous*. New York: Farrar, Straus and Giroux.

Henrich, Joseph, and Michael Muthukrishna. 2021. "The Origins and Psychology of Human Cooperation." *Annual Reviews of Psychology* 72:207–40.

Henry, P. J. 2009. "Low-status Compensation: A Theory for Understanding the Role of Status in Cultures of Honor." *Journal of Personality and Social Psychology* 97:451–66.

Hiltzik, Michael. 2021. "Exxon's Twisted Tactic to Harass Critics." *Los Angeles Times*, Oct. 27, A2.

———. 2022b. "Unvarnished Truth? Not in Chevron 'Newsroom.'" *Los Angeles Times*, Jan. 23, A2.

———. 2022a. "Broken Vows of Good Citizenship." *Los Angeles Times*, Feb. 6, A2.

Hine, Robert. 1966. *California's Utopian Colonies*. New Haven: Yale University Press.

Hinton, Alexander Laban. 2005. *Why Did They Kill? Cambodia in the Shadow of Genocide*. Berkeley: University of California Press.

———. 2021. *It Can Happen Here: White Power and the Rising Threat of Genocide in the US*. New York: New York University Press.

Ho, Arnold K., Jim Sidanius, Daniel T. Levin, and Mahzarin R. Banaji. 2011. "Evidence for Hypodescent and Racial Hierarchy in the Categorization and Perception of Biracial Individuals." *Journal of Personality and Social Psychology* 100:492–505.

Hobbes, Thomas. 1950 [1657]. *Leviathan*. New York: E. P. Dutton.

Hochschild, Arlie Russell. 2016. *Strangers in Their Own Land: Anger and Mourning on the American Right*. New York: The New Press.

Hojjat, Tahereh Alavi. 2021. *The Economics of Obesity*. Cham, Switzerland: Springer.

Hong, Yongki, and Kyle G. Ratner. 2021. "Minimal but Not Meaningless: Seemingly Arbitrary Category Labels Can Imply More than Group Membership." *Journal of Personality and Social Psychology* 120:575–600.

Hope, Matt. 2019a. "The 'Historical Jigsaw of Climate Deception': Private Notes Show How Big Oil Spread Climate Science Denial." DeSmog, July 11, https://www.desmogblog.com/2019/07/11/historical-deception-global-climate -coalition-science-denial?fbclid=IwAR13VzspUoBDU_9BD751Sr6HbUtVE _z1qW0jyLbGXbK0EDSuiGTxXrryu_w.

———. 2019b. "Revealed: How the Tobacco and Fossil Fuel Companies Fund Disinformation Campaigns throughout the World." DeSmog, Feb. 19, https:// www.desmogblog.com/2019/02/19/how-tobacco-and-fossil-fuel-companies-fund -disinformation-campaigns-around-world?fbclid=IwAR0oI640hIv9HYUrCf0AU CJKIgrqPaWfH5JHp5H5tfSGNEPyybEkAlrH71o.

Howard-Hassmann, Rhoda E. 2016. *State Food Crimes*. Cambridge: Cambridge University Press.

Howie, Brian. 2018. "Right-wing Groups Are Recruiting Students to Target Teachers." Reveal, Oct. 30, https://www.revealnews.org/article/right-wing

-groups-are-recruiting-students-to-target-teachers/?fbclid=IwAR3FhRKegY7K
-SBx8floYBHGty8ZSi8q0r7yY1_1lh6-VTKK9tZUL1UmTV8.

Hoyer, Daniel, and Jenny Reddish (eds.). 2019. *Seshat History of the Axial Age.*
Chaplin, CT: Beresta Books.

Huang, Karen, Joshua D. Greene, and Max Bazerman. 2019. "Veil-of-Ignorance
Thinking Favors the Greater Good." *Proceedings of the National Academy of
Sciences* 116:23989–95.

Hughbank, Richard J., and Dave Grossman. 2013. "The Challenge of Getting Men
to Kill: A View from Military Science." In *War, Peace, and Human Nature: The
Convergence of Evolutionary and Cultural Views,* Douglas P. Fry, ed. New York:
Oxford University Press, 495–513.

Hume, David. 1969 [1739–40]. *A Treatise on Human Nature.* New York: Penguin.

Hyde, Jesse. 2019. "Cattle Ranching Remains Top Threat to the Amazon." *Los
Angeles Times,* Oct. 6, A1, A4.

Hymel, Shelley, and Susan M. Swearer. 2015. "Four Decades of Research on School
Bullying." *American Psychologist* 70:293–99.

Ibn Khaldun. 1958. *The Muqaddimah.* Translated by Franz Rosenthal. New York:
Pantheon.

Inchauste, Gabriela, and David G. Victor (eds.). 2017. *The Political Economy of
Energy Subsidy Reform.* Washington: World Bank Group.

Jaspers, Karl. 1953. *The Origin and Goal of History.* Translated by Michael Bullock.
New Haven, CT: Yale University Press.

Jensen, Nathan. 2018. "Do Taxpayers Know They Are Handing Out Billions to
Corporations?" *New York Times,* April 24, https://www.nytimes.com/2018/04/24/
opinion/amazon-hq2-incentives-taxes.html.

Johnson, Mark. 2014. *Morality for Humans: Ethical Understanding from the
Perspective of Cognitive Science.* Chicago: University of Chicago Press.

Johnston, David Cay. 2018. *It's Even Worse Than You Think: What the Trump
Administration is Doing to America.* New York: Simon & Schuster.

———. 2021. *The Big Cheat: How Donald Trump Fleeced America and Enriched
Himself and His Family.* New York: Simon & Schuster.

Johnston, Lucas. 2013. *Religion and Sustainability: Social Movements and the
Politics of the Environment.* Bristol, CT: Equinox.

Jones, Adam. 2011. *Genocide: A Comprehensive Introduction.* 2nd edn. London:
Routledge.

Jones, Daniel N., and Delroy L. Paulhus. 2017. "Duplicity among the Dark Triad:
Three Faces of Deceit." *Journal of Personality and Social Psychology* 113:329–42.

Jones, Terry L., and Kathryn A. Klar (eds.). 2007. *California Indian Prehistory.*
Lanham, MD: Rowman & Littlefield.

Jost, John T., Jack Glaser, Arie W. Kuglanski, and Frank Sulloway. 2003. "Political
Conservatism as Motivated Social Cognition." *Psychological Bulletin* 129:339–75.

Juhasz, Antonia. 2008. *The Tyranny of Oil: The World's Most Powerful Industry-and
What We Must Do to Stop It.* New York: William Morrow.

Kachanoff, Frank J., Nour S. Kteily, Thomas H. Khullar, Hyun Joon Park, and
Donald M. Taylor. 2020. "Determining Our Destiny: Do Restrictions to Collective

Autonomy Fuel Collective Action?" *Journal of Personality and Social Psychology* 119:600–632.

Kachanoff, Frank J., Donald M. Taylor, Thomas H. Khullar, Julie Caouette, and Michael J. A. Wohl. 2019. "The Chains on All My People Are the Chains on Me: Restrictions to Collective Autonomy Undermine the Personal Autonomy and Psychological Well-Being of Group Members." *Journal of Personality and Social Psychology* 116:141–65.

Kagan, Jerome, and Sharon Lamb (eds.). 1987. *The Emergence of Morality in Young Children*. Chicago: University of Chicago Press.

Kahneman, Daniel. 2011. *Thinking, Fast and Slow*. New York: Farrar, Straus and Giroux.

Kant, Immanuel. 1978. *Anthropology from a Pragmatic Point of View*. Tr. Victor Lyle Dowdell (Ger. Orig. 1798). Carbondale: Southern Illinois University Press.

———. 2002. *Fundamentals for the Metaphysics of Morals*. Tr. Allen W. Wood. Ger. orig. 1785. New Haven: Yale University Press.

———. 2009. *An Answer to the Question: What Is Enlightenment?* New York: Penguin.

Kaufman, Scott Barry. 2018. "The Dark Core of Personality." *Scientific American* online, https://getpocket.com/explore/item/the-dark-core-of-ersonality?utm_source=fbsynd&utm_medium=social&fbclid=IwAR10V2HANAcGyID8cEmBbn qZxSBsB_8TmMV2utanlIqFWvlQG-iyeM2x8_o.

Kay, Aaron, Steven Shepherd, Craig W. Blatz, Sook Ning Chua, and Adam D. Galinsky. 2010. "For God (or) Country: The Hydraulic Relation between Government Instability and Belief in Religious Sources of Control." *Journal of Personality and Social Psychology* 99:725–39.

Keeley, Lawrence. 1996. *War before Civilization*. New York: Oxford University Press.

Kelly, Raymond. 2000. *Warless Societies and the Origin of War*. Ann Arbor: University of Michigan.

Kenrick, Douglas, Vladas Griskevicius, Steven L. Neuberg, and Mark Schaller. 2010. "Renovating the Pyramid of Needs: Contemporary Extensions Built upon Ancient Foundations." *Perspectives on Psychological Science* 5:292–314.

Kent, Eliza F. 2013. *Sacred Groves and Local Gods: Religion and Environmentalism in South India*. Oxford: Oxford University Press.

Kidder, Tracy. 2009. *Mountains beyond Mountains: The Quest of Paul Farmer, a Man Who Would Cure the World*. New York: Random House.

Kiehl, Kent A., and Joshua W. Buckholtz. 2010. "Inside the Mind of a Psychopath." *Scientific American Mind*, Sept.–Oct., 22–29.

Kiernan, Ben. 2007. *Blood and Soil: A World History of Genocide and Extermination from Sparta to Darfur*. New Haven: Yale University Press.

Kirby, Alex. 2017. "Taxpayers Give Billions in Fossil Fuel Subsidies, Lose Trillions to Related Health Costs." EcoWatch, July 25, https://www.ecowatch.com/fossil -fuel-subsidies-2467529956.html.

Kissel, Marc, and Nam Kim. 2018. "The Emergence of Human Warfare: Current Perspectives." *American Journal of Physical Anthropology* 168:doi.org/10.1002/ajpa.23751.

Kizilhan, Jan Ilhan. 2022. "Yazidi Mental Health and Collective Trauma and Terror." In *Indigenous Knowledge and Mental Health: A Global Persp[ective,* David Danto and Masood Zangeneh, eds. Cham, Switzerland: SpringerNature, 3–13.

Klaas, Brian. 2017. *The Despot's Apprentice: Donald Trump's Attack on Democracy.* New York: Hot Books.

———. 2021. "The Bad Can Drive Out the Good in Public Life." *Los Angeles Times,* Nov. 7, A26.

Koch, Charles, with Brian Hooks. 2020. *Believe in People: Bottom-up Solutions for a Top-Down World.* New York: St. Martin's Press.

Kofta, Mirosław, Wiktor Soral, and Michał Bilewicz. 2020. "What Breeds Conspiracy Antisemitism? The Role of Political Uncontrollability and Uncertainty in the Belief in Jewish Conspiracy." *Journal of Personality and Social Psychology* 118:900–918.

Kohlberg, Lawrence. 1983. *Moral Stages.* Basel: Karger.

Kong, Augustine, Gudman Thorleifsson, Michael L. Frigge, Bjarni J. Vilhjalmsson, Alexander I. Young, Thorgeir E. Thorgeirsson, Stefania Benonisdottir, Asmundur Oddsson, Bjarni V. Halldorsson, Gisli Masson, Daniel F. Gudhjartsson, Agnar Helgason, Gyda Bjornsdottir, Unnur Thorsteinsdottir, and Kari Stefansson. 2018. "The Nature of Nurture: Effects of Parental Genotypes." *Science* 359:424–28.

Korsgaard, Christine. 1996a. *Creating the Kingdom of Ends.* New York: Cambridge University Press.

———. 1996b. *The Sources of Normativity.* Cambridge: Cambridge University Press.

Kotch, Alex. 2018. "How Charles Koch Is Helping Neo-Confederates Teach College Students." *The Nation,* Mar. 21, https://www.thenation.com/article/how-charles-koch-is-helping-neo-confederates-teach-college-students/.

———. 2019. "Revealed: How US Senators Invest in Firms They Are Supposed to Regulate." *The Guardian,* 19 Sept., https://www.theguardian.com/us-news/2019/sep/19/us-senators-investments-conflict-of-interest?fbclid=IwAR0bDYDd8lJj2OndWh_onVVy3gg89ofBMdjR9cT0QoTyOYVi3xsgt0ZE AXA.

———. 2020. "Secretive Right-wing Nonprofit Plays Role in Covid-19 Organizing." Truthout, May 23, https://truthout.org/articles/secretive-right-wing-nonprofit-plays-role-in-covid-19-organizing/.

———. 2021. "Meet the Real Dark money GOP Donors Who Funded Those Who Voted to Overturn the Election." CommonDreams, Jan. 28.

Kotch, Alex, and Michael Edison Hayden. 2021. "Donors Pumped Millions into White Nationalist Group." Hate and Extremism 2021, Southern Poverty Law Center, 10–11.

Kotzur, Patrick F., and Ulrich Wagner. 2021. "The Dynamic Relationship between Contact Opportunities, Positive and Negative Intergroup Contact, and Prejudice: A Longitudinal Investigation." *Journal of Personality and Social Psychology* 120:418–41.

Kruglanski, A. W., J. J. Bélanger, and R. Gunaratna. 2019. *The Three Pillars of Radicalization: Needs, Narratives and Networks.* Oxford: Oxford University Press.

Kruglanski, Arie W., Katarzyna Jasko, Marina Chernikova, Michelle Dugas, and David Webber. 2017. "To the Fringe and Back: Violent Extremism and the Psychology of Deviance." *American Psychologist* 72:207–30.

Krugman, Paul. 2018. "Big Business Reaps Trump's Whirlwind." *New York Times,* July 5, https://www.nytimes.com/2018/07/05/opinion/trade-war-trump-business -jobs.html.

Kteily, N., and Bruneau, E. 2017. "Backlash: The Politics and Real-World Consequences of Minority Group Dehumanization." *Personality and Social Psychology Bulletin* 43:87–104.

Kteily, Nour, Emile Bruneau, Adam Waytz, and Sarah Cotterill. 2015. "The Ascent of Man: Theoretical and Empirical Evidence for Blatant Dehumanization." *Journal of Personality and Social Psychology* 109:901–31.

Kteily, N., Hodson, G. P., and Bruneau, E. 2016. "They See Us as Less than Human: Meta-Dehumanization Predicts Intergroup Conflict via Reciprocal Dehumanization." *Journal of Personality and Social Psychology* 1110:343–70.

Lachmann, Richard. 2020. *First Class Passengers on a Sinking Ship: Elite Politics and the Decline of Great Powers.* London: Verso.

Ladd, John. 1957. *The Structure of a Moral Code: A Philosophical Analysis of Ethical Discourse Applied to the Ethics of the Navaho Indians.* Cambridge: Harvard University Press.

Lahr, M. Mirazon, F. Rivera; R. K. Power, A. Mounier; B. Copsey, F. Crivellaro, J. E. Edung, J. M. Millo Fernandez, C. Kiarie, J. Lawrence, A. Leakey, E. Mbua, H. Miller, A. Muigai, D. M. Mukhongo, A. Van Baelen, R. Wood, J.-L. Schwenninger, R. Grün, H. Achyuthan, A. Wilshaw, and R. A. Foley. 2016. "Inter-group Violence among Early Holocene Hunter-gatherers of West Turkana, Kenya." *Nature* 529:394–98.

Lakoff, George. 2006. *Whose Freedom? The Battle over America's Most Important Idea.* New York: Farrer, Strauss and Giroux.

———. 2016. *Moral Politics: How Liberals and Conservatives Think.* 3rd edn. Chicago: University of Chicago Press.

Langer, Ellen. 1983. *The Psychology of Control.* Beverly Hills: Sage.

Lauter, David. 2021. "The Factions within the Political Parties." *Los Angeles Times,* Nov. 15, A2.

Leander, M. Pontus, Maximilian Agostini, Wolfgang Stroebe, Jannis Kreierkamp, Russell Spears, Toon Kuppens, Marijn Van Zomeren, Sabine Otten, and Arie W. Kruglanski. 2020. "Frustration-*Affirmation*? Thwarted Goals Motivate Compliance with Social Norms for Violence and Nonviolence." *Journal of Personality and Social Psychology* 119:249–71.

Lemay, Edward P., Jr., Nickola C. Overall, and Margaret S. Clark. 2012. "Experiences and Interpersonal Consequences of Hurt Feelings and Anger." *Journal of Personality and Social Psychology* 103:982–1006.

Leonard, Christopher. 2019. *Kochland: The Secret Histories of Koch Industries and Corporate Power in America.* New York: Simon & Schuster.

Lerner, Melvin. 1980. *Belief in a Just World: A Fundamental Delusion*. New York: Plenum.

Lerro, Bruce. 2000. *From Earth Spirits to Sky Gods: The Socioecological Origins of Monotheism, Individualism, and Hyperabstract Reasoning from the Stone Age to the Axial Iron Age*. Lanham, MD: Lexington Books.

Le Texier, Thibault. 2019. "Debunking the Stanford Prison Experiment." *American Psychologist* 74:823–39.

Levinas, Emmanuel. 1969. *Totality and Infinity*. Tr. Alphonso Lingis. Fr. Orig. 1961. Pittsburgh: Duquesne University.

———. 1985 (Fr. orig. 1982). *Ethics and Infinity*. Tr. Richard Cohen. Pittsburgh: Duquesne University Press.

———. 1989. *The Levinas Reader*. Ed. Sean Hand. Oxford: Blackwell.

———. 1991 (Fr. orig. 1978). *Otherwise than Being or Beyond Essence*. Tr. Alphonso Lingis. Dordrecht, Netherlands: Kluwer Academic Publishers.

———. 1994. *Outside the Subject*. Tr. Michael B. Smith. Stanford: Stanford University Press.

———. 1998a (Fr. orig. 1991). *Entre Nous*. Tr. Michael Smith and Barbara Harshav. New York: Columbia University Press.

———. 1998b. *Of God Who Comes to Mind*. Tr. Bettina Bergo. Fr. orig. 1986. Stanford: Stanford University Press.

Levine, Sydney, Max Kleiman-Weiner, Laura Schulz, Joshua Tenenbaum, and Fiery Cushman. 2020. "The Logic of Universalization Guides Moral Judgment." *Proceedings of the National Academy of Sciences* 117:26158–69.

Levitsky, Steven, and Daniel Ziblatt. 2018. *How Democracies Die*. New York: Crown.

Leyens, J.-P., S. Demoulin, J. Vaes, R. Gaunt, and P. M. Paladino. 2007. "Infrahumanization: The Wall of Group Differences." *Social Issues and Policy Review* 1:139–72.

Liedtke, Michael, and Jonathan Mattise. 2021. "Report Exposes Financial Secrets of Elites." *Los Angeles Times*, Oct. 4, A4.

Loki, Reynard. 2019. "ExxonMobil Is Still Bankrolling Climate Science Deniers." Truthout, Oct. 21, https://truthout.org/articles/exxonmobil-is-still-bankrolling -climate-science-deniers/.

Lopez, Ian Haney. 2017. *Dog Whistle Politics: How Coded Racial Appeals Have Reinvented Racism and Wrecked the Middle Class*. New York: Oxford University Press.

Louv, Richard. 2005. *Last Child in the Woods: Saving Children from Nature-Deficit Disorder*. Chapel Hill: Algonquin Books of Chapel Hill.

Low, Christopher, and Joram Useb. 2022. "Mental Health and the San of Southern Africa." In *Indigenous Knowledge and Mental Health: A Global Perspective*, David Danto and Masood Zangeneh, eds. Cham, Switzerland: Springer, 79–100.

Lucas, Brian J., and Nour Kteily. 2018. "(Anti-) Egalitarianism Differentially Predicts Empathy for Members of Advantaged Versus Disadvantaged Groups." *Journal of Personality and Social Psychology* 114:665:692.

Lynn, Patti, and Geoffrey Supran. 2021. "Will Congress Expose Big Oil, Just As It Did Big Tobacco in '90s?" *Los Angeles Times*, Oct. 27, A11.

Lyubomirsky, Sonja. 2007. *The How of Happiness: A Scientific Approach to Getting the Life You Want*. New York: Penguin.

———. 2014. *The Myths of Happiness: What Should Make You Happy, but Doesn't; What Shouldn't Make You Happy, but Does*. New York: Penguin.

MacIntyre, Alasdair. 1984. *After Virtue: A Study in Moral Theory*. Notre Dame, IN: Notre Dame University Press.

Mackes, Nuria, et al. 2020. "Early Childhood Deprivation is Association with Alterations in Adult Brain Structure Despite Subsequent Environmental Enrichment." *Proceedings of the National Academy of Sciences* 117:641–49.

MacLean, Nancy. 2020. *Democracy in Chains: The Deep History of the Radical Right's Stealth Plan for America*. New York: Penguin.

Madley, Benjamin. 2016. *An American Genocide: The United States and the California Indian Catastrophe, 1846–1873*. New Haven: Yale University Press.

Mahajan, Neha, Margaret A. Martinez, Natashya L. Gutierrez, Gil Diesendruck, Mahzarin R. Banaji, and Laurie R. Santos. 2011. "The Evolution of Intergroup Bias: Perceptions and Attitudes in Rhesus Macaques." *Journal of Personality and Social Psychology* 100:387–404.

Maitner, Angela T., Eliot R. Smith, and Diane M. Mackie. 2017."Intergroup Emotions Theory: Prejudice and Differentiated Emotional Reactions toward Outgroups." In *The Cambridge Handbook of the Psychology of Prejudice*, Chris G. Sibley and Fiona Kate Barlow, eds. Cambridge: Cambridge University Press, 111–30.

Mandeville, Bernard. 1988. *The Fable of the Bees: Or Private Vices, Publick Benefits*. Indianapolis: Liberty Fund.

Mani, Anandi, Sendhil Mullainathan, Eldar Sharir, and Jiaying Zhao. 2013. "Poverty Impedes Cognitive Function." *Science* 341:976–80.

Mann, Michael. 2004. *Fascists*. Cambridge: Cambridge University Press.

———. 2005. *The Dark Side of Democracy: Explaining Ethnic Cleansing*. Cambridge: Cambridge University Press.

Mann, Michael E. 2021. *The New Climate War: The Fight to Take Back Our Planet*. PublicAffairs.

Margolis, Maxine L. 2021. *Women in Fundamentalism: Modesty, Marriage, and Motherhood*. Lanham, MD: Rowman & Littlefield.

Markowitz, David, and Paul Slovic. 2020. "Social, Psychological, and Demographic Characteristics of Dehumanization toward Immigrants." *Proceedings of the National Academy of Sciences* 117:9260–69.

Mayer, Jane. 2016. *Dark Money: The Hidden History of the Billionaires Behind the Rise of the Radical Right*. New York: Doubleday.

McCarthy, Niall. 2019. "Oil and Gas Giants Spend Millions Lobbying to Block Climate Change Policies." *Forbes*, Mar. 25, https://www.forbes.com/sites/niallmccarthy /2019/03/25/oil-and-gas-giants-spend-millions-lobbying-to-block-climate-change -policies-infographic/amp/?__twitter_impression=true&fbclid=IwAR24UQzUFd VXHIiON6fJXtiCmprYrjTcRkRaIU3wAXQ6lROZlhgsbLfZWd4.

McFarland, Sam; Matthew Webb; Derek Brown. 2012. "All Humanity Is My Ingroup: A Measure and Studies of Identification with All Humanity." *Journal of Personality and Social Psychology* 103:830–53.

Mead, George Herbert. 1964. *George Herbert Mead on Social Psychology*. Ed. Anselm Strauss. Chicago: University of Chicago Press.

Mencius. 1970. *Mencius*. Tr. D. C. Lau. (Chinese original, 4th century BCE.) London: Penguin.

Mencken, H. L. 1920. "The Divine Afflatus," *New York Evening Mail*, Nov. 16, 1917, reprinted in *Prejudices*, second series, Alfred A. Knopf, 1920, 155–79.

Meyer, Theodoric, and Jacqueline Alemany. 2021. "What the New Pew Voter Study Means for the 2022 Midterms." *Washington Post*, Nov. 10.

Michaels, David. 2008. *Doubt Is Their Product: How Industry's Assault on Science Threatens Your Health*. New York: Oxford University Press.

———. 2020. *The Triumph of Doubt: Dark Money and the Science of Deception*. New York: Oxford University Press.

Milgram, Stanley. 1963. "Behavioral Study of Obedience." *Journal of Abnormal and Social Psychology* 67:371–78.

———. 1974. *Obedience to Authority: An Experimental View*. New York: Harper & Row.

Mill, John Stuart, and Jeremy Bentham. 1987. *Utilitarianism*. (Origs. Various edns in 19th century.) New York: Penguin.

Miller, Alice. 1990. *For Your Own Good: Hidden Cruelty in Child-Rearing and the Roots of Violence*. Translated by Hildegarde Hannum and Hunter Hannum. 3rd edn. New York: Farrar, Straus & Giroux.

Miller, Joan G., Matthew Wice, and Namrata Goyal. 2019. "Cultural Psychology of Moral Development." In *Handbook of Cultural Psychology*, Dov Cohen and Shinobu Kitayama, eds. New York: Guilford Press, 424–46.

Mintz, Sidney. 1985. *Sweetness and Power*. New Haven: Yale University Press.

Moll, Jorge, and Ricardo de Oliveira-Souza. 2008. "When Morality Is Hard to Like." *Scientific American Mind*, Feb.–Mar., 30–35.

Mooijman, Marlon, Wilco W. van Dijk, Naomi Ellemers, and Eric van Dijk. 2015. "Why Leaders Punish: A Power Perspective." *Journal of Personality and Social Psychology* 109:75–89.

Mooney, Chris. 2006. *The Republican War on Science*. New York: Basic Books.

Moore, R. L. 2012. *The War on Heresy*. Cambridge, MA: Harvard University Press.

Morris, Benny, and Dror Ze'evi. 2019. *The Thirty-Year Genocide: Turkey's Destruction of Its Christian Minorities 1894–1924*. Cambridge, MA: Harvard University Press.

Moses, A. Dirk (ed.). 2004. *Genocide and Settler Society: Frontier Violence and Stolen Indigenous Children in Australian History*. New York: Berghahn.

Moshagen, Morton, Benjamin E. Hilbig, and Ingo Zettler. 2018. "The Dark Core of Personality." *Psychological Review* 125 (5), doi 10.1037/rev0000111.

Mudde, Cas. 2021. "Surprised to See US Republicans Cozying Up to the European Far Right? Don't Be." *The Guardian*, Oct. 15, https://www.theguardian.com/commentisfree/2021/oct/15/us-republicans-european-far-right.

Nesbit, Jeff. 2016. *Poison Tea: How Big Oil and Big Tobacco Invented the Tea Party and Captured the GOP*. New York: St. Martin's.

Netherlands Institute for Neuroscience. 2020. "New Brain Study Shows Why Obeying Orders Can Make Us Do Terrible Things." SciTechDaily, Aug. 21, https://scitechdaily.com/new-brain-study-shows-why-obeying-orders-can-make-us-do-terrible-things/?fbclid=IwAR1MHdmrTz4o25W4YLIlS46z-pCeYQLVn1M9a-SOynzC1SDdEkOKOf-3uzE.

Neuborne, Burt. 2019. *When at Times the Mob is Swayed: A Citizen's Guide to Defending Our Republic.* New York: New Press.

Neumann, Franz. 1944. *Behemoth: The Structure and Practice of National Socialism.* Oxford: Oxford University Press.

———. 1957. *The Democratic and the Authoritarian State.* Glencoe, IL: Free Press of Glencoe.

Newman, Leonard S. (ed.). 2020. *Confronting Humanity at Its Worst: Social Psychological Perspectives on Genocide.* Oxford and New York: Oxford University Press.

Nietzsche, Friedrich. 1911. *Human, All Too Human: A Book for Free Spirits.* Edinburgh: T. Foulis.

———. 1990. *Twilight of the Idols and Anti-Christ.* Translated by R.J. Hollingdale. New York: Penguin.

Nisbett, Richard, and D. Cohen. 1996. *Cultures of Honor: The Psychology of Violence in the South.* Boulder, CO: Westview Press.

Nordhoff, Charles. 1875. *The Communistic Societies of the United States.* New York: Harper and Brothers.

Norris, Pippa, and Ronald Inglehart. 2019. *Cultural Backlash: Trump, Brexit, and Authoritarian Populism.* Cambridge: Cambridge University Press.

North, Douglass. 1990. *Institutions, Institutional Change, and Economic Performance.* Cambridge: Cambridge University Press.

Nowak, Martin A. "Five Rules for the Evolution of Cooperation." *Science* 314:1560–63.

Nussbaum, Martha. 2001. *Upheavals of Thought: The Intelligence of Emotions.* New York: Cambridge University Press.

Nwanevu, Osita. 2021. "The Democratic Party Has a Fatal Misunderstanding of the QAnon Phenomenon." *New Republic*, Feb. 5.

Nyseth Brehm, Hollie. 2017. "Re-examining Risk Factors of Genocide." *Journal of Genocide Research* 19:61–87.

———. 2020. "Moving Beyond the State: An Imperative for Genocide Prediction." *Genocide Studies and Prevention* 13:64–78.

Obschonka, Martin, Michael Stuetzer, Peter J. Rentfrow, Leigh Shaw-Taylor, Max Satchell, Rainer K. Silbereisen, Jeff Potter, and Samuel D. Gosling. 2018. "In the Shadow of Coal: How Large-Scale Industries Contributed to Present-Day Regional Differences in Personality and Well-Being." *Journal of Personality and Social Psychology* 115:903–27.

Oreskes, Naomi, and Erik M. Conway. 2010. *Merchants of Doubt: How a Handful of Scientists Obscured the Truth on Issues from Tobacco Smoke to Global Warming.* New York: Bloomsbury Press.

Orwell, George. 1950. *1984.* New York: Signet Classics

Overland, Indra. 2010. "Subsidies for Fossil Fuels and Climate Change: A Comparative Perspective." *International Journal of Environmental Studies* 67:303–17.

Oxfeld, Ellen. 2017. *Bitter and Sweet: Food, Meaning, and Modernity in Rural China.* Berkeley: University of California Press.

Parfit, Derek. 1989. *Reasons and Persons.* Oxford: Oxford University Press.

Parker, Geoffrey. 2013. *Global Crisis: War, Climate Change and Catastrophe in the Seventeenth Century.* New Haven: Yale University Press.

Parks, Craig D., and Asako B. Stone. 2010. "The Desire to Expel Unselfish Members from the Group." *Journal of Personality and Social Psychology* 99:303–10.

Parry, Ian, Simon Black, and Nate Vernon. 2021. "Still Not Getting Energy Prices Right A Global and Country Update of Fossil Fuel Subsidies." Washington, DC: International Monetary Fund.

Parth, M. N., and David Peterson. 2022. "India's Future as a Secular State Is in Jeopardy." *Los Angeles Times*, March 8, A1, A6.

Pavetitch, Melissa, and Sofia Stathi. 2021. "Meta-Humanization Reduces Prejudice, Edven Under High Intergroup Threat." *Journal of Personality and Social Psychology* 120:651–71.

Paxton, Robert O. 2004. *The Anatomy of Fascism.* New York: Knopf.

Piketty, Thomas. 2017. *Capital in the 21st Century.* Tr. Arthur Goldhammer. Cambridge, MA: Harvard University Press.

———. 2020. *Capital and Ideology.* Cambridge, MA: Harvard University Press.

Pinker, Stephen. 2011. *The Better Angels of Our Nature: Why Violence Has Declined.* New York: Viking.

Popkin, Samuel. 1979. *The Rational Peasant.* Berkeley: University of California Press.

Prime, Heather; Mark Wade; Dillon T. Browne. 2020. "Risk and Resilience in Family Well-Being During the COVID-19 Pandemic." *American Psychologist* 75:631–43.

Prunier, Gérard. 2011. *Africa's World War: Congo, the Rwandan Genocide, and the Making of a Continental Catastrophe.* New York: Oxford University Press.

Putnam, Robert. 1993. *Making Democracy Work: Civic Traditions in Modern Italy.* Princeton: Princeton University Press.

———. 2000. *Bowling Alone: The Collapse and Revival of American Community.* New York: Simon & Schuster.

Radin, Paul. 1927. *Primitive Man as Philosopher.* New York: Appleton.

Ratchnevsky, Paul. 1991. *Genghis Khan: His Life and Legacy.* Oxford: Blackwell.

Rawls, John. 1971. *A Theory of Justice.* Cambridge, MA: Harvard University Press.

———. 1993. *Political Liberalism.* New York: Columbia University Press.

———. 2001. *Justice as Fairness: A Restatement.* Cambridge, MA: Harvard University Press.

Reddish, Jenny, and Julye Bidmead. 2019. "West Asia; Iran." In *Seshat History of the World*, Daniel Hoyer and Jenny Reddish, eds. Chaplin, CT: Beresta Books, 115–44.

Revenga, Ann. 2017. "Foreword." In *The Political Economy of Energy Subsidy Reform*, Gabriela Inchauste and David G. Victor, eds. Washington: World Bank Group.

Rich, Michael D., and Jennifer Kavanagh. 2020. "How Biden Can Stop 'Truth Decay.'" *Los Angeles Times*, Nov. 19, A13.

Richerson, Peter, and Robert Boyd. 2005. *Not By Genes Alone: How Culture Transformed Human Evolution*. Chicago: University of Chicago Press.

Rickard, Stephanie J. 2018. *Spending to Win: Political Institutions, Economic Geography, and Government Subsidies*. Cambridge: Cambridge University Press.

Robarchek, Clayton, and Carole Robarchek. 1998. *Waorani: The Contexts of Violence and War*. Fort Worth, TX: Harcourt Brace.

Roberts, Sean R. 2020. *The War on the Uyghurs: China's Internal Campaign against a Muslim Minority*. Princeton: Princeton University Press.

Roberts, Steven O., Camelle Bareket-Shavity, and Michelle Wang. 2021. "The Souls of Black Folk (and the Weight of Black Ancestry) in U.S. Black Americans' Racial Caegorization." *Journal of Personality and Social Psychology* 121:1–22.

Roberts, Steven O., and Michael T. Rizzo. 2021. "The Psychology of American Racism." *American Psychologist* 76:475–87.

Romanko, Svitlana, and Bill McKibben. 2022. "Ukraine Proves It—Banks Must Stop Funding Fossil Fuels." *Los Angeles Times*, March 9, A11.

Rosenbaum, Ron. 2014. *Explaining Hitler: The Search for the Origins of His Evil*. Updated Edition. New York: Da Capo Press, Perseus Group.

Ross, Michael L. 2012. *The Oil Curse: How Petroleum Wealth Shapes the Development of Nations*. Princeton: Princeton University Press.

Rothschild, Zachary K., Mark J. Landau, Daniel Sullivan, and Lucas A. Keefer. 2012. "A Dual-Motive Model of Scapegoating: Displacing Blame to Reduce Guilt or Increase Control." *Journal of Personality and Social Psychology* 102:1148–63.

Rowland, Jenny, and Matt Lee-Ashley. 2016. "The Koch Brothers Are Now Funding the Bundy Land Seizure Agenda." ThinkProgress, Feb. 11, http://thinkprogress.org /climate/2016/02/11/3748602/koch-brothers-funding-bundy-agenda/z.

Rozin, Paul; Matthew B. Ruby; Adam B. Cohen. 2019. "Food and Eating." In *Handbook of Cultural Psychology*, Dov Cohen and Shinobu Kitayama, eds. New York: Guilford Press, 447–77.

Różycka-Tran, Joanna, Paweł Boski, and Bogdan Wojciszke. 2015. "Belief in a Zero-Sum Game as a Social Axiom: A 37-Nation Study." *Journal of Cross-Cultural Psychology* 46:525–48.

Ruan, Jianqing, Zhuan Xie, and Xiaobo Zhang. 2014. Does Rice Farming Shape Individualism and Innovation? International Food Policy Research Institute, Discussion Paper 01389.

Rummel, Rudolph. 1994. *Death by Government*. New Brunswick, New Jersey: Transaction Books.

———. 1998. *Statistics of Democide*. Munchen, Germany: LIT.

Santangelo, Paolo. 2021. *Individual Autonomy and Responsibility in Late Imperial China*. Amherst, NY: Cambria Press.

Santorelli, Lorenzo A., Christopher R. L. Thompson, Elizabeth Villegas, Jesica Svetz, Christopher Dinh, Anup Parikh, Ruchard Sucgang, Adam Kuspa, Joan E. Strassmann, David C. Queller, and Gad Shaulsky. 2008. "Facultative Cheater Mutants Reveal the Genetic Complexity of Cooperation in Social Amoebae." *Nature* 451:1107–10.

Sapolsky, Robert. 2017. *Behave: The Biology of Humans at Our Best and Worst*. New York: Penguin.

———. 2018. "Double-Edged Swords in the Biology of Conflict." *Frontiers in Psychology*, 9:2625 (online).

Sasaki, Joni Y., and Heejung S. Kim. 2011. "At the Intersection of Culture and Religion: A Cultural Analysis of Religion's Implications for Secondary Control and Social Affiliation." *Journal of Personality and Social Psychology* 101:401–14.

Saucier, Gerard, and Laura Akers. 2018. "Democidal Thinking: Patterns in the Mindset Behind Mass Killing." *Genocide Studies and Prevention* 12:80–97.

Schiff, Adam. 2021. *Midnight in Washington: How We Almost Lost Our Democracy and Still Could*. New York: Random House.

Schmidtz, David. 1991. *The Limits of Government: An Essay on the Public Goods Argument*. Boulder, CO: Westview.

Schroeder, Juliana, and Nicholas Epley. 2020. "Demeaning: Dehumanizing Others by Minimizing the Importance of Their Psychological Needs." *Journal of Personality and Social Psychology* 119:765–91.

Schulman, David. 2015. *Sons of Wichita: How the Koch Brothers Became America's Most Powerful and Private Dynasty*. New York: Grand Central Publishing.

Schulz, Richard. 1976. "Some Life and Death Consequences of Perceived Control." In *Cognition and Social Behavior*, John S. Carroll and John W. Payne (eds.). New York: Academic Press, 135–53.

Scott, James C. 1976. *The Moral Economy of the Peasant*. New Haven: Yale University Press.

———. 1985. *Weapons of the Weak*. New Haven: Yale University Press.

Scudder, Thayer. 2005. *The Future of Large Dams: Dealing with Social, Environmental, Institutional and Political Costs*. London: Earthscan.

Sen, Amartya. 1982. *Poverty and Famines: An Essay on Entitlement and Deprivation*. Oxford: Oxford University Press.

———. 2009. *The Pursuit of Justice*. Cambridge, MA: Harvard University Press.

Serpell, James (ed.). 1995. *The Domestic Dog: Its Evolution, Behaviour, and Interactions with People*. Cambridge: Cambridge University Press.

Shaw, Martin. 2003. *War and Genocide; Organized Killing in Modern Society*. Cambridge: Polity Press.

———. 2013. *Genocide and International Relations: Changing Patterns in the Transitions of the Late Modern World*. Cambridge: Cambridge University Press.

Shin, Yeon Soon, and Yael, Niv. 2021. "Biased Evaluations Emerge from Inferring Hidden Causes." *Nature Human Behaviour* 5:1180–89.

Shweder, Richard. 1991. *Thinking Through Cultures: Explorations in Cultural Psychology*. Cambridge, MA: Harvard University Press.

Shweder, Richard, N. C. Much, M. Mahaptra, and L. Park. 1997. "The 'Big Three' of Morality (Autonomy, Community, and Divinity), and the 'Big Three' Explanations of Suffering, As Well." In *Morality and Health*, A. Brandt and Paul Rozin, eds. New York: Routledge, 119–69.

Sibley, Chris G., and Fiona Kate Barlow (eds.). 2017. *The Cambridge Handbook of the Psychology of Prejudice*. Cambridge: Cambridge University Press.

Sidanius, Jim, Sarah Cottrell, Jennifer Sheehy-Skeffington, Nour Kteily, and Héctor Carvacho. 2017. "Social Dominance Theory: Explorations in the Psychology of Oppression." In *The Cambridge Handbook of the Psychology of Prejudice*, Chris G. Sibley and Fiona Kate Barlow, eds. Cambridge: Cambridge University Press, 149–87.

Sidgwick, Henry. 1902. *Outlines of the History of Ethics*. London: Macmillan.

———. 1907. *The Methods of Ethics*. London: Macmillan.

Silva, Abigail, Nazia Sayed, and Maureen R. Benjamins. 2021. "Inequities in Selected Causes of Death: HIV, Homicide, and Opioid." In *Unequal Cities: Structural Racism and the Death Gap in America's Largest Cities*, Maureen R. Benjamins and Fernando G. De Maio, eds. Baltimore, MD: Johns Hopkins University Press, 123–38.

Silva, Abigail, Nazia Sayed, Fernando G. De Maio, and Mureen R. Benjamins. 2021. "Inequities in the 10 Leading Causes of Death." In *Unequal Cities: Structural Racism and the Death Gap in America's Largest Cities*, Maureen R. Benjamins and Fernando G. De Maio, eds. Baltimore, MD: Johns Hopkins University Press, 100–22.

Simon, Dan. 2021. "Who Voted for Hitler?" *The Nation*, Jan. 15.

Sinatra, Gale M., and Barbara K. Hofer. 2021. *Science Denial: Why It Happens and What to Do about It*. New York: Oxford University Press.

Slobodian, Quinn. 2018. *Globalists: The End of Empire and the Birth of Neoliberalism*. Cambridge, MA: Harvard University Press.

Slovic, Paul, C. K. Mertz, David M. Markowitz, Andrew Quist, and Daniel Västfjäll. 2020. "Virtuous Violence from the War Room to Death Row." *Proceedings of the National Academy of Sciences* 117:20474–82.

Sluga, Hans. 1993. *Heidegger's Crisis: Philosophy and Politics in Nazi Germany*. Cambridge, MA: Harvard University Press.

Smith, Adam. 1910 [1776]. *The Wealth of Nations*. New York: E. P. Dutton.

Smith, David Livingstone. 2011. *Less Than Human: Why We Demean, Enslave and Exterminate Others*. New York: St. Martin's Press.

———. 2020. *On Inhumanity: Dehumanization and How to Resist It*. New York: Oxford University Press.

———. 2021. *Making Monsters: The Uncanny Power of Dehumanization*. Cambridge: Harvard University Press.

Snyder, Timothy. 2015. *Black Earth: The Holocaust as History and Warning*. New York: Tim Duggan Books.

———. 2017. *On Tyranny*. New York: Tim Duggan Books.

———. 2018. *The Road to Unfreedom: Russia, Europe, America*. London: The Bodley Head (division of Penguin Random House).

———. 2021. "Tyranny's Playbook." *Los Angeles Times*, Oct. 3, A17.

Speth, James Gustave. 2021. *They Knew: The US Federal Government's Fifty-Year Role in Causing the Climate Crisis*. Cambridge, MA: MIT Press.

Sponsel, Leslie. 2012. *Spiritual Ecology: A Quiet Revolution*. Santa Barbara, CA: Praeger.

Stanley, Jason. 2020. *How Fascism Works: The Politics of Us and Them*. With a new preface. New York: Random House.

Stanton, Gregory. 2013. "The Ten Stages of Genocide." Posting, Genocide Watch website: http://genocidewatch.net/genocide-2/8-stages-of-genocide/.

Starr, Douglas. 2018. "Human Nature, Observed." *Science* 359:510–13.

Staub, Ervin. 1989. *The Roots of Evil: The Origins of Genocide and Other Group Violence*. New York: Cambridge University Press.

———. 2003. *The Psychology of Good and Evil*. Cambridge: Cambridge University Press.

———. 2011. *Overcoming Evil: Genocide, Violent Conflict, and Terrorism*. New York: Oxford University Press.

———. 2018. "Preventing Violence and Promoting Active Bystandership and Peace: My Life in Research and Applications." *Peace and Conflict: Journal of Peace Psychology* 24:95–111.

Stedman, John Gabriel. 1988. *Narrative of a Five Years' Expedition against the Revolted Negroes of Surinam*. Ed. Richard Price and Sally Price. Baltimore, MD: Johns Hopkins University Press. (Orig. ms 1790; orig. publ. 1806–1813.)

Sternberg, Robert J., and Karin Sternberg. 2008. *The Nature of Hate*. Cambridge: Cambridge University Press.

Stiglitz, Joseph E. 2019. *People, Power, and Profits*. New York: W. W. Norton.

Stiglitz, Joseph E., Jean-Paul Fitoussi, and Martine Durand. 2019. *Measuring What Counts: The Global Movement for Well-Being*. New York: The New Press.

Sullivan, Paul. 1989. *Unfinished Conversations*. New Haven: Yale University Press.

Sun, Lena, and Janet Eilperin. 2017. "CDC Gets List of Forbidden Words: Fetus, Transgender, Diversity." *Washington Post*, Dec. 15, https://www.washingtonpost.com/national/health-science/cdc-gets-list-of-forbidden-words-fetus-transgender-diversity/2017/12/15/f503837a-e1cf-11e7-89e8-edec16379010_story.html?utm_term=.8aef9ac3d868.

Sussman, Robert Wald. 2014. *The Myth of Race: The Troubling Persistence of an Unscientific Idea*. Cambridge, MA: Harvard University Press.

Swann, William B., Jr., et al. 2014. "What Makes a Group Worth Dying For? Identity Fusion Fosters Perception of Familial Ties, Promoting Self-Sacrifice." *Journal of Personality and Social Psychology* 106:912–26.

Talhelm, Thomas, and Shigehiro Oishi. 2019. "Culture and Ecology." In *Handbook of Cultural Psychology*, Dov Cohen and Shinobu Kitayama, eds. New York: Guilford Press, 119–43.

Tannahill, Brynn. 2021. *American Fascism: How the GOP is Subverting Democracy*. N.p.: Transgress Press.

Tatz, Colin, and Winton Higgins. 2016. *The Magnitude of Genocide*. Santa Barbara: Praeger, "an imprint of ABC-CLIO."

Tavris, Carol. 1982. *Anger, the Misunderstood Emotion*. New York: Simon & Schuster.

Taylor, Kathleen. 2009. *Cruelty: Human Evil and the Human Brain*. Oxford: Oxford University Press.

Taylor, Steve. 2021. "The Problem of Pathocracy." *The Psychologist* 34:40–45.

Te Brake, Wayne. 2017. *Religious War and Religious Peace in Early Modern Europe.* Cambridge: Cambridge University Press.

Thurow, Lester. 1980. *The Zero-Sum Society: Distribution and the Possibilities for Economic Change.* New York: Basic Books.

Tierney, John, and Roy E. Baumeister. 2019. *The Power of Bad, and How to Overcome It.* New York: Penguin (Allen Lane).

Tomasello, Michael. 2016. *A Natural History of Human Morality.* Cambridge, MA: Harvard University Press.

———. 2018. "How Children Come to Understand False Beliefs: A Shared Intentionality Account." *Proceedings of the National Academy of Sciences* 115:8491–98.

———. 2019. *Becoming Human: A Theory of Ontogeny.* Cambridge, MA: Harvard University Press.

Totten, Samuel, and Paul R. Bartrop. 2008. *Dictionary of Genocide.* Westport, CT: Greenwood.

Traverso, Enzo. 2019. *The New Faces of Fascism.* (French original, 2017.) London: Verso.

Travis, Hannibal. 2019. "The Long Genocide in Upper Mesopotamia: Minority Population Destruction amidst Nation-Building and 'International Security.' *Genocide Studies International* 13:92–131.

Turbet, Martin, et al. 2021. "Day-Night Cloud Asymmetry Prevent Oceans on Venus but Not on Earth." *Nature* 598:276–80.

Turchin, Peter. 2016. *Ages of Discord.* Chaplin, CT: Beresta Books.

———. 2018. "Evolutionary Pathways to Statehood: Old Theories and New Data." Talk, University of California, Riverside, March 1.

Turchin, Peter, and Sergey Zefedov. 2009. *Secular Cycles.* Princeton: Princeton University Press.

Turney-High, Harry Holbert. 1949. *Primitive War: Its Practices and Concepts.* Columbia, SC: University of South Carolina Press.

Twain, Mark (Samuel Clemens). 1913. *Roughing It.* New York: Harper & Bros.

Udupa, Sahana, Iginio Gagliardone, and Peter Hervik. 2021. "Hate Cultures in the Digital Age: The Global Conjuncture of Extreme Speech." In *Digital Hate: The Global Conjuncture of Extreme Speech*, Sahana Udupa, Iginio Gagliardone, and Peter Hervik, eds. Bloomington, IN: Indiana University Press, 1–19.

Uskul, Ayes K., Susan E. Cross, Ceren Günsoy, and Pelin Gul. 2019."Cultures of Honor." In *Handbook of Cultural Psychology*, Dov Cohen and Shinobu Kitayama, eds. New York: Guilford Press, 793–821.

Villa Rojas, Alfonso. 1945. *The Maya of East Central Quintana Roo.* Washington, DC: Carnegie Institution of Washington. Publ. 559.

Voorhees, Burton, Dwight Read, and Liane Gabora. 2020. "Identity, Kinship, and the Evolution of Cooperation." *Current Anthropology* 61:194–218.

Waller, James. 2002. *Becoming Evil: How Ordinary People Commit Genocide and Mass Killing.* Oxford: Oxford University Press.

———. 2016. *Confronting Evil: Engaging Our Responsibility to Prevent Genocide.* New York: Oxford University Press.

Weber, Max. 1978. *Economy and Society: An Outline of Interpretive Sociology*, vol. 1–2. Edited and translated by G. Roth and C. Wittich. [German original 1922.] Berkeley: University of California Press.

Werner, Emmy, and Ruth S. Smith. 1982. *Vulnerable but Invincible: A Longitudinal Study of Resilient Children and Youth.* New York: McGraw-Hill.

———. 2001. *Journeys from Childhood to Midlife: Risk, Resilience, and Recovery.* Ithaca, NY: Cornell University Press.

White, Shannon, Juliana Schroeder, and Jane L. Risen. 2021. "When 'Enemies' Become Close: Relationship Formation among Palestinians and Jewish Israelis at a Youth Camp." *Journal of Personality and Social Psychology* 121:76–95.

Whitehouse, Harvey, Peter François, Enrico Cioni; Jill Levine, Daniel Hoyer, Jenny Reddish, and Peter Turchin. 2019. "Conclusion: Was There Ever an Axial Age?" In *Seshat History of the Axial Age*, Daniel Hoyer and Jenny Reddish, eds. Chaplin, CT: Beresta Books, 395–407.

Wilber, Del Quentin. 2021. "An Oath Keeper's Wife Feels the Sting of Jan. 6." *Los Angeles Times*, Nov. 12, A1, A6–7.

Williams, Roger. 1956. *Biochemical Individuality.* New York: Wiley.

Winerman, Lea. 2017. "4 Questions for Alison Gopnik." *Monitor on Psychology*, March, 33–34.

Wordsworth, William. "Rob Roy's Grave." Poetry Atlas, http://www.poetryatlas.com /poetry/poem/2458/rob-roy%26%23039%3Bs-grave.html.

World Health Organization of the United Nations. 2021. "Violence against Women."

Xunzi. 1999. *Xunzi.* Tr. John Knoblock. Changsha and Beijing, China: Hunan People's Publishing House and Foreign Language Press.

Zajonc, Robert. 1980. "Feeling and Thinking: Preferences Need No Inferences." *American Psychologist* 35(2):151–75.

Zaki, Jamil. 2019. *The War for Kindness: Building Empathy in a Fractured World.* New York: Crown.

Zeki, Semir, and John Paul Romaya. 2008. "Neural Correlates of Hate." *PLoS One* 3 (10):e3556.

Zhao, Xuan, and Nicholas Epley. 2021. "Insufficiently Complimentary?: Underestimating the Positive Impact of Compliments Creates a Barrier to Expressing Them." *Journal of Personality and Social Psychology* 121:239–56.

Zimbardo, Philip. 2008. *The Lucifer Effect: Understanding How Good People Turn Evil.* New York: Random House.

Zitek, Emily M., Alexander H. Jordan, Benoît Monin, and Federick R. Leach. 2010. "Victim Entitlement to Behave Selfishly." *Journal of Personality and Social Psychology* 98:245–55.

Index

About the Authors

E. N. Anderson, PhD, is professor of anthropology, emeritus, at the University of California, Riverside. He received his PhD in anthropology from the University of California, Berkeley, in 1967. He has done research on ethnobiology, cultural ecology, political ecology, and medical anthropology in several areas, especially Hong Kong, British Columbia, California, and the Yucatan Peninsula of Mexico. His books include *The Food of China* (1988), *Ecologies of the Heart* (1996), *Political Ecology of a Yucatec Maya Community* (2005), *The Pursuit of Ecotopia* (2010), *Caring for Place* (2014), *Everyone Eats* (2014), *Food and Environment in Early and Medieval China* (2014), and with Barbara A. Anderson, *Warning Signs of Genocide* (2013), *Halting Genocide in America* (2017), and *Complying with Genocide: The Wolf You Feed* (2020).

Barbara A. Anderson, DrPH, CNM, FAAN, is professor of nursing, emerita, at Frontier Nursing University. She has done research on health-care decision-making among Cambodian refugees on the Cambodia border and among resettled refugees in the United States. She is a public health specialist and nurse-midwife with extensive academic teaching and program consultation. Her consultation work has focused on Southeast Asia and Africa. Her books include *Reproductive Health* (2005), *Caring for the Vulnerable* (2008, 2012, 2016, 2020), *Best Practices in Midwifery* (2012, 2017), *DNP Capstone Projects* (2015), *The Maternal Health Crisis in America* (American Journal of Nursing first place award in maternal health, 2019), and with E. N. Anderson, *Warning Signs of Genocide* (2013), *Halting Genocide in America* (2017) and *Complying with Genocide: The Wolf You Feed* (2020).